T0158855

"Should I Go Walkabout" Again (a Motorhome Adventure)

Diary 3—Part 2 of "The Big Lap"

JOHN TIMMS

AuthorHouse™ UK
1663 Liberty Drive
Bloomington, IN 47403 USA
www.authorhouse.co.uk
Phone: 0800.197.4150

Published by AuthorHouse 11/09/2018

ISBN: 978-1-7283-8066-7 (sc)
ISBN: 978-1-7283-8082-7 (e)

Print information available on the last page.

authorHOUSE®

INTRODUCTION –Diary 3

This is not a travel documentary although you will get a lot of information about Australia and a great deal of detail about a few places. This book is more about being confused, the things that went wrong, the things or places that surprised us and those that disappointed us. It also touches on living with your partner twenty-four seven, along with two dogs and what joy those two dogs gave us when we arrived at, for example, a deserted beach. Sometimes when things went wrong I cried and so did my friends but their tears were those of laughter as I continued to send them out our weekly diary via email. It's about the accidents that happened to our vehicles to us and the dogs, unusual physical ailments and boredom which is not what you see on the television when you listen to travel shows. Here in Australia the interviewers always seem to find happy travellers who are sitting on the edge of beautiful beaches with close friends, sipping wine as they watch the sun sink over the horizon and they are all such happy campers. I haven't yet met these people and if I ever try to sit near the beach at sunset, in a warm climate, my only companions are mosquitoes and sandflies! I could spray myself all over with some sort of near lethal mosquito repellent of course but I hate the smell and can't get away from myself quickly enough. So, this is what happened to us (me my husband and the dogs) on this second part of our odyssey around Australia as part two of 'The Big Lap' from the Nullarbor Plain.

We had travelled for over seven months to get to Bremer Bay on the southern coast of Western Australia and now had to traverse the Nullarbor Plain in South Australia along the coastal route to Victoria through inland New South Wales and back up to Currumbin on the Queensland Gold Coast. Another three months on the road.

It is strange to be home at last, the gypsy life is addictive. Do we need a house?

Two years later we still had the travel bug and took one final extended journey to Bowen in North Queensland then travelled down in land through Queensland, New South Wales and Victoria across to explore Tasmania for a few months and complete the Continent. Now what!

Should I Tour Australia?

By
Lisa(Eizabeth) Timms

DEDICATED TO MY DEAR WIFE
WHO SHARED THESE MEMORIES WITH ME
BUT WHO DIED SUDDENLY
ON 5th November 2015.

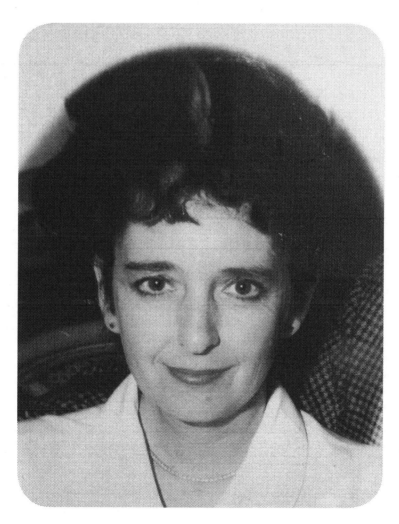

Chapter 1

Should I "Go Walkabout" Again (A Motorhome Adventure) Part 2 of "The Big Lap"- Diary 3

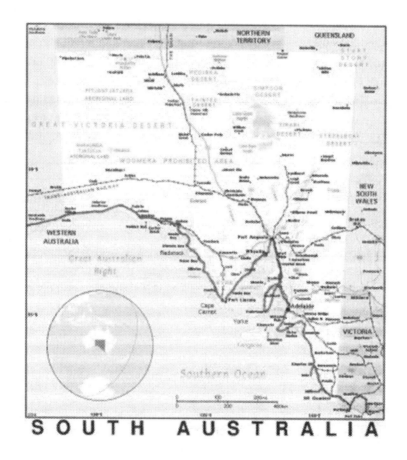

Last stop Bremer Bay, Western Australia (We had set off from Currumbin in Queensland up to Rockhampton, across Central Queensland into Northern Territory down to Uluru. Back up to Darwin, across to Kimberley to Broome and down the Western Australian coast via Perth and Margaret River to Bremer Bay.

We set off again tomorrow and the television news tells us that we are in for some rough weather with storms and possibly quite severe winds tomorrow and Wednesday when we are due to visit a small coastal town that was singled out on the news as being one of those places that will be hardest hit with the bad weather. We have been so lucky so far and I just hope our luck lasts out.

One of the campers who we had talked to on New Year's Eve left before we did the following morning. Then we left and when we arrived at Ravensthorpe we noticed that the camper had backed his trailer into the back of our Ute! He must have known he'd hit us but had driven off. His friends next to him no doubt knew about it as well but how on earth can we prove it! Now we've had drivers damage the back and front of the Ute quite badly and we do not have their details which will mean that I have to claim on insurance and will get penalised presumably by increased annual costs.

Well we got here without rain, battling locusts instead. What a day! John had gastroenteritis last night so hadn't had much sleep, one of our rented homes flooded, my son's car blew up on an island off Brisbane and had to be towed home and my back hurt so much that after half an hour of travelling I had to ask John to stop as my eyes were glazing over and I felt very sick. I thought I'd got his bug but it seems not, just something wrong with my back. Whilst people were trying to reach us on the mobile, we were out of range and it was just lucky that I called my son as soon as the mobile was working again as he told me that a plumber had been organised to stop the flooding and he was going to arrange for a water extractor. I could see dollar signs flashing before my eyes and quite rightly too because at **Jerramungup** we managed to get hold of our insurance company and I was told that it would cost $1000 to suck the water out of the carpet and to put dehumidifiers in to dry the concrete floor beneath! The insurance company will cover that. However, I was also told that they would not cover the cost of the plumber and I feel an argument coming on as we have no idea where the leak is coming from, only that water is seeping through from upstairs and coming down by the double patio doors downstairs. Unfortunately a huge semi-trailer pulled up adjacent to our van doors and windows with caged sheep destined for the abattoir as I was trying to concentrate on the questions I was being asked.

We are in a caravan park at Ravensthorpe now but neither of us feels like eating and we just collapsed with relief on arrival! The evening news on television is giving us 'severe weather warning' briefs for this whole area and now say that Thursday will be the worst day which is the day we leave here for Esperance which is also included in the warning.

We went into **Ravensthorpe** and it is a delightful small town. Just going to the local supermarket which doubles up as a hardware store became an event as everyone was so friendly and it was quite amusing being stuck in a long queue listening to everyone, most of whom knew each other. I had a chat with a young boy who is the eldest of three boys on the benefits of being the eldest. 'I get to go out fishing with my Dad' he told me. The younger two boys were very lively but their mother told me that they were being very well behaved today. The minute she said that the middle child did the disappearing act! I t*old the elder boy that being the eldest meant that he got thrust into maturity a lot quicker and that he would learn to be more responsible earlier than the other two but that it not always a bad thing and he grinned at me and agreed. He was a lovely young lad. A very tall gentleman found himself holding the door open for what seemed a never-ending string of shoppers with their bags laden and as I went out under his arm I said 'Didn't we use to play oranges and lemons years ago?' Then I realised that he needed to get out the door himself with two huge boxes of groceries so we swapped places and he said 'You have no idea how grateful I am'. I'm surprised he could move his arm.

Anyway, John is completely better today but my back has become so bad that I cannot sit properly so John has gone off to see **Hopetoun** with the camera and the dogs. I am shut in the van (we normally rarely close our door) because of the rain. Just before he left we heard a warning on the radio which became more and more detailed, telling us that we have half a days warning to get away from the ocean, to be careful if you are in big trucks or caravans, to pass messages on to relatives or phone the emergency services if you know of anyone camping in remote areas because we are in for some very violent weather. Telephone numbers were provided for assistance (non life threatening because for those you dial the normal emergency number), for updates on road conditions in case tress or floods have cut them off and web site addresses. John listened to most of it before heading towards the coast. Apparently there is a lot of traffic already moving away from the coast so the roads are busy and extra care must be taken. So before we leave here tomorrow we will have to phone the information line to find out if we can get to Esperance or not. We just pray that tree branches do not damage our vehicles or us. Luckily in this park the trees, although tall, are more of the sapling variety but as they said on the radio some thinner branches can spear vehicles.

In the north a cyclone is crossing the coast as I type this and even the port at Port Headland has stopped all shipping from arriving or leaving and has closed down. Apparently it is expected that the weather here will be just as severe as the different weather fronts merge.

Our telephone calls this morning revealed that the insurance company is going to have to replace our carpet in our rented house, the toilet leak has been fixed but we need further work done on it and then we received another call from the agency who looks after our other rented property to say that the tenants had phoned to say that their toilet is leaking again despite work being done on it for the same problem about five months ago. It's odd that we are having 'toilet problems' because the first thing you see when you arrive at the reception area in this van park are a heap of toilets being used as pot plants! The old toilets vary in height and shape and they line the path to reception. They are not very attractive despite their flowers!

No choreographer could imitate the dance of delight that the trees are displaying as we watch them through the rain dripping down our van windows. We never got as far as Esperance which was probably just as well as they have received over 100ml of rainfall in just three hours this afternoon.

John had a restless night. I didn't, although he did wake me up when he moved the van in the middle of the night. He had already moved the Ute, dogs within, by this time. We had prepared the van for a quick getaway in case of flooding. We had already moved the van once but were in a low lying area of the park and John was trying to frighten me with talk of getting electrical equipment, such as our van heater, off the floor in case the flooding came up inside the van. He seemed to believe that I would be able to drive the Ute in such an eventuality but having been caught once before in a creek that flooded I already knew the futility of that. I recall thinking that I'd got caught in rising water and by the time that I'd thought that the water was seat high and I'd had trouble opening the car door but having got out I couldn't walk against the water as it was so ferocious and two men had helped me to safety. It happens so fast that you cannot 'think' about it.

So, I had gone to bed and had pulled up the blinds so that John could see out of his rear vision mirror and there was no-one beside us anyway, when I awoke to see lights flashing beside me and as I was half naked I didn't want to sit up! I had gone to bed fully dressed ready for a quick take-off but just couldn't sleep like that so had peeled off this and that until I had felt comfortable. Grabbing the quilt cover around me I hesitantly sat up and saw that we were outside the caravan park toilets and looking behind me confirmed that the Ute was missing so he had already moved that and then I went back to sleep. Apparently John had shifted the van back and forth before he was satisfied with its position less flood prone, which explains the flashing lights of the toilet block.

As we were ready to leave we set off earlier than usual but one of my sons saw a T.V bulletin and phoned me and all I can really recall of the conversation is the word 'Stop'. We were about four kilometres from a roadhouse and we did stop and bought a coffee, saw the headlines in the paper and decided to find somewhere to put the bus. Headlines such as 'State's south-east braced for 'Once in a generation' storm' and words such as 'Defence force on standby as Weather Bureau warns of gale-force winds and torrential rain the like of which has not been seen in decades expected to batter towns from Esperance to Meekatharra' convinced John that we would go no further as we were right in the midst of the area. The most worrying part is that even the weather forecasters did not know what to expect as cyclone Isobel that had crossed the north coast merged with a deep surface trough through eastern Australia. The newspaper quoted 'It has created an explosive development. The combination has effectively given the atmosphere a turbo-charge…' So here we are and the poor dogs have no understanding as to why we have kept them locked in the back of the Ute. Jack thinks it is wonderful weather and wants to play but Callie is quite happy to return to it after the necessary toilet walks. They have hardly been out of the Ute because of the driving wind and rain. Just feeding them became a master performance! I'm pretty well prepared with gun boots (wellies), PVC coat with hood and waterproof trousers but having got all this gear on I have more of a problem getting them off, especially the boots, without flinging water all over our carpet and lounge suite. We have hangers with dripping wet clothes now hanging in our shower. We have also been so cold that I have been wrapped in my winter quilt whilst reading this afternoon. I had thought of having a nice hot shower but I don't know where to put the dripping clothes.

Until this afternoon I was so laid back about it all but the winds have frightened me so I've now had a whiskey and lemonade and am really laid back!

9.20pm

The van is rocking about. The wind is howling and sharp noises alert us as things hit the van. The rain is so loud we that we have to repeat what we say to each other as we cannot hear properly. We heard the six o'clock weather report as it was first up on the news and we found out that some areas of Esperance have lost electricity and some places are flooded. Apologies were made by the news announcer because they were experiencing difficulties and then we lost all radio stations so now we have no idea what is going on elsewhere and feel very cut off. The third time I phoned the caravan park to say we wouldn't make it today the phone was finally answered. Apparently they have lots of room there! Not surprising really because I expect many people got out of caravan parks in Esperance yesterday or this morning. I think I was told that their reception area had got water in it.

After his last walk Jack howled for at least twenty minutes because he didn't want to be back in the Ute. It was irritating, frustrating but more to the point pitiful as he just doesn't understand as he doesn't care about the cold or the wet weather. Callie is quite happy to jump back in as she hates it. Earlier in the afternoon I had thought that the rain and wind had eased but it was just teasing us. After dinner John said he thought it was easing but it returned again with a vengeance. We couldn't get warm no matter what we wore or wrapped ourselves in. I ended up having a hot shower, digging out winter pyjamas and winter socks and together with a thick jumper, thick towelling dressing gown and a winter quilt wrapped around me I have managed to stay warm. John complained that even his nose is cold. We have been jumping up and down to try and get our circulation moving. 'We are helpless against nature' was John's most recent comment as we glanced up from our books and looked at each other when fear overtook us once again. We've both had indigestion tonight as we try to outwardly stay calm but inwardly our stomachs are taught with tension.

I resorted to an expletive tonight and shouted 'Piss off rain' but it didn't make me feel any better. It's John's turn to take the dog out for their final walk tonight, in the dark, in the mud, in howling rain and dodging flying debris. At least he won't have to cope with me returning which always ends up with me hysterically laughing. My back has been so painful for the last few days that I cannot bend properly and have trouble sitting or lying on my back but I cannot stand around all day! So, I get one boot off by using the other foot but then I'm stuck in the doorway trying not to drip water on the carpet in a very small area. I get my coat off and hang it on a hanger almost above my head so I'm now getting wet anyway and John pulls my waterproof trousers down, takes off the other boot and releases that leg from the trousers and I slot that foot into a slipper and then it's the turn of my other leg. I push the trousers under the coat and hang to hang on the bottom of the same hanger and make a quick dash to the shower cubicle to hang them up and then stack my boots near the door amongst his three pairs of saturated shoes. He wore a hat today to try and keep his head dry but it flew away. He found it and that is also hanging in the shower along with another jacket. Also in the shower is a bucket of hand washing and another bucket that we keep all our shower items in when travelling, such as shampoos, nail brush, shower plug, shower cap, my shower gloves (great for a harsh scrub down) and a soap container. You can imagine the chaos when I decided I'd have to have a shower to get warm tonight as I had to empty the shower first! Everything feels wet even if it isn't and sometimes when I think I am dry I find that my jumper has wet sleeves or collar and I hadn't realised and I've now dampened the winter quilt that I was wrapping around myself. A leak in the front of the van has appeared and has soaked John's box of C.D's. I've been repairing the box tonight. John's past reading any more of Bill Clinton's autobiography and I'm over reading about Keith Richard and Mick Jagger's early career but neither of us feels safe enough to get into bed. Both books contain so many names that our heads are spinning. The windows sound like they are going to cave in as I write so the storm seems to be getting worse. John had just dozed off on the settee but the noise woke him instantly. I think that by the time we get settled down on a normal sunny day again we are going to feel the full force of our tension. We will really feel exhausted, as at the moment we are living on adrenalin. The flight or fight syndrome, but we cannot fight and it is the worst type of stress. We were up very early this morning despite a very late night and it seems it will be the same tonight.

We wonder what we will face if we get to Esperance tomorrow but right at the moment I could think of nothing better than helping someone clean up their home from the flooding because it would use up some of my pent up energy and feeling of helplessness. Now I can't get up as my back's ceased up. 'John, help!'

5th January 2007

My bed got wet last night through a gap in the window. I'm trying to dry quilts and sheets out in our 'hot' cupboard. John later finds that the step inside the van is saturated and as it is carpeted he works out an ingenious way of 'sweeping' the water out with a brush and I notice that he is using the back of the brush and pressure. I find some public toilets with paper towels and we take some of them and try and soak up the rest and put cardboard on top. Local people are coming and dumping their rubbish in the bins here by our bus and there is now rubbish everywhere and giant ants are proliferating and I'm wondering whether rats will be the next to arrive.

We're stuck as the road is closed between Ravensthorpe and Esperance. The Oldfield Bridge has collapsed behind us and another towards Esperance is going to be checked by engineers apparently. We hear talk of its possible collapse if vehicles go over it. We see cars going down the road ignoring the signs and returning. The petrol station by us does not sell milk, or bread. The guy that runs it was going to try and get through to Esperance to get some today but has found out he can't, not even on the dirt roads using his four wheel drive vehicle. We believe that he's getting some information but he's not very communicative so we can't find out anything through him.

We have a semi trailer (with forty wheels) near us who has tankers full of white wine so it has been suggested that we find a hose and connect it so that we can all get 'pissed'. Another couple have their coach and trailer behind us and they too have been on the road since May. He used his HF radio to get through to my son Kevin to tell him we are safe but it starts with a recorded message whilst the phone tries to connect to the satellite signal as the message is being played. Kevin, thinking it was a hoax call put the phone down cutting off the call. A couple of minutes later he tried again for me and the line was so bad that Kevin thought that the guy had said 'brother' and retorted 'What's my brother's name?' I got on the phone and told him that we are safe but have neither communication nor electricity and that we are marooned and he suddenly realised that it was a serious call and thanked the guy who had helped us. We believe that we will be stuck here for three to four days whilst they repair the bridge!

Esperance has now received 150ml of rain water and the town is flooded and people were evacuated from camp sites last night so we're probably better off here. The dogs don't think so as they are soaked and miserable and are now outside as they are so fed up with being trapped in the Ute. We have a couple of channels on the radio now so at least we can hear that Australia has won the Ashes test!

We stop anyone who passes by in a vehicle in the hope that they have some news of what is happening. Two men turn up who have arrived via dirt roads in a four wheel drive from a mine that they work at. We see the men drinking with the owner of the garage and they get noisier as the evening goes on and we settle down for another night wondering what the morning will bring.

The morning brings helicopters flying overhead and we are not sure if they are filming for the T.V news or if they are connected to government agencies and whether we might get some relief drops of milk, bread or some communication. Later a plane flies very low overhead and John runs outside to wave and says he feels like we are marooned on an island and are cut of from civilisation. The couple who have a coach have a small car which they tow in a trailer and the guy goes back and forth to check the bridges and we hear from him that it is the first bridge that is unsafe and not the second as we thought and that there is also a huge fallen tree blocking the bridge. The only part of the bridge that is not covered is the side where the foundations appear to have been washed away. I make up some skimmed milk out of a packet that I had bought before we set off, for emergencies such as this. We still have a little bread and bottled water and feel lucky. However we are getting low on dog food so it's a good thing they like rice and pasta!

Around lunchtime a road vehicle turns up and I am ecstatic because it had to have got here from Esperance. A little while later a vehicle drives up and a road worker at last gives us some information. He tells us that they are cutting up the tree to get it off the bridge so that the road will be open but he does not seem to know if heavy vehicles can go over it. We decide to pack up and chance it because there is still no electricity in the area and no phones will work. We have seen so many people driving up to the public pay phone which is dead.

The truck driver and the other couple are not so sure that we are doing the right thing. The truck driver says that he will follow us but makes no move so we presume that they are all waiting to see if we return before trying themselves. When we drove up to the bridge the guys cutting up the tree look a bit shocked but we sail over the bridge waving to them. We haven't actually been given the go ahead to go over it. We have just over one hundred kilometres to get to Esperance and we cannot get there fast enough. We see rows and rows of tall, spindly trees uprooted by the wind. Further along we see huge fir trees lying on the ground with their huge root balls facing adjacent to the road and an elderly guy trying to cut one up with a chain saw. If he's going to chop them all up and remove the wood he will be working until next year to complete the work. We suddenly hit a road block and veer around it and I look back and see a huge 'Road Closed' sign. John keeps talking to me over the two-way radio, pointing out the flooded fields and the second bridge and flooded roads. All I can think of is getting to a hospital as I am feeling so ill.

Chapter 2

Esperance

We arrived at the van park and parked the vehicle and John took me straight to hospital as I had such severe back and stomach pains and had been self-medicating myself whilst we had been marooned and nothing I took had worked on top of which I hadn't been to the loo for about eight days because my back ache is making me so tense! I am booked in for a battery of tests but am told I can go home until Monday and to only eat a very light diet such as soup. The doctor mentions my pancreas whereas I think I have the ulcers back and soft tissue damage in my back from falling down the stairs twice so we are at odds. I find his questions odd and I don't think we communicate very well and it is because I am seeing two of him as my vision is blurred and I am having difficulty in following his directions. He asks me to tell him what has happened from the present day going backwards and I am totally unable to do so – all I want is a something to knock me out such as morphine! It's like when a dentist asks you questions when you have a mouth full of instruments! I ask the doctor what date it is and what day as I have no idea anymore and he keeps asking me when I arrived in Esperance and I keep telling him 'Just now. I've just arrived. I've been marooned'. He asks me where but I cannot recall and even if I could I wouldn't have been able to pronounce the name, just as a local in this caravan park told me today that she can never say it either. I've already told him that I had duodenal ulcers and had a second test before leaving home to ensure they had gone and then he asks me if I've ever had a camera put down my throat and I look at him aghast wondering whether he is really a doctor or a cleaner. How does he think they found the ulcers?

We get back to the park at around tea time and I stagger around trying to get the inside set up whilst John does outside and feeds the dogs who are so delighted to get here where it is dry and where they can lie on grass instead of wet mud. The caravan park got its electricity back on last night. We see some T.V news and are horrified at the sight of what was a bridge that we had gone over just prior to stopping. Half or more of the bridge is missing including the surrounding earth. Also forty metres of the road has gone and this is the main highway! One report said that it could take months to get the bridge rebuilt. To get to Albany now you would have to go inland to Kalgoorlie (369ks) and turn left to Merredin (295ks) and then try to cut down secondary roads to Albany (about 462ks) or go through Merredin and on to Perth and down the highway to Albany from that direction (about 669ks).

This morning we phoned my kids and our friends who we were supposed to be catching up with to tell them the road is closed and they are presently at Wave Rock which we did not go to, mainly because it would have meant a four hundred round journey with the two dogs and we would have had to have done it in a day. It is an amazing feature but we tossed the idea around and thought it would have been just too much for Jack. However, if you are in the area, make the trip. If we had gone there, we wouldn't have been able to get here to Esperance and we would have regretted that more so now I'm glad we skipped it.

We are not sure now how long we are going to be here. I do recall the doctor repeating the fact that they are only a country hospital which I presume means that they offer limited services but as we cannot go backwards as the road is closed and the desert is in front of us we have little choice but to rely on this hospital for whatever services can be offered.

We are not so sure that we are going to stay in the caravan park though and after the hospital tomorrow we are going to look at other parks. The amenities block is limited as is the hot water in the showers and there is only one washing machine working with cold water fill only. We also cannot empty our black water tank which is now becoming a necessity. There are many residents here and everyone is so friendly and we have a large site so we won't move unless we are impressed with another park but we have to deal with our black water so will have to pack up anyway.

I also phoned my friend in Victoria today and she was telling me about the terrible bush fires there and how even Port Fairy on the coast had been affected which is the very place we wish to get to, to complete our trip around the circumference of Australia on ordinary roads. There are places we cannot get to in our two wheel drive vehicle which includes the far northern section of Australia and in particular, Cape York.

We've had a very quiet day today trying to get the washing done in the one machine and we actually have a sheet and a pillowcase that have mould growing on them so I have a huge bucket of washing soaking which will have to be done tomorrow. I had had to add *items that have been through the washing machine and have come out just as dirty. How I rely on hot water and good washing facilities and take them for granted! The joys of being on the road!

I cannot recall what happened yesterday other than the fact that we did a huge grocery shop and spent the evening swatting flying ants in the van (that's what they looked like anyway). Every time we thought we had got rid of them more would appear on the sink, in the sink, in the kettle, on the ceiling, tables, and chairs and on us. Oh yes and we've decided to stay here having seen a couple of other parks because we have so much space here and because everyone is so very friendly.

Today John dropped me off at the hospital and I'm lying on the bed with this thick-set, middle-aged, swarthy looking man gliding whatever it is they glide over my abdomen, whilst he stared at his screen as though my insides are the most fascinating T.V program that he has seen in years and I ask him questions but he doesn't seem to have the ability to say very much except 'Breathe in, breathe out. Breathe in, breath out'. At one point he said 'Breathe in' and

I mouthed 'I am' because he had forgotten to tell me to 'breathe out' and his face crumpled up with laughter. He hadn't had so much fun in years.

'Oh that happens sometimes' he said chuckling away. 'Okay, now breathe in.'

'I still am!' I glared at him.

At the end I asked him if there was anything wrong with my pancreas. 'Not as far as I can see'.

'There's nothing wrong with my stomach is there' I stated.

'Oh, I don't know. These will go to and be checked. There's not much of you.'

I made the mistake of telling John that he had said 'There's not much of you' when he picked me up.

'What have you got left?' he asked. 'I know you've got a heart and lungs. You've got that pancreas and liver and kidneys.'

'Yeah and a bladder and I've got that damned bowel too'.

'You're streamlined for speed' he said.

'Pardon'

'Like a racing car, stripped down for speed'.

That made me laugh taking into account my present condition. Just driving into town and back had left me in agony! Actually I can walk and I'd had enough of the van by this evening so instead of giving the dogs their dinner we took them to the beach. Even though it was already half an hour after their normal dinner time they didn't seem to mind. Actually Callie ran along the beach and Jack, John and I walked along the seafront promenade. The grass banks have given way in the storm and pipes are exposed and some broken and it is very difficult to get down onto the beach but it didn't stop Callie who had a ball playing on her own. It was really beautiful despite being battered.

The local council is already hard at work bringing in tons of sand to replace the sand that has been washed away. Apparently a team of scientific experts have judged a beach called Lucky Bay near Esperance as the whitest beach in Australia. Tallebudgera Beach which is just down the road from our house at the Gold Coast came second!

The competition was sparked by friendly rivalry and a claim that Hyams Beach in New South Wales had the whitest sand. Thus it was that in my first tome called 'Should I tour Australia' I told you a fib as I quoted Hyams Beach in that and it certainly was startlingly white but it came in fifth. Anyway, if you get one of these leaflets here telling you how they test it and judge it, I have to warn you that first they spelt Tallebudgera incorrectly, secondly that they said it was near the Gold Coast and it's 'at' rather than 'near' the Gold Coast and thirdly there was the following quote which is absolutely ridiculous as far as Tallebudgera is concerned. 'The fact that the winning beaches are pretty remote from major population centres would have worked in their favour to stay pristine and white'. This was apparently stated by a senior research officer with the Department of Agriculture and Food in Western Australia. He obviously hasn't travelled to the vastly overpopulated Gold Coast! As the sand samples had to be the beach rather than distant sand dunes I would guess that we have several hundred thousand people who have constant access to that beach! He must be too busy inspecting quartz and coral based sand (all the contenders apparently in this competition gave samples of quartz based sand) to know his Australian geography.

When we reached the pier we put the dogs in the car and went to watch the fishermen and a young boy called out to me, telling me to go and look at the playful sea lion. What a show this wild sea lion put on. It was outstanding and wonderful. He loved the attention and no-one was feeding it or anything. It played hide and seek and would then roll on one side and look at us and then submerge and keep still and suddenly pop its nose out and duck again. It swam back and forth in various ways as though showing off.

So, other than seeing the town and the shops and finding a bakery that serves superb chocolate éclairs and coffee we have really only seen the seafront and pier so far. Before leaving for the beach I asked the park owner where the nearest shop was and was asked what I needed, followed by an immediate offer for one of the men to be organised to drive me there because of my back! That is what I mean about them being friendly here. I reminded her that I had John here to drive me around but I was quite stunned by the offer. We are about seven kilometres out of town and the nearest shops are at a place called **Pink Lake** and there is indeed a pink lake here. Actually, there are several but I'm not sure if that is because of the flooding.

Oh yes, I remember what we did yesterday other than shopping. We went to see **Bandy Creek Harbour** where the fishing boats come in and I bought some fresh fish for dinner as I was getting sick of tomato soup which is all I had been able to stomach. (It wasn't until I was reading The Weekend Australian march 31-April 1, 2007 that I read that nobody should have been eating the fish from around Christmas onwards when thousands of birds started falling from the sky. It took three months for the W.A. government to offer free blood tests for residents and for the rainwater tanks, soil samples and seabed to be tested and a multi-million dollar export industry has been forced to stop shipping lead carbonate through the Esperance port. Marine sediment readings in one area have shown lead readings seventy-two times higher and nickel levels more than one hundred and fifty times higher than recommended levels. The community has been told not to eat any local seafood and as there are high lead and nickel levels found in rain water tanks they are not to drink the water from tanks either. I couldn't have chosen a worse dinner considering my stomach problems.)

Anyway, back to the harbour - a footbridge collapsed in the storm and tons of mud and silt poured into the harbour (and is still pouring in) along with trees. Boats had got stuck on the newly formed sand banks and a viewing platform collapsed with people on it but luckily no-one was hurt. The harbour is ruined and the commercial fishermen are going to be so badly affected. On our way back home we saw a large fire which seemed incongruous as it appeared to be a grass fire. Apparently about 300 hectares of land was destroyed and it was caused by a power line.

The area from Esperance to Ravensthorpe and surrounding districts have been classified as a 'Natural disaster zone' now so there is financial assistance for personal hardship, loan interest subsidies, assistance for farmers along with money from the State Government for road repairs. No-one yet knows how many sheep were lost but apparently it is possibly around 10,000

I bought a Barbara Taylor Bradford hardback book today for three dollars from the camping shop. That's cheaper than the second hand book store. This business of my saying that you should equate sterling to dollars as I've mentioned in the past, comes from our average cost of living when we lived and worked in England for nine months, about nine years ago. Remember when reading this in the future, rates of exchange and the cost of living have drastically changed, so my following comments would not necessarily apply now regarding Australia v UK.

Despite John being a highly qualified accountant he was not employable in the major cities as he was too old, being over sixty one years of age, according to the specialist agencies! So we lived and worked in Devon and the wages were lousy but the vegetables were cheap and certainly the rental market prices were so much cheaper than London that it's not worth comparing. We did manage to secure a cheap rental, that being a three bedroom furnished flat (unit to us Aussies) with stunning views over a harbour for one hundred pounds a week, plus rates (yes I know that's unheard of in Australia, paying for the rates on rental properties and it was a shock to us too), plus electricity when it came to the heating. The meter ate up pound coins at such a rate that we purchased a gas fire heater. We were lucky to get a three bedroom flat for that price and the position was a huge bonus. During our stay I kept a record of everything we spent on food (I even kept the dockets from the supermarkets) and as I was working in an Estate Agents (Real Estate office to us), I was well aware of the cost of housing, interest rates and rental prices. Housing and petrol were dearer but cars, electrical goods and many foods were cheaper and when I worked it all out after returning home I realised that with the abysmal wages we were earning because we were not in a major city, we might just as well have read the pound sterling symbol as an Australian dollar symbol.

So, although people who sell their terrace homes in the U.K and emigrate here find that they can buy an enormous detached house, a couple of cars and a boat out of the proceeds and still have money to spare, they soon find that the wages are lower in comparison to sterling and they end up asset rich in Australia and cash poor. However, if they wish to return to the U.K they often find themselves in trouble because as house prices are usually rising simultaneously, converting their Australian dollars back to sterling can be a shock and they can find that the terrace home they used to live in is suddenly out of the question as they don't have enough money! So when I talk of wages of $100,000 per annum being good here, in sterling it is about forty odd grand. But when you look at that in terms of housing, food and other living costs the same amount in pounds sterling is going to buy you about the same overall per annum in the U.K. It's great for young people who go to London and live in a youth hostel and save a lot of money and then come back home here with it though.

As I can't sit down, I'm either standing or walking most of the time and I'm going to get fit and lose some flab whether I like it or not! I spent most of the afternoon walking around town and found some more bargains! John took the dogs to the beach and did some 'running repairs' to the motor home windows and blinds. I've also booked a visit to a sports masseuse/rehabilitation practitioner tomorrow.

We both enjoyed looking at the old buildings sited alongside the Information Centre in town where we went into the art galleries, craft shops and gift shops.

We had a running battle with ants this morning. They had discovered my crystallised ginger on the lounge table on one side of the van and were all around the sink on the other side of the van. I attacked the sink problem from the outside with outdoor surface spray as they were running up the connector hosepipe. We seem to have won the battle and I told John that I've had enough of fighting infestations of locusts, flying ants and now normal ants all within the last couple of weeks! No more, enough is enough.

John went out this morning to drive along the coast as far as he could. Unfortunately the road has been closed along the forty kilometre scenic drive but he thoroughly enjoyed his trip and said on his return that he was 'beached out'.

This afternoon he dropped me at the massage therapist where I found out that my back is injured, most likely from when I fell down the van steps and that is affecting my lower left back and I was my muscles were so tight that it was quite painful having the work done on them. My right shoulder are and upper back were also bad which is probably because when I do sit down I do so in a very awkward fashion. I got stretched and pulled and twisted and it was great! With a letter in hand from the masseuse, I visit the doctor tomorrow.

Meanwhile John had gone to the Museum, mainly to see the sky lab bits and pieces that fell on Esperance. Actually, they weren't all 'bits' as the collection included a tank and big chunks of metal. He said that there was a fair bit to see at the Museum and he could have stayed much longer but had to return to pick me up.

We went back to the pier and this time the sea lion was basking on the beach but he was certainly keeping an eye on us. We treated ourselves to hot chocolate pudding with hot chocolate sauce, a mound of ice cream and another mound of fresh cream from the van on the sea front. It was sublime. I couldn't work in that van because I'd want one every day!

Yesterday, still dreaming of chocolate pudding, we decided to try my back out and John took me to some of the beaches near town that he had seen before. We looked at **West Beach** and **Blue Haven Beach** and went down onto **Salmon Beach**. All are different and all are stunning. West Beach is large and there are steps down onto it as there are at Blue Haven Beach which is a much smaller beach. Salmon Beach was a huge bay and the waves were turbulent. It didn't stop the dogs though who had a great time until Callie got picked up by a wave, tossed into Jack who went under and then crashed her onto the sand under the water! Callie had been swimming out for a stick that John was throwing to her and he wasn't throwing it very far out so she was basically chasing the waves in and was standing on the sand most of the time until this rogue wave came in. Jack came up to me looking completely dazed and seemed to have a problem with a front leg last night. Callie was funny because she still looked for the stick and would pick it up and drop it immediately as if she thought it had caused the problem. I believe I read somewhere that dogs have a short-term memory of about four minutes and she carried on like this for about that length of time and then all of a sudden she wanted John to play with her again!

One of the things I like about Esperance is that they seem to be dog-friendly here and when we saw other beaches they were also allowed on them, on leashes. Salmon Beach was a designated dog beach so that they could run freely.

Looking out to the many islands off the coast along the way we could see the heat haze so photographs would not have come out too well but I did get a shot of a couple of larger islands nearer to the beach. It suddenly heated up yesterday and today is very hot.

John has gone to the Cape Le Grand National Park today. I decided last night that if I wait until I can get there we will be here for weeks as the short trip we did yesterday left me in so much pain and I had trouble eating again because of back and stomach pain. We received a text message from our friends who are already in South Australia and it helped me to make this decision because I couldn't stop thinking about how far we still have to go and I want to get across that desert. Although it's not called a desert but the Nullarbor Plain, to me it's the same thing. I phoned them this morning and they told us that we could get across it in three very full days but with Jack that will not be possible.

Oh no, another power cut and on a day when it's due to be about 40C and it feels that way now. I have just made the stuffing for a large chicken that I'm due to cook in a high-dome frying pan this afternoon and as it's lunchtime now I hope it gets sorted out quickly. I also hope it's not due to a fire again because the fire brigade were very worried about people going into the National Park today. I'm starting to drip already without the air conditioner on so I'm off to hose the dogs and go to the pool.

Cape Le Grand National Park

John reckons that the first part of the journey would have bored me rigid and that although he only had to go about sixty kilometres the road seemed endless. There is a small fee to enter this National Park and he paid the pensioner rate of five dollars per car. The first beach that he came to was Le Grand Beach which stretched off into the distance and it was a superb beach for children as the water was calm and very clear, in fact it was sparkling.

On the way to Hellfire Bay he came to Frenchman's Peak which he could have climbed if he had had a couple of hours to spare and it hadn't been so hot. A sign warns that it is two hours of 'hard' walking. Hellfire Bay was another beautiful but smaller beach with wonderful huge rocks and boulders around and people were climbing over the rocks and fishing. He walked over the rocks and around the corner to take a photo of Little Hellfire Bay.

Thistle Cove came next and instead of taking the shorter route to get to the beach, he climbed over the rocks taking many photographs along the way. He returned to this bay later which I will mention in a minute.

Lucky Bay, with the whitest sand in Australia, was the last bay that he went to and he said that he was disappointed as it had so much seaweed on the beach and so many people were there. He believes that the seaweed was brought in by the storm. (When I saw the photographs I thought it was stunning!)

He decided that he would much rather return to Thistle Cove for his lunch and as the beach was only minutes away he felt it worth back-tracking. Apparently there was a whale carcass on the beach or in the water somewhere there because there was a notice warning people not to swim as it was attracting a lot of sharks. However, he ignored the warnings as he could not resist the temptation to have a swim at this glorious bay. It could have been the last I saw of him! He found out afterwards that the carcass was up at the other end of the beach. He said it was such an idyllic beach and there was nobody else there (hardly surprising) so it was a stunning place to eat his lunch after his swim.

So I've been 'photo travelling' and whilst he was doing all this I got a lot of jobs done and hardly sat down and thus did not have back ache all day, nor stomach ache. I also enjoyed going in the pool several times. My back is hurting now because I've been downloading the photos and writing this so I'm off so toodle-oo.

Chapter 3

THE NULLARBOR PLAIN

According to our leaflet 'The Nullarbor Plain is one of most unique tracts of unspoilt wilderness on the face of this planet' and crossing it is one of the world's great road journeys. The name is derived from the Latin 'nullus arbor' which means 'no tree'. It has an average rainfall of 20cm! Is that right? Well, having done it once It's enough for me and I won't be doing it again!

It's over twelve hundred kilometres since I last wrote to you but I was just too tired to write during the journey. Our first day was slow because we had to drive a couple of hundred kilometres just to get to **Norseman** and when we got there we had to get a key for the dump point from the Information Centre (which was free for us as we are CMCA members) to get rid of our black water waste. What a relief it was to clean out that tank as it was full to near overflowing! We also had to go back and get a key for the toilets and I seemed to spend most of my time either collecting keys or returning them.

A little girl approached and her mother admonished here and called her back. She and her husband were having a 'domestic' and he seemed fed up with problems with his vehicle and was getting verbally more irate with some colourful language. Mum was very pregnant and I began to wonder if that was the only reason she was still with him! Eventually she had to sit in the car whilst he used a screwdriver under the bonnet and whatever he did he was successful and they were on their way. Waiting for John I became inordinately inquisitive about this family as their vehicle seemed to be crammed with stuff.

We didn't much like the look of Norseman so decided not to stay the night there but get on the road and begin the arduous journey and at first it did not seem so bad. We stopped just after the **Fraser Range Station** and there was plenty of room and no-one else was there. (We had read that we would never be alone but this was not the case for us as we camped alone for three nights.) There were a lot of huge black ants around which the dogs didn't like and we were none too happy when we found small ants in our food cupboard! The joys of travelling! John said that we should be sitting outside with a glass of wine but whenever we do in the evening we get bitten by mosquitoes! We were parked right beside a concrete table with concrete benches and they were off the ground on a concrete slab and Jack found that a great place to sleep but both of them got into the Ute without us suggesting it in the morning and we believe it was because of the ants.

One bonus of being there was the view of the stars and I stood outside with John and it was an awesome sight. For the first time in my life I saw the 'Milky Way' very clearly and I now know why it is so named. I saw a satellite but John was trying to find a comet that we should have been able to see but failed to find. There were just so many stars! We can see them elsewhere of course but I had been told that I must look at them when crossing the Nullarbor because the air is so clear.

2nd Night - Free Camped

We had quite a few trees around us and when we were leaving the following morning I was directing John around the trees when I felt a large ant on my leg inside my jeans. I pulled my trousers down just as a car towing a caravan passed and they looked at me and smiled! I never did get rid of it and it bit me all up my leg as I was driving.

The road to Balladonia was really pretty and just after where we had camped I saw a camping spot by a lake. I wouldn't have wanted to have parked there with the dogs because the water was a pinky colour and I'm not sure it would have been good for them to have drunk any of it, which no doubt they would have done but it would have been a pleasant place to camp without them. I'm trusting that there weren't too many mosquitoes there of course! Another stone hit my windscreen and I'm glad I haven't bothered to get it repaired yet as I now have three nasty chips in it. John had a bird fly into the front of the bus and kill itself.

We saw a sign for a sheep station which had a caravan park and the sign invited us to 'stop for a cuppa'. There were still trees around although they were getting smaller in places. Some of the soil was a pretty pink/red colour and there was some of a red/brown mixture, the trees were so green and these colours set against the pale grey and bright green shrubs and the clear blue sky provided wonderful palette of colours. The journey was not flat either with quite a few hills around. We saw signs for emergency telephones which was reassuring because only satellite phones get any signals across the Nullarbor and we haven't got one.

When we got to **Balladonia** we bought a coffee and went to sit outside – right next to the couple I had been interested in the day before. I started talking to the guy and he told me that he had broken down eighty kilometres past Balladonia, jumped down from his vehicle and a wire went into his foot. A truck driver stopped after several cars had passed them without stopping. He said that his wife was also in labour and I asked him where they had been aiming for and he said Melbourne! She told me that she is eight and a half months pregnant and they had their little girl, who seemed to be about two and a half to three years old as well. I asked where they had come from and he told me Kalgoorlie (inland from Norseman) and that he had sold his vehicle and the people at the road house had looked after them and had arranged for his trailer to be towed to Kalgoorlie. When I asked why there he told me that they were waiting for a plane which was coming to collect them and take them both to the Kalgoorlie hospital as it seemed that the baby was coming early as well as the fact that he was limping badly. I just looked at him and said 'You two are a catastrophe' and he burst out laughing. He said that he might stay a while at Kalgoorlie because a guy driving an ice-cream van there was earning seventy thousand a year! They were much happier and relaxed.

The Eyre Highway between Balladonia and **Caiguna** has the longest straight stretch of road in Australia(approximately 147 alms) and on the very flattest part I saw three vehicles driving towards me with their headlights on. Considering that you can see a vehicle about ten kilometres away and apparently at night about forty kilometres away it seemed ridiculous. The sun sparkled like flashing lights off the windscreens as it was and I kept having to put my sun glasses back on so every time I saw another car with their lights on I flashed them. The drivers all waved their thanks, probably believing that a speed trap was ahead! Either that or they were very friendly. Whatever, it amused me and made me giggle to have so many drivers wave to me!

The road seemed endless after Caiguna with no trees to look at, only the odd patch of dry grass and scrubby shrub. On a trip like this you read every sign, whatever it says but one which I wasn't expecting when we left Caiguna was 'Central West Time Zone. Advance Clocks 45 Minutes'. Not much point really because time doesn't matter to us here and the time zone will probably change anyway when we get into South Australia. Another sign warned us to watch out for Emus, Kangaroos and Camels.

Our second night was spent past the **Cocklebiddy** Motel at another off-road site. This time we got inundated with moths and did not see many ants in the van so I wondered if they had gone and wondered what they thought when they got to the ground and wondered where the heck they were! As they run along a scent trail they must be running around in circles trying to find it! I cooked all the fruit and vegetables that evening prior to reaching the Border Village quarantine station the following day. I now had a huge pile of mashed potato in one bowl, another full of onion, carrot, celery, sprouts and any other vegetable that was left. I also had another bowl full of stewed Pink Lady apples along with two punnets of fresh blueberries and having cooked it I found a kiwi fruit in the back of the fridge so sliced that up and mixed it in. Exhausted when I went to bed I didn't wake up until 9.30am. This was the second morning I had awoken at that time so I must be finding the driving tiring. We were looking forward to actually crossing the Western Australia/South Australia border. It has taken us five months to get around Western Australia!

We were also looking forward to reaching the Great Australian Bight which is believed to be the longest stretch of sea cliffs in the world stretching 1160km. The dogs will just be happy to get to civilisation as they don't seem to be happy staying in the bush. Jack barks every so often as though he is warning whatever he imagines could be 'out there'. It's not a normal bark but a half-hearted sort of bark so we just reassure him and he relaxes. It was extremely cold last night so Callie wouldn't have been too happy as she hates the cold.

As the journey goes on and on and on I am so pleased I purchased a new C.D player before leaving because when the track changes it wakes me up. I suddenly saw an eagle. It flew in front of me, landed on a scrubby tree branch and watched me as I drove slowly past. I am driving in front most of the time now because I can't see the road-trains coming when I am behind John and their sudden passing makes me jittery. John, of course, can see over the top of me. However, I drive too fast all the time so every so often when I can no longer see him I am forced to slow down and wait for him. It was during one of these moments that I spotted the pretty, pink lake and that I saw the eagle so it has its advantages.

I was listening to Paul Simon singing 'Homeward Bound' and shouted with glee 'We are, we are'! I am still seeing water across the road ahead of me and yesterday I was having mirages about off road parking signs where we could pull over for a rest! We stopped at the **Madura** Hotel as we were looking for gas for the van and we decided to buy a coffee. It cost four dollars each, we had to make it ourselves in a paper cup and the carton milk tasted as though it had gone off. It was so foul that I gave it back to the attendant!

We again stopped, this time at **Mundrabilla** Roadhouse for lunch. We had seen heaps of traffic going the other way including caravans and motor homes but we had hardly had any traffic on our side of the road for the entire trip. However, when I did want to overtake the mirage effect on the road looked like the road was dipping, as though there was a dip and then a hill ahead and I felt that it was unsafe to overtake as I couldn't see whether anyone was coming the other way or not. Every time I chanced it, it turned out that the road was absolutely clear and flat! It was truly weird and rather unnerving.

Eucla, which is just before the border is a funny sort of place. It's quite pretty but I missed the turn off to the petrol station and so did the guy in front of me who stopped and asked the way. I had led John on a round - about route but we got there in the end.

3rd Day - En Route - Coffee Break

At last we got to the WA/SA **Border Village** and there was a sign telling us that we didn't need to stop there and that we would go through quarantine at Ceduna. All that cooking last night!

Anyway, I took photos of the border crossing, mainly because the sun had magically disappeared and it was cloudy all of a sudden. Before the Nullarbor Hotel/Motel we saw a sign for **The Great Australian Bight Marine Park** so we went off road to have a look at the sea. We stopped near the edge of some cliffs where a couple of other small vans had pulled up for the night but we were concerned about staying there because of the dogs. If Callie got off her lead she would take a leap right over the edge of the cliffs, or slip down because there were warnings about how unsafe it was near the edge. We drove back towards the road and set up camp away from the other campers and those cliffs. However the sea and cliffs were a wonderful sight as they are so steep and majestic.

I heated up some of the potato and vegetables in a covered microwave dish for dinner (John put the generator on so that I could use the microwave) and topping it with fried eggs for dinner. We followed that with stewed fruit and glasses of water as we both felt dehydrated. We were bloated after all that food.

On this our third night we had giant, flying cockroaches along with the moths again. I was sitting outside and wondered what was on my leg and it wasn't until I saw one on the screen door that I decided to have a look. We were getting worried about our water level for washing up and showers – in fact we were desperate for long hot showers. We had continually asked if we could get some water when buying petrol but had been told we couldn't have any which is contrary to what we had read. We realised we should have paid for a shower because you can do that and the prices vary from roadhouse to roadhouse. We had looked at a caravan park at a roadhouse but even if you paid to stay there, only electricity was supplied (by a very loud generator which would drive you nuts) but there was no water connection and it was so very bleak. At least where we were it was not bleak and we could hear the sea crashing against those cliffs as we drifted off to sleep.

There are so many photo opportunities between the Border Village and Nullarbor that we started to skip them because we really wanted to get to the end of this trip by the end of this, our fourth day. What with petrol stops, dog stops, coffee and lunch breaks, camera stops and the time I had to stop because my front right headlight and frame had completely fallen out and was hanging by the wires, the time was passing all too quickly. Just before Nullarbor we hit an extra large road train which was taking up the whole road. Actually there were two of them and they were accompanied by vehicles with flashing lights and policemen on motorbikes. We were longing for a coffee as we hadn't had one all morning and here we were not being able to go more than eighty kilometres an hour and sometimes much less. It was painful and everybody coming the other way had to get right off the road. At last we saw a sign indicating that we had only five kilometres to go and saying that 'Drowsy Drivers Die'. At this rate we would fall asleep. Another sign said 'Nullarbor Plain Western End of Treeless Plain'.

The road trains stopped at **Nullarbor** so we thought that we would have the chance to get in front of them. John found out that the gas pump wouldn't work properly. I ran into the toilet with the dog's water container and their small bowl and painfully slowly I managed to fill up the container by using the sink tap. It was one of those taps that you press and hold and when you let go it turns off so I had to hold it all the time. Dogs watered, I got them out for a 'pee' walk, got them back in again and went back to the loo so that I could have one too. Then I saw the policemen coming out of the roadhouse and rushed up to one of them and asked if they were leaving. They were and John had just found out the same fact. We ran to our vehicles and got out only just in time so that we were ahead of them.

Further down the road John saw a sign for "Head of Bight' and got on the radio and said that was really couldn't go past it as we'd probably never be back again. I screamed back 'I can (go past it). We'll end up behind that road train again.' My prayers were answered as the road was closed!! Then my headlight fell off again and this time we had to do sturdier urgent repairs, all the time praying that the road train would not catch us up. We drove into the **Yalata Mission** but it appeared closed and they don't sell fuel or anything. I believe you can sometimes buy some Aboriginal art but it looked very deserted to us. John had lost interest immediately as he was looking for gas.

I know my headlight still works because I flashed the next vehicle to have its headlights on and the driver waved to me! Actually, it's odd how many people do not check their lights because we saw so many vehicles with only one headlight working. I thought it was illegal to have headlights on during the day unless visibility warrants their use.

I asked John if he was happy to go on to Nundroo Roadhouse without a break and he retorted 'Let's just get somewhere instead of nowhere'. I took a couple of photos over my steering wheel of what the endless road looked like for something to do.

We had to stop at **Nundroo** as we both needed fuel. I had organised the dogs and had tied them up in the shade whilst John had filled the bus tank with gas but when we went inside and he tried to pay, the elderly gentleman behind the counter had trouble with the bankcard transaction. I ended up offering mine and this time he managed but he was so slow and didn't seem to know what digits to press on his till. It was quite a sophisticated piece of machinery which put orders straight through to the kitchen but even when someone paid in cash he was peering at the keys and then at the screen and was telling it to stop making noises!

There was a thick set man who appeared to be standing to one side and I thought he'd ordered something and by the time our bank card transaction went through there was a long queue and some people had ice creams in their hands which would have started to melt. We were going to order lunch but I told John to wait and just pay for the gas and move the bus out of the way which he did. I went to the back of the queue as I wanted to ask what fillings were available for a sandwich. We get to the front and I order lunch, plus two flat white coffees and pass my bank card over. This time things went a bit smoother except for the till getting scolded again. The thick set man then ordered something and I thought 'Good grief, he's patient, he must have been waiting all that time!' The gentleman behind the counter, having put the cash in the till, said he would go and get whatever it was himself as it would be quicker and then proceeded to serve other people. This went on and on and I had no idea what this guy was waiting for and grimaced and grinned at him in sympathy. That was obviously a grave mistake as I was to find out.

Whilst all this had been going on, John had been and filled up my car with petrol and I had to pay the bill for this too now. However, when I approached the counter there was this sudden roar from behind and a string of verbal abuse. 'Are you going to use that thing again? You town people are all the same with your bank card things. Don't you have any patience? Can't you let other people get served?' I told him that I had done just that by going to the back of the queue. Then I reminded the still very gentle man behind the counter that this man was waiting for something and it was obvious by his face that he had completely forgotten.

I went into the dining room and gave up paying for the fuel for the moment. When his wife brought our food I told her that we'd also ordered coffees and she said 'My husband will get those for you'.

I replied 'Are you sure? He's very busy'.

She looked in the shop and he was nowhere in sight. He suddenly appeared and asked me where his customer had gone but I didn't have a clue. His wife asked me if I wanted the coffee made with all milk and said I suppose so and then I told her that the lettuce I'd ordered wasn't in the sandwich and she replied that she didn't even know we were eating in the dining room and immediately returned with the correct sandwich on a plate.

Eventually the two men found each other and disappeared outside and the guy had apparently paid for a slab (case) of beer which must have been stored in an outbuilding or something. By this time I had completely gone off food but managed to swallow half of my sandwich and John finished the rest for me. To cap it off, as we left I saw a sign which said 'Under New Management' (which didn't surprise me at all) and 'Free coffee for drivers'. They did not bother to tell us that.

Incidentally, there is another thing that is not promoted very much and that is the fact that you can get two cents off per litre at several petrol stations if you ask for a leaflet. When I asked one girl she had never heard of it but the owner (or manager) came out and grudgingly found one under the counter. I only saw them displayed at one roadhouse. However, another roadhouse was twelve cents cheaper per litre and the owner told us that the others put their prices up ten cents and give you two cents back and he had a good point if he could afford to sell his petrol twelve cents cheaper.

So we were still trying to reach Ceduna and get through the quarantine border which we had been warned could take ages when we caught up with the road train again. I couldn't take that again so suggested to John that we stop for another drink and we pulled into an off road parking site. I opened the Ute door and the car immediately filled with flies and when I went to the back the dogs were covered. I grabbed my fly net and pulled it over my hat but one even got underneath that. I got the dogs to follow me to the van which John had parked further along near a barbecue table, hoping that there were less flies there. I got a drink, came out of the van and the dogs water was full of drowning ants. I was glad to get back on the road again and as flies do not like the cold air conditioner I put it on high and opened my window directing all air vents towards my open window and all but one disappeared.

The check point was easy. 'Any eskies in the back or is your stuff all in the van?' 'I've got empty eskies in the Ute and all food is in the van. 'That's okay then, bye'.

So I went to the van and another guy had already looked into the fridge and seen all the stewed fruit etc and he was already leaving. We'd been warned that they were so thorough that they even looked into porta-potties and I said to John that they could look down our loo as much as they liked – they were welcome to it!

Through **Ceduna** town at last and when John stopped for more gas I phoned ahead to a caravan park that had been suggested to us, at Streaky Bay on the Eyre Peninsular. By this time we were all overheated, particularly the dogs, exhausted and dehydrated. Jack had given up crying at having to get back in the Ute. The girl at the caravan park told me that it would take about an hour and twenty minutes to get to the park but that the office would be open until 8pm. Before she rang off I asked her what time it was (I was too tired to have remembered to look at my phone which changes automatically. When she told me I was stunned because we had gone through another time zone without knowing it and we now had to move our watches forward by an hour and a half!

This means that we are now half an hour earlier than Kevin and Helen in Queensland and only half ahead of Colin instead of two hours behind. Now I have no idea what time it is in England again – it's driving me round the twist as I need to call Christine as I didn't get to speak to her at Christmas.

The rest of the journey was pleasant although we were in no mood to really enjoy it as we were so tired. Having radio programs back again I turned to Radio National and enjoyed an address by a Harvard University Professor to Melbourne University Undergraduates. What I liked in particular was when he said that 'Being puzzled is a gift' rather than knowing the answers. Take an issue and question and question and return to the issue over and over again, taking it to a more sophisticated level. I do that when I have a problem or have a major decision to make. I will often discuss it with other people to get a different perspective. I had thought I was a slow decision maker but I now I feel a bit better about my methods!

As for 'being puzzled is a gift' then I'm truly gifted! I often wonder what life itself is all about, why I'm here, what I am supposed to be doing and what is it all for? I puzzle about why I have this opportunity to travel and not work and wonder what on earth I have done to deserve this indolent life and what good will it do for anyone other than myself and John. I feel that there has to be a reason which is perhaps why I write this diary – I'm not sure. I'm still puzzled about it!

Chapter 4

STREAKY BAY S.A. (South Australia)

So we finally arrived at Streaky Bay, fed the dogs, levelled the van, got a couple of chairs out and sat outside with a drink in hand feeling completely dazed. The beach is a few steps away and we booked in for two nights although we don't recall much about the first night other than the fact that we watched the news and found that there is severe flooding at the other end of the peninsular.

4th Day En Route - Endless Great Australian Bight

Today, after making phone calls our neighbour informed us that we are marooned on the Eyre Peninsular. The only way out is back across the Nullarbor Plain. Ha, ha, ha, ha – sorry I'm becoming hysterical.

The news is not good but we are hoping to move off tomorrow morning a little further around this coastline. The Eyre Peninsular is, according to our latest information leaflet, the size of Tasmania where I could happily spend two to three months so we feel that we need to keep moving and just hope that the flooding has cleared by the time we want to leave it!

We called into the Streaky Bay Hotel today to have a sticky beak (nose) and first went to the public bar which was the first door we found and were not that impressed but persevered as it had been recommended to us and eventually entered the dining area and saw a lovely lounge. I told one of the staff that it was the first time since I arrived in Australia that I felt that a Hotel was similar to what I had been used to in England before I emigrated. It was truly so comfortable and the menu was sufficient and very reasonably priced. The salad bar looked excellent and included a fish salad and I asked the price and was told it only cost eight dollars. A main course of steak, for example, with a sauce costs eighteen dollars. That's John and me sorted but we were not hungry and we had the dogs outside and were supposed to be shopping for fresh vegetables, milk and bread and the weekend paper. We found out that the paper does not arrive until 4pm on a Saturday, if we want today's news! John walked back to town along the beach this afternoon, with the dogs.

It is a small town with all the basic necessities, with a good foreshore park, beach and jetty. Most of what we want to see is a little further along the coast so we are quite happy to keep moving. We know when we are in a place where we want to stop and it has to feel absolutely right for some reason, like when you've found the house you want to buy even though it might not have all that you thought you wanted. It is instinctive and if we find a place like that then we'll stop a few days and I'll get the washing done and John will have a game of golf and we'll literally have a few days holiday rather than travelling.

21st January 2007

We left Streaky bay today and visited **Murphy's Haystacks** first which are a series of rock formations that resemble haystacks. An early pastoralist was recommending farrowing of the land and pointed to the distant 'haystacks' as an example of what good farrowing could produce as he thought they were haystacks. As they were on Murphy's land, other coach drivers would call them Murphy's Haystacks as they passed by. They are on private land, two kilometres from the main road and they have a charge of two dollars per person for the upkeep of the car park via an honesty box. Callie adored one of the rocks for some reason and wouldn't leave it alone and wanted to climb it and she went whichever way she could find to try and do so but it was too steep for her. She's a funny dog as she wouldn't go down some steps on a previous trip in a place called 'Hanging Rock' so she senses something that we do not understand and we of course, have no idea why she loved this particular rock!

Next we called in at **Port Kenny**, but it was a sad place to look at. It seemed much neglected and run down.

Murphy's Haystacks

Our next stop was **Venus Bay** which we had been advised not to stay at because it's not very good. The caravan park is right on the calm bay and was ideal for people keen on fishing and boating but in the distance we could see cliffs and the sea was crashing in waves in two different directions. We had lunch at the caravan park kiosk and picked up some free tourist leaflets. I was watching some large birds which had bills with a slight hook to them and asked what they were. A guy there told me that what most people call sea gulls, those being the normal white small ones are actually Cape Pigeons and the large brown and white ones that I

driving along the edge of this lake for quite a while. Further on again we saw another lake that was almost white and it looked like a salt lake. The road was not straight for a change and we had no traffic at all on our side of the road during the 140 kilometres that we travelled here. We are only staying one night here but it was certainly worth our while making the effort instead of continuing on to Port Lincoln.

After we had settled into the caravan park we went to have a look at the town. There's not much of it but you can buy the necessities. We drove around the harbour and there is access to the water almost all the way along. We stopped at a boat ramp first to chat with the pelicans and for the dogs to have a swim and then got in and out of the car all the way along the roadway, finding tiny beaches and walkways all the way around. We only saw one tiny beach occupied with a guy sunbathing and a couple of people snorkelling. Coffin Bay is well known for their oysters but today they are farmed Japanese Pacific oysters rather than the original industry here when native oysters were dredged. The demand for Coffin Bay oysters seems to be growing.

We also did the obligatory trip up to the town Lookout but it was worth it as it gave us a wide view of the harbour which meanders around the town.

After we returned John went off to visit the **Coffin Bay National Park** but he only went as far as a two wheel drive can go. It's about forty kilometres long and includes the Coffin Bay Peninsula and the **Whidbey Wilderness Area** being, in total, about thirty-one thousand hectares. Great Southern Ocean crashes against the unstable limestone cliffs and the seas can be dangerous with strong rips, freak waves and large swells. What a contrast to the serene waters of the harbour we saw earlier in the day. There is about twenty kilometres of sealed road and an entrance fee via an honesty box system. There are a lot of islands off the coast here but are off limits unless you have written permission.

Now, back to that name of Coffin and whence it got its name. It is named after an Admiral Sir Isaac Coffin, Bart, born in 1759 in Boston (USA) and joined the British Navy at the age of 14. He was commanding a cutter by the age of 19 and by 22 was captain of the 74 gun Shrewsbury. He not only travelled widely but survived a shipwreck, saw action in the American Revolution and jumped overboard to save the life of a seaman. Unfortunately this heroic effort upset an old injury and he wasn't fit enough for active service again. He became Resident Commissioner of Sheerness Naval Dockyards in Kent (England), was appointed Admiral in 1802 and a Baronet in 1804 and retired in 1808. Then he got married and became a member of the British Parliament, both events occurring in 1811 and served eight years as an MP. He died in 1839, in Cheltenham in England at the age of eighty and I reckon that's not a bad age in those days.

John enjoyed the **National Park** as the journey was interesting with winding roads, wonderful views, particularly at the end when he saw the views of **Golden Island** and **Point Avoid**. Yangie Bay was mainly a calm inlet where people were camping and it was rather uninspiring whereas the surf side was magnificent. I'm looking forward to downloading the photographs in a minute. Pity you can't be here to see them too.

John has got half the people in the park Comet watching at the moment as he has a pair of binoculars but you really don't need them as it is so large (a very long tail) that it is clearly visible with the naked eye. Apparently there are some wonderful photographs of it in the paper, as well as on the web and people are phoning into the radio programs talking about it but I have no idea what the name of the comet is! (I was later to find out that it was called **Comet McNaught**. Tonight is apparently the last night we will ever see it again. That reminds me, as well as having Goggle Earth there is also going to be a Goggle Universe where you can dial up into the largest telescopes and view the solar system. I'll never get John off the computer! Apparently Steven Hawkins has booked himself a flight on Richard Branson's space flights and this year will go in one of those planes where you become weightless and fly around inside a padded fuselage. Considering he can only move his eyelids it will be an amazing experience for him.

I was listening today to New Dimensions Radio National Summer program on the state of the oceans and the life therein. It was a discussion on the fact that there are so many places in America for example where dolphins, otters, manta rays and all types of fish are now extinct but people living today do not realise that they were ever there so they don't worry about it. Marine life has changed dramatically with each generation.

Apparently it is very hard to get people involved to protect places or things to which we don't relate to emotionally or which have little or no value to us. It is therefore important to let people know what we did have and what has been lost and more importantly, what is left that is worth protecting and why it is important to do that. For example, in the struggle to protect whales, it wasn't the fact that people realised that we needed them for our own survival, nor that they were at risk of disappearing from the world but more the fact that people felt that whales should have a place in the world, that their disappearance would somehow leave us poorer in ways that transcend material concerns. People had an emotional connection to whales and that fuelled the international effort to save them.

A large part of the program concerned fish farming, not so much the fresh water fish farming but the dangers of marine farming. Apparently the farmed salmon that I buy is a horrific example. They are fed crushed fish and so many fish have to be caught and crushed to get just one kilo of salmon that it contributes to the shortage of the fish in the oceans that we are experiencing today. Also they are fed hormones and some sort of pesticides and they are packed together like sardines in a tin and their waste accumulates on the ocean floors. Instead of salmon farming helping to provide the fish that we demand, it is contributing to the loss of fish in the oceans! By the time I had finished listening I knew I could never buy farmed salmon again. I have been hearing from other sources about the shortage of tuna at the moment and I'm getting a bit peeved as tuna and salmon are two of my favourite fish! The price of fish certainly does directly affect me so suddenly I care.

Apparently despite the damage done to the world's oceans there is still a great deal to protect and the sea can recover. If we reduce the fishing pressure the fish will come back and if we stop destructive practices the big fish will come back and there is still time to correct the damage to our oceans. Apparently you can go to a web site for more information about the world's oceans and future of life in the sea at info@newdimensions.org (program 31/21). Today's lesson is now over, class dismissed (sorry but it sounded a bit like that, didn't it).

Chapter 5

PORT LINCOLN

We couldn't go to the caravan park nearest town because they do not accept dogs so had to go about ten kilometres the other side at North Shields and the dogs have done us proud again. At this park (which is cheap) we were given a huge beachfront site, right near to the toilets and laundry (handy and they were spotless), with wonderful views of an island, hills behind and Port Lincoln along across the bay which looks incredible at night because of the lights. The town centre lights are mainly red and orange with five distinct white lights spaced along the length of the town (or so it looks like from here). The residential and marina area to the left of the town, as we view it, are mainly a blue colour with speckles of many other colours. The sunsets over part of the water and the hills that we can see out of our window from our settee are lovely.

Port Lincoln is gearing up for the annual 'Tunarama' Festival and we are leaving tomorrow as it is getting too busy. However, for those with children it would be a delight as there are sand sculpture competitions, camel rides, a fun fair, an Underwater Fantasyland, a music band for the kids, fireworks, and prawn tossing for the five to ten year olds and the Kingfish Toss for the eleven to sixteen year olds. There is also the Teddy Bear's Parade, Tiny Tots, Little Princess and Mr Muscle.

For the adults there is the Tuna Toss! There is a Keg Roll, Slippery Pole and Tug of War, presumably for everyone as well as a street procession. There are helicopter rides and Arts and Heritage Trail, a Fun Run, Swim Thru and a Triathlon as well as Sail Past and Blessing of the Fleet. The men may appreciate the Beach Babe's competition and everyone should enjoy the Sydney 32 yachts race.

A seafood feast at the Gala Awards and the dancing may interest you and there are several awards to be presented. There will be sixties music to dance to and a mini auction. There will also be a competition called the Battle of the Bands at a nightclub tonight and a Citizens Breakfast/Australia Day Celebrations on the foreshore tomorrow (Friday). At the Yacht Club there will be a Seafood and Wine Expo on Saturday. There is so much happening that there is an A4 size booklet provided with 32 pages! When we arrived at the park we were told that we could have the sea front site for two nights or choose another site and stay longer. We chose the two days on the sea front and have no regrets as we are ready to move on as I am a little worried about how much we yet have to see and how quickly the days are passing.

We had our own seafood feast that night as we had found out that there are two fresh fish outlets on the edge of town and the first one we came to accepted our credit card (we've found most of them normally want cash only) and we decided to stock up. I was surprised at the final bill as it was so low! It was the best fish I have tasted for a long time.

Port Lincoln is quite a nice town and we've driven the suggested tourist routes and have stocked up again as there are all the shops you could need but there is little left for us to discover and we wonder if we are becoming blasé or perhaps are just tired. We have seen so many wonderful views recently that we are almost 'viewed out'. We certainly do not like towns and traffic and find it quite unnerving. I held up the traffic this morning so that a lovely young woman could back out, mainly because she had three beautiful young girls in the back of the car and the traffic was hurtling around a bend exactly where the rear of her car was heading so that she could get out. Goodness knows how we'll manage when we get home!

TUMBY BAY & PORT NEILL – today is Australia Day

We stopped to have a look at Tumby Bay and took a few photos of the beach, the jetty and from a lookout. We also emptied our black water in a motor home park opposite the cemetery (enough to make them turn in their graves). The motor home park did not appear to have any facilities whatsoever other than the dump point and I cannot imagine anyone wanting to stay in such desolate surroundings.

On to Port Neill where we were asked at the caravan park how many nights we are staying, which is quite normal but were told that if we only stayed one night then we wouldn't get the same site as if we'd stayed longer. Our site is dirty and dusty and we are not impressed. We have been to another lookout and paddled in the sea at quite a nice seafront park where a sunshade is provided for shade and were surprised at how warm the water is. Jack must have appreciated it because he went further out than he usually does and really seemed to enjoy walking around. Just as well because his front leg collapsed earlier and he squealed in pain. John had a walk around the other side of our van park and found a deserted beach but there really isn't that much to see here for the traveller but very relaxing for the annual family holiday, especially if you like fishing or lawn bowls as there is a club in town.

We visited a gallery/op shop but the one place I had come to see was closed. I am going again tomorrow morning when we leave as it is a place that I have either seen on television or read about where they electroplate fragile organic items. They do it to gum leaves and nuts but I'm not so sure about the seahorses that they do. Sea horses are farmed for the domestic and export industries but to treat them as a commodity to make jewellery, for example, out of them turns my stomach. However, all the pieces are electroplated in copper and nickel and oxidized (I'm reading off the back of a leaflet here) to create colours which are unique to every piece. They have a website if you are interested www.tanplaters.com.au

I was listening to the radio today – yes I know, here she goes again. However, it's important for European visitors to know that you do not go to our outback wilderness in our summer because you will be heading into temperatures of 50C on most days and you won't cope with it. It is causing headaches for some property owners who are now getting visitors all year around because of these daft travellers who do not do their research before setting forth. It is all very well to want to experience the 'real Australia' and perhaps see where Burk and Wills (two of our many famous explorers) died by visiting such places as Innamincka but please ensure that you only visit during our winter months such as June, July and August. You can visit the Burk & Wills Dig Tree and their grave sites.

Also realise that any electrical power comes from generators and is very expensive. Everyone has to be self-sufficient to live there and that includes pumping their own water from the under the ground. If the people who live there need a service technician for their solar panels or inverters of some such thing it costs them around $2300 just to get somebody to come out from Broken Hill which is over 600 kilometres away and that is just to look at it! Air fares, accommodation and time have to be worked out before they will even come out!

Don't travel alone, always carry two spare tyres and lots of water, a satellite phone and preferably a CB radio so that you can talk to the locals if you do break down and if you do break down never, ever leave your car. In fact be prepared to lose at least two tyres on some of the outback roads.

However there are showers and toilets provided by the town community for whoever does arrive at Innamincka and you can camp down on the common along Coopers Creek. There's a new motel and three places for home stays. One place finds tyres for people, provides the Laundromat and serves cappuccinos! Multi-faceted businesses out here!

There are a lot of water holes to visit and rocky outcrops with Aboriginal carvings. Visitors who find an Aboriginal site must not disturb it as it is an offence so don't move rocks or pick up stones but just take those memories with you. There is only one waterhole though that has been known to always have water since white man arrived and because Burke and Wills did not rely on the Aboriginals knowledge they did not survive. They were obviously experienced explorers and if they didn't survive what hope have you got if you don't know your facts before you come to a place like this, especially in our summer!

As we are mainly sticking to the coastline, our next stop will be Whyalla and it is taking us enough time just to get around the coastline of Eyre Peninsular, let alone go inland.

The shop was shut in the morning and I was annoyed as it was advertised as being open. As I've been disappointed with this side of the peninsular so far, that would have been a highlight for me.

ARNO BAY

We called in en route to have a look at the town and beachfront. There's quite a large hotel on the front, a golf club, general store, jetty and clean public toilets with soap and paper towels! As it started to rain whilst we were there we did not hang around.

COWELL

Before we turned off I saw a sign which said 'township' and that is the first time that I have heard that term. I presume it means a small town or village and I like the term.

The township of Cowell was bustling and pretty. There seemed to be several hotels with the Franklin Harbour Hotel near the foreshore looking quite majestic. It was a busy Saturday morning and all the shops seemed to be doing a roaring trade. Either they are laid back at Cowell or just too busy because they still have their Christmas decorations up in town. There are some really nice buildings in the main street which leads straight down to the jetty, car park, boat ramp and a caravan park. We stopped there and made our own 'instant' coffee despite the fact that we had passed a pavement café in town which seemed very popular. On the way out of town I was looking for a motel that has a showroom selling jade pieces and jewellery and it was nearly opposite the garage where John filled the bus up with gas. Cowell has one of the largest **jade deposits** in the world and I enjoyed the visit and saw some pieces of rock with the different colours inside and was told that it is the black jade that is rare.

Cowell is also becoming known for its oysters and John bought a dozen of them from the garage whilst he was there for six dollars! We now only have a hundred and five kilometres to drive to get to Whyalla where we are stopping.

WHYALLA - South Australia's third largest city

When we arrived at the caravan park we were told that Whyalla is a 'funny town'. It is, it's really odd! How it can be called a 'city' I'll never understand! However, on our first night we had other things on our mind. I had heard a wind warning for Whyalla on the radio and we have a seafront site and that night was so windy that the van rocked around and when it became really severe we had to put the dogs into the car. Actually, we didn't have to put them in, just open the back door and they bolted in, even Jack! There is debate about the name but one of the suggestions is that it is Aboriginal for 'windy place' and I think that suits it perfectly! We were told that it is not always like this but it hasn't stopped since we arrived. We are quite glad that we only paid for three nights.

There is a large modern shopping centre nowhere near the town and seven day trading is allowed although we did find the smaller stores shut. The town itself seems old, very daggy and is quite depressing. Two blocks are designated as one way street and the two together make up the main street and as you head down there is a Harvey Norman shop facing you. It seems out of place. There is a Post Office, bakery, butchers, hairdressers, Real Estate agency and other small shops and it's all very drab. We went around three times and still could not make head nor tail of it.

Nearby is the foreshore park and Marina which is quite nice and we certainly enjoyed our coffees at the café by the Surf Life Saving Club. We had been up to the **Hummock Hill Lookout** and from there you have 360 degree views of the town, suburbs, the coastline and the steelworks. That area is horrific and red dust blows everywhere so that all the town buildings, roads, kerbs and presumably people if they hang around too long, are red!

Hundreds of thousands of giant cuttlefish come here to spawn between May and August and Whyalla has been called the '**Cuttlefish Capital of the World**'. You can tour the steel works, there is a Maritime Museum, cinemas and a health and leisure centre. The latter is a good idea as the sea is shallow and where it seems to get deeper, because the colour becomes darker, the lifeguard tells us that it is actually because there is so much seaweed beneath the water. The beach also has a fair bit of seaweed on it and the tide goes out a heck of a long way. I'm waiting for it at the moment to try and get a photo of it!

We are taking advantage of some of the shops such as Spotlight and Super Cheap Auto to get things that we have long been avoiding buying. For example, we are going to a hardware store tomorrow as we've been told that they'll cut some timber for us and we want some replacement pieces to put on the ground for the ramps to sit on as ours are either worn out or lost. It is turning out to be a stop where we just get 'stuff' done. I'm not doing the washing though because I'm frightened that it will blow away.

Now for a completely different subject, relevant to our travels. It's our medical box and back to the issue of water. John and I are still suffering stomach problems despite the fact that we are both now drinking bottled water bought in 15 litre containers from the supermarket. If you buy them from one of the big supermarkets they are very cheap and we fill up our small water bottles with them. The water here at this caravan park irritates my eyes when I have a shower and a local told us it's not very good so we feel we are not wasting our money. We eat well and we also drink enough water.

The point that I'm trying to get to is that we eat so many fruits, vegetables, lean meats, grain breads, good cereals and drink water and both of us are suffering from what we suspect is travellers tummy, as termed by the doctors. We either cannot go to the toilet at all for days or cannot get off it and it affects our quality of life as we either cannot sleep properly because we are so uncomfortable or feel exhausted or daren't eat when the other way.

The result is that our large medical box is now packed with products. We started off with a normal supply of emergency supplies and then we were buying tablets for heartburn relief, mild laxatives, tablets to stop gastroenteritis, tablets on prescription to give your digestive system a reminder and then we progressed to eardrops from constant water in our ears when up North and then eye drops because of the sand and grit blowing into our eyes (the dogs have had the same problems with bowels, ears and eyes) but the one thing I have given up on is creams for mosquito bites as the quickest way to ease them is with a block of ice! My warning here is to buy a big plastic box from one of those cheap shops and leave plenty of room to add stuff to it!

It is also hard to feel feminine when you live in a confined space and spend so much time saying 'Pardon me' as you belch or pass wind constantly for days and if we hadn't had our own loo I would never have made it to the park toilets at times so get a porta loo for emergency use if you have the room. It can also be really cold at night if you do need the loo and many off road sites do not have any facilities, not even water.

After my last trip someone asked me if I had Impetigo and I replied 'No, every one of those scars is a bite from a different part of Australia'. Sometimes the bites go sceptic and I find a bar of antiseptic soap, moistened slightly and rubbed on, seems to help stop the itching (after the ice) and clears them up. However, my arms and bottom of my legs are covered in scars and I've had bites on my ears, eyelid, forehead and nose but only when I've had spray on and they have had nowhere else tasty to go to. Being that the scars are white and the suntan is - well tan - means that the scars show up. We were certainly not prepared for all this when we left home.

Our last day at Whyalla turned out to be a beautifully warm day with a gently cooling sea breeze. The sea actually came right in fairly early in the evening so I sat outside with a whiskey and lemonade trying to ape those advertisements I'd seen on the T.V. However, I was cooking stewed fruit and had to keep checking on it and then the dogs returned from their walk with John and slapped their wet tails around my legs in greeting. However, I went back outside several times in the evening and it really was lovely and there were no biting insects to spoil these precious moments. It was the first time I had seen people on the beach other than those walking dogs.

We are plagued by ants. I put a bottle of water on the lounge table and it was suddenly surrounded by them. John put a coffee cup on the other table and it was immediately surrounded and they are in our fridge again. We are losing the battle because every time we get rid of them in one place they turn up in another and our crockery cupboards was teeming with them this morning. They hate my disinfectant so our van is sprayed all over the place.

Chapter 6

PORT AUGUSTA

Well we only really saw a few streets and the Information Centre where we enjoyed a very good mug of coffee each. We gave up because there was too much traffic, too many policemen everywhere – just too overwhelming. We had found the caravan park that we were supposed to be going to and had gone for a walk by the river and had sunk in the sand and our shoes were caked and Jack was finding it particularly hard going. If this was going to be their daily walkies route then it wasn't going to be much fun. The real reason though is that the Flinders Ranges looked absolutely magnificent and we need to go there with a four wheel drive vehicle and without dogs. The ranges are so vast and so high and huge and they really are an awesome sight and I would think that you could spend many, many weeks there. We need to do a separate trip for that area as with Kakadu National Park.

We decided to move on to Port Pirie. It was a very hot day and we stopped for lunch at Port Germaine where we found covered barbecue tables near the jetty in a parkland area but the heat made us all feel a bit rough. **Port Germaine** has a lot of old buildings, many shops that are closed. John remarked that at least it was better than Port Augusta! Port Augusta is a thriving town whereas Port Germaine, which used to be thriving, is now very quiet.

From there to Port Pirie there would have been nothing to see (except for the railway line running parallel to the road) if it weren't for the ranges on our left but they were much smaller in height. There were a lot of semi-trailers and trucks travelling both ways on the highway so we hadn't exactly got away from the traffic and pulled over to let three go past us and I was doing the speed limit.

The caravan park at **Port Pirie** sounds like it is on the beach but there isn't much of a beach, mainly rocks. There are a couple of other parks in town. John went into town this morning to get various types of ant baits because despite finding a dead mouse yesterday and spraying profusely, out fridge was inundated with them this morning and we had to throw some stewed fruit out despite it being fully wrapped in cling film. They still seem to love my organic fresh carrots!

Today we had a visitor at lunchtime by which time I had dried copious amounts of washing which I had done last night, cleaned the fridge out, done the ironing and mended whatever needed mending. Our visitor was a half-sister of a friend of ours who lives here. It was like seeing double and the odd thing is that she is an identical twin herself so all three siblings look alike. She bought me a ceramic gift that she had made herself and she chose a card that I had made that she loved. I had made it from a photo that I had taken and she asked John and I to sign and date the card and said that she wouldn't use it but would always keep it.

We ended up having a very late lunch and John has just gone out for a drive to try and find something to look at other than take a tour of the world's largest lead smelter! A full page is dedicated to this in the tourist booklet for Port Pirie and it includes in its article that they are trying to reduce 'fugitive emissions' which impact on the blood lead levels in the community and that it is 'a significant environmental and health issue that impacts on both the Smelter and the community of Port Pirie'. They are hoping that 95% of children aged nought to four years old have a certain low level by 2010. Not sure what happens to the other 5% of kids that age, nor anyone older than four years of age – is it too late for them? Suffice to say that we wish to leave and we don't drink the water. I saw some people fishing but I wouldn't fancy eating their catch.

Everyone we speak to tells us there is nothing to see but John is so restless and has nothing else to do. I want to get on with making some more cards, prepare the dinner have a shower and sit outside with my book and have a whiskey and lemonade, as soon as it is cool enough to go outside and away from the air conditioning! I also need to download photographs but John has taken the camera so I can escape that chore, and it is becoming a chore. It's nice to take a few photos now and again but with all this touring it is a constant battle to keep up with them.

So John went off to see what he could find and first he went to **Telowie Gorge** which was approximately ten kilometres on dirt roads and a two kilometre return walk to the gorge and back. It was pretty but not exceptional. It was very hot and there were signs about it being a high risk area for bush fires. Dogs are not allowed.

Next he went to see the villages of **Nelshaby** and **Napperby** but there wasn't much to see. He couldn't resist having a look at **Weeroona Island** which could be seen from the highway leading to Port Pirie. It is a dome-shaped island and to get there you drive a dirt causeway which is subject to flooding on high tides. The island is covered in dirt roads and is in the early stages of a development with blocks of land for sale. There are various types of housing scattered around the place and wonderful views of the sea and the Southern Flinders Ranges.

Tomorrow we head to Port Victoria which is when we will be well down the Yorke Peninsula. I'm not sure where the Peninsula actually starts from because Port Broughton is included in the Yorke Peninsula booklet and that town is only fifty-seven kilometres from here but it's not actually on the peninsula. The peninsula is shaped like a boot.

It was 35C here today and it is due to be 36C tomorrow and I cannot stand it as it is such a dry heat. Even John is having a problem with the mosquitoes and sand flies I have about five more bites.

PORT BROUGHTON, WALLAROO & KADINA

As soon as we had left Port Pirie and its surrounds the scenery started to improve. John and I both had hay fever type symptoms this morning until we got well away from it. We got off to a bad start with Jack as he seemed to be having trouble on his first walk of the day and promptly vomited a lot on our return. I had taken him down a track to the rocky foreshore as I could hear a guy singing opera and we had been told that we would be woken up by him some mornings as he swum around the bay. He was doing an over arm stroke but obviously kept his face out of the water as he sung his heart out. What a wonderful way to start the day!

We hosed Jack down to cool him off and worried about how he would cope with the heat today and as we were about to leave I took his chain off to get him into the car and got shouted at by the park manager. I felt like strangling him. Most managers or owners would calmly ask 'Is there a reason why your dog is off the lead?' and had he done that, by the time he had walked the distance from where he was, Jack would have been in the Ute. On our arrival he had actually said to us when he handed over the park rules 'Once you've read the rules you will think you are in a Nazi concentration camp'. I cannot stand it when people use words like that loosely as I can remember the guy that cut my hair as a child having the numbers on his arm and that was when I first heard about the camps. He was one of the lucky ones and survived but I don't think any of his family did.

When we arrived at Port Broughton, which is a lovely small seaside township, we wondered why on earth we had stopped at Port Pirie. The main street was very attractive and there was a coffee shop with bougainvilleas growing up posts outside it, a Hotel Broughton on the corner and at the end of the street the war memorial with parkland and the sea beyond. It seemed such a happy little place. We made a coffee and sat on a bench on the foreshore in the shade after the dogs had had a swim to cool down, watching the boats, looking at the jetty and soaking up the relaxed atmosphere as the waves lapped against the beach. There were a lot of barbecue tables and benches provided all along the beachfront and the public toilets were painted with frescoes. There are two caravan parks there to choose from. When we were leaving to go to Kadina I saw two lovely churches and one of the caravan parks which looked really nice, seemed quite large and it is very close to the beach. They had a vast amount of vans stored there so it must be a popular place for people to come for their annual holidays. Just beyond that were some new building blocks so the town is growing.

We drove through **Alford** and John spotted it but I missed it (I must have blinked). Kadina was an enormous surprise and we were both exclaiming aloud. There was no warning that we were entering a huge country town because the scene was so rural when we parked the bus and John got into the Ute. We saw the original part of town first and the town park which is square-shaped with houses and other buildings all around it and then we saw what we thought was the main street but then there seemed to be more shops and lo and behold we came to a modern section with a large Woolworths store, Target store and other shops. It seemed to go on and on and we were going around in circles, or rather blocks, getting lost. Kadina is a major supply centre for the Yorke Peninsula.

Amazing Sandstone Pillars

We found the road to Wallaroo and saw the jetty and boat ramp where there is a ferry service but I have no idea where it takes people to. We then tried to find **North Beach** which was great fun because there are major residential canal developments taking shape and we had to go a long way round and eventually along a road of huge, modern, newly built homes to find it. We saw a caravan park near the beach and were glad that we hadn't had to try and find it with our big van.

When we did find North Beach we experienced another shock as we found that we could drive onto it, that it was an absolutely enormous beach both in length and width as the tide was out and that there were carports on the beach for cars! There was also a thirty kilometre speed limit sign! We drove down to the water and the dogs had a wonderful time and John paddled whilst I took photographs. It was a magnificent beach and well worth finding.

Wallaroo has its own township and so has North Beach apparently as we saw a sign stating so but we never got that far.

We returned to the van and we both drove into the town and parked by the park and that is where we had our picnic lunch as it was lovely with large trees providing shade. The park had an old artillery piece on it and an old railway engine, a playground for children and many benches for resting.

There were some strikingly different styles of homes in town with some being quite old. Many buildings and homes had been built out of sandstone and I was really impressed. It is a lovely town and everywhere was so well cared for and so clean. A bonus for me was the sight of a beautiful cottage with roses growing wildly over the front door and across the walls either side. The front garden was a stunning cottage garden and I wished that I hadn't been driving at the time and could have stopped to get a photograph.

The next town we came to was **Moonta** - 'Australia's Little Cornwall'. Apparently a man called Shepherd Paddy Ryan found copper there in 1861 which led to the Moonta Mining Co. being established and it became one of the richest copper mines in Australia. Most of the miners were Cornish. John saw a sign which I missed, to Moonta Bay. I didn't even realise it was on the coast! We passed a beautiful old church and it was certainly pretty in places. Anyway, we drove on because we wanted to get to our destination. As we drove on passing parched farmland I saw a sign welcoming us to the Yorke Peninsula so now I know where it begins, just past Moonta.

I didn't see much of **Maitland** either because I received a telephone call on my mobile, whilst driving through town and had to pull over after my discussion with the insurance company over the flooding of a room in a rental house of ours. I can only recall it looking quite nice and our confusion in finding the road that we were to take next. The road surface was really rough and I wondered if we'd have been better off on a gravel road as even the road surface that had been renewed was rough but it was quite a pretty journey.

By the time we reached **Port Victoria** John said he'd had enough of driving for one day. We hadn't driven a huge distance but with the stops and the heat we were glad to book into a van park, hose Jack down, get the air conditioner on and get cold drinks. By the time we had set things up I was so hot that I stuck my head and neck under the shower rose and turned the cold water tap on high!

We have been making friends very quickly with a couple in front of us and it amazes me how much information complete strangers can share with each other. We only met them this afternoon but we know so much about each other's families that it is quite ridiculous. They love staying in Queensland and we gave them information on a park they hadn't heard of and so forth. No doubt we'll get advice off them in the morning on where to go on the rest of this peninsula because they had a holiday home here for many years and have only bought their caravan this year.

Did I tell you that I was talking to a guy recently who had met a young British couple in Darwin and they had taken two days to drive to Katherine, which was where he was talking to them? They told him that they were flying out from Sydney in two days time but were not sure if they were going in the right direction! He was too stunned to speak and went to get his map of Australia. He asked them where Darwin is and then told them to point out where Katherine is and said 'That took you two days to drive. See how far you've driven on this map? Now find Sydney'. If you are due to fly out of Sydney in two days time you had better start driving as fast as you can and never, ever stop until you reach the airport but I doubt you'll make it.' He was more stunned with their response which was 'But we want to see Cairns on the way'.

We were advised to come this far down the peninsula and I'm glad that we have because most of the points that we want to go to at the end of the peninsula are only about half an hour's drive in each direction and it has been seriously hot today.

We stopped at **Minlaton** en- route, it has a nice main road as you come through with a lot of sandstone homes. It's got everything you need including a sports store, bank, shoe shop, grocery store, electrical shop, pharmacy, churches, café, information/craft centre plus a

National Trust museum. Whilst John got gas I found a parking place outside the Harry Butler Memorial which is a building with full glass windows. There in all its glory was his tiny aircraft (Captain Butler was a pioneer aviator), the Red Devil, a 1916 Bristol monoplane and its bright red paintwork shone.

We arrived at **Point Turton**, our final destination before lunch which is unheard of for us! It was nice to have the whole afternoon to relax. I spent most of the day trying to get hold of one of my sons because the kid's dad broke his femur yesterday and is back in hospital again so I had other things on my mind, like how far away from them we are.

The caravan park is adjacent to the jetty and boat ramp and overlooks Hardwicke Bay and is very popular with families, people who like fishing or who have boats. The area is becoming popular for people wanting holiday or retirement homes. There is a general store, open seven days a week, which sells fuel, groceries, bait, alcohol and is also a 'take-away' café.

Marion Bay and Corny Point

Marion Bay was first up and we were disappointed in it. The restaurant which I thought was on the beach wasn't, the area was tatty, the toilets weren't on the beachfront and there were no barbecue facilities that we could not find anywhere to shelter from the sun. We tried to get to **Stenhouse Bay** but it was in the National Park and when John went into the Tourist Information Centre near the toll gate, he was told that what we could see from there was about it! We drove along the road which passes Formby Bay and I think we should have taken the dirt road named after it because from a distance it looked fabulous. However, we continued on in the hope that there was another access point but there wasn't and we continued along the bitumen to Corny Point and Corny Point! Yes there are two places with the same name, the first being where the shop is and the second at the headland. We were desperate for shade and parked under some trees outside a house! The dogs had had a couple of swims so they were happy but as John said to me 'If anyone asked me about it I'd tell them not to bother coming to these areas'. None of what we saw was what you could call pretty, there was no shade anywhere and the flies drove us nuts. It was good to get back to Point Turton and we drove around the area and along the beachfront before coming back to the van.

Today we set off for the other side of the Peninsula via **Warooka** and **Yorketown**, taking the wrong road and ending up at **Port Giles**. We loved some of the old buildings that we had seen at the inland towns, particularly in Yorketown and we saw lots and lots of flowers there and especially liked all the roses and hibiscus bushes growing in people's gardens but Port Giles was dominated by the huge and very ugly grain terminal.

We headed for Edithburgh where we had meant to arrive! It was established in 1869 and it was the first town on the southern side of Yorke Peninsula. There used to be a large salt industry there and en route we had been puzzled at the sight of so many dams that looked like salt plains. We were disappointed that we couldn't get down to the beach but there were a lot of barbecue tables provided along the front and we found some shade and let the dogs stretch their legs whilst we had a coffee. There was a caravan park at the end of the road and I wondered if there was easier beach access from there. The place is growing with some new housing, mainly large monstrosities.

We went back through Port Giles and passed through **Wool Bay**. There were a few old houses around and cliffs to deal with again if you wanted to get down to the beach.

Stansbury we liked particularly when we saw the beach and harbour and we stopped there for a while and ate our lunch. We were relieved to find some shade again and there were a lot of tables provided along the front as well as shade sails at the jetty. At the end was what seemed to be a very popular FPA caravan park as people were queuing up to get in! I was amused by the IGA grocery store as it also had bakery items, cards, gifts, Manchester (haberdashery), electrical appliances, clothes, photo processing and fish and diving accessories – talk about multi-faceted! There were a mixture of homes here with quite a few modern lowset houses (bungalows) of various types. The first beach we came to was not that pretty looking but then we came into the town and realised how pretty the place is. There were a lot of trees along the front, a big hotel and there were a lot of sandstone (and sandstone faced) homes and some beautiful flower gardens again. The council has planted flowers all along the front too and we thought it a much prettier place than Edithburgh. Where we were a very good barbecue was provided and there were toilets further up near the caravan park. As we sat eating our lunch we talked about the fact that you need a boat if you come to this Peninsula more than you need a four wheel drive. It seems that everyone but us has a boat in our caravan park and I believe that some places are only accessible by boat and not by four wheel drive. The world is your oyster here with a boat, quite literally as they do have oysters here and they are farmed locally. There are so many deserted beaches and islands that we can see that we can't reach.

We were extremely lucky today because we had a beautiful cool breeze blowing on us whilst we ate lunch and we know that Adelaide was heading for temperatures of around 40C today. (When we did get back to our caravan park on the other side of the Peninsula it was so hot that people were talking about it.) We had escaped the extreme heat all day.

We continued driving along the coastline but between towns all we could see were flat fields which mainly produce wheat. We were now heading for **Port Vincent**.

The residential area was quite nice but the sea was a long way out, a really pretty town centre because of all the sandstone buildings, although we preferred Stansbury. However, we found what we wanted when we got to the other side near the harbour. There was a lovely beach with deeper water, a hotel, a kiosk on the beach with a café providing fish and chips, the Port Vincent Institute being a lovely building built in 1910 beautifully maintained, right next to it an FPA foreshore caravan park. Next to the kiosk there was a large covered area with tables and benches and a lower covered area of bench seating providing plenty of shade.

Hardwick Bay had a lot of houses on the beachfront, all with water tanks and most with tractors to tow their boats in and out of the water. There were a lot of new homes but they were in keeping with the area being 'beach-shack' style with only part having a few large modern homes.

We accomplished what we wanted to see and although we left late we still got home mid afternoon and it had been a very relaxed and pleasant day. We did not go to Ardrossan as we will have to drive through it anyway when we leave tomorrow, on our way to **Port Wakefield**. We had originally thought we would be staying on the other side but are now wondering if we will make Adelaide tomorrow. It might be a good idea if I phoned a van park to see if they can fit us in because there are not too many parks close in to town where dogs are allowed, let alone room for a big rig like ours.

Before leaving the caravan park I went to thank the owner because we had not been given any rules on arrival. That has to be the first time that has happened and as I said to her, it was the cleanest park we had been to. Nobody let their dogs off their leads, nobody dropped any litter whatsoever, everyone was quiet after ten o'clock at night, nobody was noisy in the mornings, and everyone recycled all their rubbish plus the toilets and laundry were always left spotless as were all the sites. At most parks you are given a list of rules like this and there are always those that abuse them and chuck their cigarette ends on the ground or whatever.

We went via **Ardrossan**, didn't think much of it but it was good to stop on the seafront and have a coffee and look at the cliffs.

ADELAIDE

Yes, we made it to Adelaide and it was a pleasant journey until we hit the smog about sixty-one kilometres from Adelaide. When you looked ahead it was horrific but it may have been dust blowing off the arid farmland and having been in such clear air for so long it was quite a shock. Then there was the traffic because it was terrifying. There were so many road trains which were going so fast and even though they had a free lane to pass, they would wait until they were right up your bum before pulling out to overtake and then chuck the gravel and grit into your vehicle. My poor windscreen has hundreds of minute chips that look like raindrops! We couldn't go too fast as there were wind warnings on the radio, which we didn't need as even my car was being rocked around so we travelled at only eighty to ninety kilometres an hour instead of the maximum speed limit of 110kph despite the very good, straight dual carriageway. Jack had his head out of the window once when a road train went past and he must have been frightened as he shot back inside and didn't put his head out for the rest of the journey.

I was in front and knew that we had to turn right at a five way intersection, which I did but had gone about one kilometre when I realised we were on the wrong road. John, who was a way behind me did a u-turn but I had to go up to a shopping centre and try and get across three

lanes of traffic on both sides of the road to do so and then had to try and catch up with him
again. There was nowhere for him to pull over safely but he did! So I take the next left and
know that we are on the right road when I see in my rear view mirror that John has suddenly
swept across the dual carriage way, which is teeming with traffic, and has turned right into
a minor residential road. I'm yelling at him on the two-way 'What are you doing? We are on
the right road. Stick to the main road' but his two-way isn't working.

I knew that he knew the name of the road we needed to be on and the fact that we had to take
a certain road to the left further along this road so that is exactly what I did. I also knew that
he wouldn't know where to go once he was in this second road so I would have to pull over
and wait for him. The kerbs were very high to deter people from pulling over onto the strip
beside the road which is exactly what I needed to do. When I came to a roundabout I became
really worried and having gone around it I found an access road to a company car park, went
up it, did a u-turn and sat at the exit so that I could see John coming. It was 37C and I knew
that the dogs would be suffering every minute I waited. This is what I have on my tape.

'He's following me and he suddenly veers off into a side street because his two-way won't
work but he's following me and I've got the directions so what's his phone got to do with the
price of eggs. I've gone into a business area and done a u-turn and a taxi followed me, doing
exactly the same and now I'm blocking him! So I go back out and round the roundabout and
come back again and I'm still sitting here ten minutes later with no sign of him and he hasn't
changed his batteries. I can't reach him by phone and I don't know where he is. He could have
gone around the block and got lost so there's no good me going all the way back looking for
him as it would be just my luck that I'd see him across six lanes of traffic hurtling along on
the other side. What do you do with a man who veers off a main road in the wrong direction
when he's following you? Would he think to look for the other mobile that hasn't had reception
because it will probably work here in Adelaide and phone me?

(Later) Still no sign of him, the dogs are hot, I want a wee, we've just got to Adelaide and I've
lost him.

Still no sign of him and it's now a quarter of an hour. How long do I wait? I don't know where
to look for him. My engines still running as well, do I turn it off at the exit to the car park?

(Later) I've turned it off. Oh, I'm dying for a pee and I'm so hot and I'm sure Jack and Callie
must be in a bad way with this heat. I don't know what to do, there's no sign of him. Oh blast,
someone is coming and they want to come out.

I went around the roundabout and I've gone right into the company grounds this time and I'm
going to get the dogs out and walk near the road.'

I had turned the engine off, got one leg out of the car and John went sailing past! I managed
to turn on the ignition quickly enough to blast him on the horn – many times!

I found him way up the other end of the road and how he's managed to pull over I've no idea. His only complaint about that was that someone had parked in a stupid position in front of him! His two-way still wasn't working.

When we arrived at the park and I got in the van there were batteries everywhere. I took out the ones that were in the handset, put some in and it worked beautifully. He had thought that I had both mobiles with me for some reason. He had been waiting for me to come back and look for him!!!

The effect of the heat on me was not good and I felt really weird and it was rather frightening. Stress from the heat and from losing him, mixed with frustration I suppose. When I did go to bed I was feeling very dizzy and sick and it frightened both John and I but the air conditioning stopped the nausea and I slept until half past nine this morning. I asked John to go and get me some milk because I could not face the car and traffic again. I hate traffic with a vengeance now.

Chapter 7

ADELAIDE CITY

I read somewhere that Adelaide is the only city in the world surrounded by parkland. Another brochure says that Adelaide is known as a city within a park. There are actually 29 parks covering forty-five percent of the city. The layout of the city centre is amazing and almost symmetrical with an oval park in the middle and four square parks towards each corner. The streets are in blocks with five main streets running north-south and eleven streets running east-west. There are four roads crossing the Torrens Lake and River Torrens at the northern end of the city connecting it to North Adelaide. There is parkland on both sides of the lake and just before the river on the city centre side there are the Botanical Gardens, Adelaide Zoo, Torrens Parade Ground, National Wine Centre, Royal Adelaide Hospital, Art Gallery, Museum and Library and University. There is also Parliament House, Government House, a Festival Centre and a Convention Centre. On the other side of the water, on the North Adelaide side there is the City of Adelaide Golf Links, the Adelaide Oval, the University Oval, Tennis Courts and St Peters Cathedral is also in North Adelaide. As I said before, surrounding both of these areas are parks, plus the Victoria Park Racecourse and a cemetery! There are so many parks and churches and shops and fine buildings to see that it would take us months.

Today we took the dogs with us having found out that the nearest kennels were actually vets and they were going to cage the dogs. We found an underground car park (getting lost both on the way in and on the way out because we found the free maps provided hardly ever give street names except for in the city centre itself). The dogs settled down to sleep with a bowl of water beside them and we woke them up on our return. The car park was cheap, they were happier and cooler together and felt safe in their familiar surroundings.

Having found the General Post Office which was a very impressive building and interesting in itself, we picked up our post and headed for the Rundle Mall which was

Rundle Mall Goes On Forever

very much longer than it had appeared on our town map. It was also fascinating with many arcades and side streets. We had our customary cup of coffee sitting in the mall listening to the buskers and people watching. I got my last Christmas card amongst the post – well I should think it's the last one as it is now February! Then we wondered around looking at statues (including Queen Victoria), works of art, a fountain, and shops of course, the town parks and the many churches including St Francis Xavier Cathedral.

Next it was off to the city market which was close to our car park to collect freshly baked crusty bread, meat and fruit and vegetables. I bought a joint of beef and four pieces of veal and thought my twenty dollar note wouldn't cover it but then she asked me for around twelve dollars and I was staggered. Likewise with the fruit and vegetables, as I think the lot came to about eight dollars. The plums we bought we so delicious I think they'll all be gone by tomorrow! The only dear purchase were apples for John as I decided he should have the best variety instead of the cheapest that he would have bought. The market had so many cheeses and deli items that we could have stayed and tasted and purchase so much more but we thought the dogs had been left rather too long. We were quite tired by then so we called it a day and returned home for a very late lunch as we hadn't had the time to eat out. This is pretty daft as Adelaide has the reputation of having more restaurants per head than any other Australian city and some streets are devoted to dining whether it be in cafes, restaurants or pubs. There are apparently some great seafood and Asian restaurants. As there are local wineries, wine is taken seriously here and there are large selections. The birth of Australia's most famous wine, Grange is only fifteen minutes from the city centre.

It was a lovely day and I think the city is beautiful. It was originally planned in 1837 by a Colonel William Light and he did a mighty fine job of it. The roads are so wide, tree lined, there is so much available parking and the traffic flows beautifully as does the pedestrian traffic as you only have to walk a few metres for pedestrian lights wherever you are. If you don't wish to walk all the time there are trains, buses, the Glenelg tram and bright yellow buses travel the main streets and go to all the main attractions and you can hop on and off them for free. The buses are all run on natural gas and the City is proud of it's 'green' transport system.

Today we headed off to find 'Eagle on the Hill' and Mt Lofty. I had spent the morning shopping and John had been repairing a frame on top of the motorhome which he had ripped out when he drove under some trees by the ocean on our way to Adelaide. We needed a complete change of scenery so headed for the hills.

We didn't know what 'Eagle on the Hill' was and it turned out to be an off-road site where presumably you should be able to have a good view of the city and ocean but we couldn't see a thing because of the trees and bushes, so it was a complete waste of time. We were advised by a cyclist to go back to the freeway and look for a sign further along for the turn off for Mt Lofty.

It is in a National Park although there were no signs indicating that dogs were not allowed but we left them in the car with some water and went to explore. It's a good job we did because we entered the Information Centre and through some more glass doors leading to a superb viewing area. I took some pretty lousy photographs of the city and the coastline and the hills. The reason they are lousy is that it was too hazy although it was not that hot today. At 727m (or 710.1m according to a different leaflet) Mt Lofty is South Australia's third highest peak so local people enjoy snow up there every year or so. If you walk around to the side of the restaurant you can see some lovely views of the hinterland.

We went into the restaurant and had a coffee and returned to the Information Desk for information about the Port area of Adelaide and the South Australian Maritime Museum which we are going to visit tomorrow. There are no underground car parks in that area but if we go in the morning we should be able to park the car in some shade provided by some buildings. It opens at 10am and we could be in there a couple of hours so we had to ensure that the dogs would not get too hot if we were to leave them in the Ute. By midday when the sun will be overhead or in the wrong direction and there won't be any shade.

We returned on the old road and it seemed to go on forever, John was driving down a switchback road and the drop off the edge of the road was on my side of the car! I kept yawning so that my ears would pop in order to hear again. We got caught up in the peak hour traffic and got completely stuck at some lights. For some unfathomable reason, the filter lights allowing people to turn right across the traffic at the junction does not function during rush hour in the evening. I have seen other signs at other lights that state that they do not light up in the morning rush hour. If it is to allow people to get into the city easily and out of the city in the evenings it just does not make sense because it ensures that drivers have to play Russian roulette to get across the intersections. It requires the two drivers at the front of the queue to move over the line and then to both do a mad dash, side by side, across the junction between light changes. That is possible as long as you can trust that the traffic coming towards you on the opposite side is going to stop when the lights turn amber. If anybody ignores the amber and doesn't stop then you are going to be wiped out on your passenger side and could easily be killed. When we turned up at this intersection we had to wait for about six changes of lights before it was our turn to watch the lights assiduously and press foot to accelerator so hard that we could shoot off as if we had been catapulted across the road, so you can imagine the frustration of the drivers who had piled up behind us. The city 'minders' might be proud of the fact that they have few traffic jams in the city but they obviously are oblivious to what is going on out in the suburbs during rush hour or purposely ignore the dangerous conditions. No way in the world could I live in a city that allows such conditions even though it is very lovely to look at. Life is too precious.

Yesterday we exhausted ourselves. We got off to a late start as we were on the phone until ten o'clock as we have a close member of our family in hospital not doing too well and then we got lost again on the way into town. How we can get lost I have no idea but last night realised that if we had been using the map of Adelaide. With our Hemma Map we would have found our way around a lot easier than by using the tourist maps which are free.

We started by going to **The Port** and visiting the South Australian Maritime Museum where we stayed for an hour and a half, most of that time in the lower level where they have built copies of cabins from the 1840's, have passenger lists and vessel databases and you are invited to lie on any one of the bunks and listen to the stories of the people who spent so many weeks aboard getting from England to Adelaide. You experience the conditions the settlers experienced. You hear the anguished details of a woman's life on board and the death of her two children within twenty-four hours for example. You hear about the food (what there was of it), the lack of medical assistance and the different experiences of passengers depending on which ship they travelled. I lay and a bunk with my eyes closed and it was an experience that will live with me forever. There were also recreations of cabins from 1910 and the 1950's. I stayed down there and looked at everything and used the databases and found out that a paternal relative had come out to Australia in 1912 on the ship 'Orama'. I could not get a copy of a sketch or photo of it as it was torpedoed in 1917. Another ship was built afterwards with the same name. As I have a very unusual maiden name (there is no-one with the same name in the Queensland telephone directory) I was quite surprised. I was even more surprised to find four moire people with the same name in later years. John had a ball looking up his name.

On the middle level where the entrance to the museum is there are many old ship's figureheads on display and a full scale reproduction of a sailing ketch which you can go on and down inside. The 'kitchen' (you could hardly call it a galley) was just big enough for one person to stand in. There were a lot of other exhibits on the upper level which John enjoyed but I was still downstairs in the hold of the ship in my mind and could not concentrate on anything else. I went outside and took some photos of the buildings around, bought a cup of coffee and sat at the pavement tables outside in the shade. The dogs could see me and they were still fine and parked in the shade. There was a shop next door with some remarkable sketches and photos and memorabilia and I admired many old ships and bought a card for my son for his Birthday. He loves old ships so he'll like it much more than a normal Birthday card.

Our ticket included entry to the lighthouse. So after John had had his coffee and visited the shop (he didn't comment on the ships but did comment on the saucy old photographs) we clambered up to the top with John only hitting his head once, at the only place where there was a large warning. Exiting the stairwell at the top was the hardest part and coming back down I had to tilt my pelvis forward to get through the hatch as my bum was catching. Being a size twelve to fourteen there's a warning for anyone bigger. John being longer and leaner didn't do too bad but did consider coming down backwards which I advised him not to do but to please watch his head!

The dogs had already had a walk around the block in between our tours but now it was their turn to hit the beach. They didn't get much chance for the first half hour though as we headed for Outer Harbor and shouldn't have bothered. We didn't stop but turned around meaning that it was a completely wasted journey and our first stop was at Largs Bay. We continued down the coast to **Semaphore, Tennyson, Grange, Henley Beach**, **West Beach** and finally **Glenelg** and they are all so different that I will give you a quick description on them in a minute. It was a lovely trip and a wonderful day until John decided that we should return home via North Adelaide. He tells me that it was lovely to see but I have no idea as I was the map reader and he would say 'Look at that. Which road do I take next?'

'What road are we on'. He would tell me and I'd respond 'We can't possibly be because we have just turned into so-an-so road. Which way are we going, tell me the next street.' He'd tell me and I'd respond that we were going in completely the wrong direction. What complicated things was that I was trying to get back into the City to go home our usual way not knowing that he wanted to go home via a different route. This meant that we ran around and around with John veering across lanes of traffic, going around blocks and doing u-turns where it is not permitted before we stopped and found out that we were both trying to head in different directions. We saw one church several times and went around and around a square several times by which time my eyes were so sore from trying to read the names on the map and he was losing patience. Once I knew which direction he wanted to go, rather than the direction that I wanted to go, it was a piece of cake and he thanked me for getting us home.

'What's for dinner?' he asked. 'You're not getting any' I responded 'You can have the remains of my cheese sandwich from lunch and I'm having a large glass of whiskey and lemonade. Perhaps you will take me to see North Adelaide sometime seeing as you think it is so lovely!' When I looked at the Hema map last night I found out that there are three streets all called Brougham Place all going in different directions with Brougham Gardens in the middle. No wonder we had been along that road so many times! Mills Terrace is also odd as you go up it and turn right, then left, then right and then left and you are still in it but running adjacent is Mills Hill Street, so if John just said 'Mills Hill' I could well have been in the wrong street. There is so much to see between North Adelaide and the City as well and North Adelaide being also surrounded by parks, we wonder how long we are going to stay. We believe that we will just stick to our planned weeks stay and continue on as we can't possibly see it all. Every street has a building or church or park that you want to take a photograph of, let alone all the attractions there are to visit and did I mention the Markets – loads of them. Adelaide is known as the Festival State too but I've decided not to look at the calendar of events because I'm sure there will be something in the arts arena that I'll want to see.

Well, I took 113 photographs yesterday, 64 of them of Port Adelaide, the Museum and the lighthouse alone so I'd better face them and clear my camera. These digital cameras are a boon for me – I love them and I save a fortune not paying for photos that I wouldn't want printed.

The Semaphore Palais on the seafront is a hotel but is really more like a pub and people were sitting inside and outside enjoying afternoon drinks. When I came out of the toilet I saw a notice board which was covered with letters of thanks and photographs from people who had held their Wedding or Engagement receptions there and a multitude of other celebrations. There was a marquee on the beachfront and people were scurrying around setting it up for yet another occasion. The parkland on the front is lovely and we sat under a large tree to have a picnic lunch and the dogs went for a swim in the sea. There is a children's playground and a small water park with tubes and slides to enjoy. The main street is attractive and the beach endless.

HENLEY

There is a beachfront square and Henley is one of the original settlements of Adelaide. There is the obligatory jetty and many cafes and restaurants and of course the beach and we liked the place.

GRANGE

We liked Grange and when we were trying to find a way around to look at something along the front we happened to end up in a seafront road where there was a row of beautiful old buildings. A terrace, three stories high with ironwork features and tiny front gardens and it was so beautiful that we took photos and talked to some local people who were strolling by. They told us that they pass them every day and wish they owned one of the flats, so they have been broken up into individual units. It's within walking distance of the jetty if you walk along the front towards Henley Beach.

At this stage I must mention that the coastal road itself is lovely, lined with Norfolk Pine trees and many large palm trees. Most of the towns have tree-lined roads and they not only provide the shade needed, they are very beautiful.

We drove on through Henley Beach and West Beach to Glenelg. I would tell you more about these places if my tape recorder hadn't suddenly died on me. I've tried new batteries and a new tape but to no avail and it is very frustrating!

GLENELG

This is a large town with a tram line starting right near the seafront, going straight down the main shopping street (Jetty Road) and on to the City centre. Judging from the amount of building going on, Glenelg is very popular for locals and visitors alike.

It has been popular for a long time because the first European settlers to arrive near what was to become Adelaide landed here in 1836 from England. They camped here whilst Adelaide was surveyed and it was in Glenelg that the colony's government was proclaimed on December 28th in 1836.

With a sea inlet it provides safe harbour for the boats (and there were many there today) and the bonus of a long lake system which is has a great deal of parkland along side. We stopped there to make a cup of coffee and for the dogs to cool off again in the calm water.

We stopped again at the parkland where the HMS Buffalo Restaurant and Museum is. It is a replica of the vessel that brought the first European settlers to South Australia. I had no idea it was a replica as it appeared to be so ancient.

We drove around the centre and even in the car the main road, lined with shops seemed amazingly long and there are many historic buildings to look at along the way. One of the tour leaflets tells us that there are over two hundred and fifty speciality shops and they still seem to be building and expanding. On weekends, weather permitting, they hold an art and craft market along the seafront.

So it was that from this bustling place we headed off for North Adelaide and in comparison the latter seemed quiet and sedate even if we were not, as I've already mentioned. It was a full day and a very good day sightseeing, full of contrasts and easy to travel to for those who have good maps!

Have I told you about the difference between the night and day temperatures here? On the day that it was forty degrees Celsius (the day before we arrived) it apparently dropped to about twelve Celsius overnight. Anyway, the first night we were really cold and put our dressing gowns over our duvets but on the second night we were too hot and had the air conditioner on. It is the first time in Australia that I have asked John 'Did you spot the night time temperatures on the television tonight?' It can vary so much between day and night. We have been lucky with the weather as it has not been too hot during the day since we arrived.

I had an encounter with a cop this morning. Well that's not quite true but I looked up and saw a red light, having not noticed the amber light, and screeched to a halt over the line right opposite the police headquarters where the cop was crossing my lane of traffic. Had I gone through the lights then there wouldn't have been much of the cop left to worry about as I'd have hit him. My light turned green just as I saw him put all his flashing lights on but he was in a lane where he had to turn left and I was turning right at the same intersection. Two cars went through when my light turned green and then it turned amber again and meanwhile this cop was holding up all the traffic in his lane. I didn't move and waited for my light to turn red! He turned his flashing lights off and left. I'm not sure whether he realised that I'm normally a careful driver or whether he saw my number plates and realised that I was from Queensland and thought 'Oh, a Banana Bender, that explains everything'.

Having been on a useless journey because the suburban shops don't open until 11am on a Sunday I returned to the van and we all went into the city and this time tried just following the city centre signs and it was a breeze! We came to North Adelaide, skirted around the city and tried to enter the car park where we had parked the other day but it was closed so we had to find street parking. This varies enormously on a Sunday from half and hour, an hour, two hours or all day free depending on where you park. We parked in a side street outside someone's house so we didn't have to abide by any rules and there was a tree to provide the dogs with shade. John and I then went and sat in a bus shelter for half an hour. We were waiting for the

City Sights free bus. There are many free buses in Adelaide but the one we were to catch was supposed to have a T.V screen with information about all the sights and a very helpful bus driver. We had neither as the T.V didn't work and I heard another couple say 'The driver must be sick of tourists because she's really miserable'. Anyway, we went around the perimeter of the city and had the chance to see the buildings and gardens and it only took around twenty-six minutes. We were parked near Chinatown where we could smell the aromas which set off our taste buds. However, it was getting hot so we went back to the car, woke the dogs up and drove towards home, stopping for lunch on the way. We returned via North Adelaide and it really is lovely and this time we saw some of the pubs and cafes. The city had been bustling with people and cars (which had surprised me because I had thought that most people would be at one of the various markets or at the beach), but North Adelaide was elegant and serene and people could dine in peace. The trees in Jeffcott Road were absolutely glorious, heading up to Wellington Square, and some of the buildings in Pennington Terrace were magnificent – huge old mansions.

We're off tomorrow so I'm cooking a chook as usual so that we have cooked chicken in hand for easy meals. I've been a brick this week as I've I roasted a joint of beef as well the other day! Two roast dinners in one week is almost worth a celebration when we're on the road. It gives me an escape route though when I'm tired like last night. John had the rest of the cold beef and fried himself some sliced potato. A funny meal to my way of thinking, but he enjoyed it. I had a fried egg on toast later, which was quite enough to satisfy me but wouldn't have satisfied him. He would have looked at me in astonishment and asked where the rest of his dinner was!

I am celebrating because our family member has suddenly become lucid again and because John has told me that Adelaide is the last big city that I have to face before getting home as we are going to avoid Melbourne and Sydney. That is glorious news!

John has just been reading about the place we are to stop at next and was saying that he could not understand that the word Victor Harbor could have been misspelt as there is only one way of spelling the name. I asked him to read it out loud to me. 'In 1837, Captain Richard Crozier in the HMS Victor......was to give Victor Harbor its name, although the misspelling was the work of a government official and is perpetuated in the spelling of all South Australian harbours today.'

'It's not Victor they are talking about, it must be harbour' I suggested and so it was. Now I've got to check if I've written the word 'harbour' anywhere else since entering South Australia because neither of us have noticed this before! How daft is that though? Someone misspells a word and they keep doing it!

Well I got my computer to do a word search and the 'Harbour' it missed was in South Australia when I wrote about Outer Harbor, so I've found that myself and corrected it and if there's any more then it's just too bad.

Chapter 8

VICTOR HARBOR

I like this story so I'm going to tell you before I forget. In April of 1802 our Captain Matthew Flinders was snooping about in his ship called Investigator when he came across Nicolas Baudin from France in his ship Le Geographe so Flinders named the bay Encounter Bay. Anyway, England and France were at war at that time but as they were on the other side of the world they didn't care a hoot and shared breakfast together, had a natter, swapped maps and went on their way! Very civilised don't you think?

Bliss, dinners over and I haven't got to think about what my other half would like for dinner for hours and hours and hours! We have a lovely large site and there is loads of room for the dogs to play and whilst we were setting up a guy in a coach a few sites away (there's no-one else around) came up to remind us that we were next door to each other in Darwin! That seems so long ago now. He and his wife are young and have three very young girls and apparently sold three homes they had, invested the money, bought the bus, At our last park in Adelaide there were a couple next to us and he is a Sheriff Clerk at the court apparently, whatever that is. Apparently they had worked there for nine months before and this time had returned for a year. 'Have van, can travel to work' or so it seems to be but unlike the majority of the population they take their home with them!

Victor Harbor is lovely and so are the people we've met in the shops or on the street. Everyone seems to love living here and it reflects in their attitude. So we went into town this morning and explored, came home for lunch and read the weekend paper for a while and were both falling asleep. I have an excuse as I've got out of the habit of sleeping properly since our relation became so ill and cannot seem to get to sleep before 2am at the earliest and waking six hours later having got up several times in the night. That has reflected in my health as I feel exhausted and run down, especially as I now no longer have to worry and the full effects of the stress is allowed to come to the surface.

John reckoned we should get out and wake up and I agreed so we headed for Port Elliot (only a few kilometres away), **Middleton** and Goolwa to see the mouth of the River Murray and go over to Hindmarsh Island. A couple of things happened whilst John was driving and he reckoned that I was more awake than him. That was until I saw a church that we had spotted this morning in town, high on the hill, which is in impressive sight and mumbled to John 'It's still there, the church, it hasn't moved since this morning'. I've obviously been in too much traffic!

We came to **Port Elliot** first but didn't stop there until out return journey. I liked Port Elliot and would rather live there and come into Victor Harbour to do my shopping because it's quite busy here.

Goolwa had some beautiful old buildings but our visit to **Hindmarsh Island** was a bit disappointing because the River Murray outlet is being dredged and is completely blocked with sand at the moment! However, in all, the journey was pretty, interesting and we saw some lovely sea views.

We spent a long time at Port Elliot on the way back as we found **Horseshoe Bay** which is very pretty and we could see **The Sisters Islands** and a much bigger island called **Pullen Island** further out in **Encounter Bay**. Apparently Horseshoe Bay used to be a busy port. It became one in 1851 and by 1856, seventy-nine ships were entering it but so many ships were lost between 1853 and 1864 that it was officially closed for port use in 1866. We went up to the headland and took photos of the bay, the islands and from the other side of the headland, of Victor Harbor and the coastline beyond.

I also found an organic fruit and vegetable shop at Port Elliot and was able to get some lovely broccoli, bananas, kiwi fruit, apples, avocados. Having been seeking good produce in vain for so long I was like a kid in a candy store. Which reminds me, another stop on our way back was a shop that sold chocolate, nuts and lollies (sweets) some of which I haven't seen since I left England. I can't remember seeing 'sprinkles' nor some mints that I saw which are green and white striped with chocolate in the middle. I was good and only purchased coffee beans covered in dark chocolate, which we ate on and off on the way home. We still have a lot left and they only cost three dollars a bag

We followed the Fleurieu Way route from Victor Harbor to Cape Jervis (part of the coastal strip is called Lands End) first stopping at **Newland Hill** to take photos. The scenery was totally rural from them on and the hills were undulating and pretty and some of it was beautifully green although the rest was parched. We were really impressed with the stands of pine trees that had obviously been planted to act as wind breaks across farmland and they also lined some of the roads and almost joined overhead in places. Parts of the countryside reminded us of Devon in the U.K and it was much prettier than we had expected. It was basically cattle and sheep country and there were a lot of pretty pink and yellow wild flowers lining the roadways. Nearer to Cape Jervis there were plantation forests and then it opened up again into fields of cattle, some of which were pure black and the sight of windmills in the distance and the sea. We continued to see wonderfully undulating hills until finally we turned left at **Delamere** to head to **Cape Jervis** where you can catch the Sea Link ferry to **Kangaroo Island**. We contemplated doing the trip to Kangaroo Island, but it was too expensive especially to take the motor home! We suddenly saw a field of kid goats, the red roof of an Anglican Church and some beautiful trees with rich, red blossoms and it was a perfect scene. We saw a sign outside a farm saying that they had Boysenberries for sale and I cannot recall when I last saw them for sale at a farm gate. We stopped about five kilometres short of Cape Jervis for a photo opportunity and when I got out of the car I nearly got knocked off my feet with the cool wind.

We watched the ferry go out but it was all very slow and laborious which is probably why they charge so much. I compare this to the vehicle ferries in Moreton Bay, Queensland where everyone is on in a flash, the ferries run at regular intervals and think of the distances those ferries have to travel as they kangaroo hop from island to island until they get to Russell Island. We used to travel with our car for a total cost of around fifty dollars and only two dollars one way as a passenger and yet it would cost us (car and two people) $308 return to get to Kangaroo Island and then we'd have to stay somewhere and buy food.

We were talking to a couple from Ireland who told us that it only cost forty Euros to get from Ireland to England and they couldn't believe the one way price to Kangaroo Island when they saw it in the Lonely Planet guide book. Another lady was looking for something to eat and a cup of coffee but the kiosk was closed until 2.30pm so we sat there to have our picnic lunch. John walked down into the terminal and told me that there was a café with a lounge with glass window overlooking the water.

Our next stop was at **Second Valley** which had some pretty, old buildings on the main road. We drove down to look at the caravan park and jetty. There is a tiny beach where you can take dogs but rather oddly a sign saying that horses are not allowed?

We stopped again where there was a photo opportunity, just before **Lady Bay** (and oddly enough I was to meet and chat with an elderly man who lives there the following day in a different town). The Bay here is called **Yankalilla Bay** and we found that there were three beach shacks down on the edge of the beach. That is what you call 'beachside living' as one of them was on the beach.

At **Normanville** we were greeted with a construction site! All new townhouses, a new hotel, units and houses and some very ugly development to our left called South Shores. We were unimpressed with the town so followed the road to the jetty and the beach. There was a beach café, the Surf life Saving Club and a permanent caravan selling take-a-way food and ice creams. It wouldn't be a place that we would wish to stay at. We even saw a café called 'Seagull's Droppings' – how revolting! There were about four older cottages on the road down to the beach and a few older homes on our way out of town towards Yankalilla but other than that it was brick-and-tile lowset land and very boring.

Yankalilla

Normanville almost merges into this pretty little town although it was not apparent on the map or perhaps it was the other way around because there are a lot of new homes being built on the outskirts.

I had been looking for the shrine of Our Lady of Yankalilla when I was in Adelaide and couldn't find it! I spotted the Anglican Church as soon as we came into the township and was delighted but knew nothing about why it was a shrine. On August 24th 1994 a number of parishioners were startled to see an image of the Blessed Virgin Mary on the wall near the altar and informed the parish priest who called in the diocesan bishop. The Bishop advised caution and for two years all was quiet until an Adelaide newspaper ran an article about it and the church got swamped with Australian and overseas tourists. The Bishop of Murray formally blessed the church as a shrine calling it 'Our Lady of Yankalilla' and it was the world's newest Marian Shrine and the first in Australia. It was first called 'Australia's Lourdes' in 1997 in a feature in 'The Bulletin' (a national magazine).

I was quietly reading information about all this when John said 'You haven't even been inside the church yet' (obvious impatience) so I asked for a fifty cent piece for the Church. Then he told me that someone was praying and that I was making too much noise!

I had also rushed him a bit that day (so he tells me) although we loitered around by the ferry for ages and I do not recall anything being rushed. We both thought though that it would take us most of the day to get around our route with stops for photographs, dogs and cups of coffee but we left home late and got home around three o'clock, despite the fact that we doubled back and went up **The Bluff** (headland) when we got back to Victor Harbor.

John delayed my entry to the church further by pointing out a font which had been brought over by the Vicar of Salisbury Cathedral in 1877. When I did get inside I looked mainly at the wall and moved around a bit because I could not see the image of the Mother and Child. What I saw was a mother holding her dead son in her arms and I was moved beyond words and 'felt' such searing grief that I was choking back my tears. I felt sort of 'tiny' and 'worthless' in the face of this feeling. I could not see her face and for some reason I wanted to. I could see a rose at her feet. After I had got home I read a leaflet that I had bought and there I read that 'In addition to the Apparition's primary image of the Mother and Child, a 'pieta' is clearly visible (i.e. Mary holding the crucified Jesus in her arms). There is a rose discretely placed at her feet to signify and confirm Mary's presence here and emerging on the right side of the Apparition are some letters seemingly forming the word 'PEACE'. There is a lot more information but I can't write it all down.

Apparently on April 24 2000, Easter Monday, at 6.40 four people saw the Madonna standing over the small statue of the Mother and Child in the Rosary Garden and it was the same time as her appearances at Medjugorje in Bosnia-Herzegovina'.

I came out to look at a postcard which depicted the image of Mother and Child to see what it was that I could not see on the wall. John was suddenly there saying 'The dogs and I have decided that you've had long enough'. Well, that did it! Choked up as I was already all I could think of was what a pompous ass he was when I had found the Shrine that I had wanted to find for so long. We had been there for no more than twenty minutes to half an hour. I hadn't had time to read the leaflet and had felt hassled by him even before going inside. To add insult to injury he then added 'You've seen the leaflets, you've been in and out of the church and you've said your prayer'. The latter made me speechless with rage for many reasons but also because I had been praying for him and his children to find each other in love (they have been estranged for years), as well as for him and my children and that had taken me all of four to five minutes, mainly because I knew he was waiting! On top of that the dogs were running around the church ground like idiots.

Perhaps it had something to do with the fact that I'd missed Valentine's Day too! I had been reminded when I saw the red card in the shopping bag as he unloaded the car when we had got home from the shops the day before. I had sort of heard it in the background on the television the night before too and thought 'Oh, is it tomorrow?' and then it had gone out of my head. In the morning he gave me the card and I didn't have one for him and I make cards! In the car I composed some words to him and secretly wrote them down on the lines of 'Valleys and lakes and never-ending trails…..' etc with the first letter of each word spelling out the word Valentine and talking of our journey. Despite writing it down it never got transferred to a card though because I still was too angry by the time we got home! As I cannot express anger, my stomach got upset and I couldn't eat for twenty-four hours. This is what I mean about it not all being wine and sunsets when travelling together twenty-four hours a day, seven days a week for a year.

On the way back we stopped at a junction where there was a lovely hotel for sale called Leonard's Mill Hotel and a beautiful cottage, both of which I wanted to take photographs of. There was a small stream on opposite the cottage and I noticed the name of it was River Parananacooka – what a mouthful! This is an aboriginal name meaning "main river at Second Valley".

Feeling washed out, I put the plug in our small bath and sat there cross-legged and thought of Mary as a person for the first time. A mother who watched her son tortured, crucified and who held him in her arms once dead. Then I realised yet again that there are millions of mothers who have held their dead babies and children in their arms through whatever cause and how lucky I am not to have had to experience that.

I could hear crashing and banging from the kitchen area and asked Mary to quieten John down and it suddenly went quiet and I felt that I could see her face and she was smiling at me and I smiled back, woman to woman in understanding. Maybe I was hallucinating but I don't think so and her smile that I could see in my mind's eye made me want to giggle. She was a woman, just the same as me and I've never before really thought much about her. Most religions do but I haven't despite my (chosen) religious education.

So this morning, as soon as John appeared, I was out the door and back to Yankalilla. I drove slowly as it there is so much beautiful scenery to see and stopped to take photos of wild flowers, blossoms on trees and even of the cows that I stopped to say hello to. I also saw a turning to the right to **Mt Alma** with warnings that the road was only for cars not any trucks or caravans as it was so steep and winding. Up I went and on and on until I came to a T-junction, not having noticed anywhere to stop on my side of the road. I turned around and on the way down there were a couple of places (and I also stopped where I probably shouldn't have done as there were so many continuous double white lines in the middle of the road) and took a heap of photos.

When I reached Yankalilla I first went to the Tourist Information Centre and had a long talk with the young woman there, starting with her views on the Shrine and the visions and then about her own house which used to be owned by Buddhists. She told me how peaceful it is and how the guest bedroom had been the room that the head Buddhist (I don't know his title) used to love to meditate in. Apparently, when she has visitors they can never understand why they sleep so well and for so long, particularly as the sunlight streams into the window in the morning right onto the bed and yet they don't wake up until very late. She has one friend who does not sleep well who actually told her that she needed to come down and stay just to get some sleep again.

I went next door for a coffee and an elderly man ended up on my table talking to me about the Gold Coast, Mt Tambourine where his son lives, the fact that he likes the Glasshouse Mountain area and that he has a son in the town of Seventeen Seventy all of which are in Queensland. He has a lady friend who lives in Mackay who was flooded in the recent floods and she is moving here. He told me that since the road has been sealed into Seventeen Seventy the place has been ruined and that there are now fast food restaurants and a big main caravan park. There was a small park there when I went there many, many years ago but the roads were just dust then and I had to have my car engine replaced because of the roads after getting home. So we had a chat and a laugh and then he brought up the war in Iraq and what he thinks of President Bush, we weren't laughing any more but agreeing with each other and went our own way. I at last got to the church.

This time I had a little more time to look at the information which led me to look at the stain glass windows, one of which is of Mary but which was placed there one hundred years before the images appeared. It is only a tiny church so there are not many windows and most depict local scenery in the background, so the lady at the Information Centre told me. I went outside to look at a huge mural of Mary which is absolutely beautiful and which I hadn't seen the day before. I also went to the Rosary Garden and saw the statue of Mother and Child. I looked at everything and yet was probably not there any longer than the day before but this time I was really taking in my surrounds. There are many notes on the walls being prayers for sick and afflicted people and may people say that they have been cured after praying to Mary. Mary Mackillop has stayed in the building next door. One miracle is needed to approve a Beautification and two for Sainthood and in Mary's case one miracle has been approved. Many people come and stay there apparently from all over the world. Suffice to say that it is worth visiting, it is very beautiful and peaceful and I drove all the way home smiling, at peace and thanking Mary for allowing me such a wonderful morning. A couple of hours later I was able to eat again.

Greeted By A Lobster Coming Into Town

When I got home I walked in the door and John immediately asked me 'Where's the car battery charger?' (we have ordered a new one for inside the van) and the fact that he had been in the middle of a conversation to a friend and the phone battery had run out cutting their conversation dead, and then without taking a breath, how much money he could have made if he had invested $50,000 dollars last December in shares (he has been running a phantom experiment as we don't have the money to invest), followed by how much my petrol consumption has been and then the water usage by our tenants for our home in Currumbin! I stood just inside the door dumbstruck! My head had been in an entirely different place! A real 'Men are from Mars and Women are from Venus' moment.

So I suggested to John that he go out without me and the dogs for a while and I would take my turn 'dog-sitting'. He has been thinking about crossing a causeway to an island and it is far too hot and far too great a distance for Jack who is not very well again. It would also give me the chance to download the photos and do the diary.

Well, John crossed the the causeway and took a one and a half kilometre walk around and over **Granite Island** (Nulcoowarra) home of little penguins and had a wonderful time. On the walk he was passed by the only horse-drawn (Clydesdale) tram in Australia, if not in the world and regrets that he did not have a camera. He had some magnificent views of the coastline of fantastic granite rock shapes and there is a modern restaurant on the other side for thirsty and hungry walkers and yachties. The granite outcrop which forms the island and the Bluff were part of a rock formation buried ten kilometres below the ground level millions of years ago. The surrounding land eroded over this long period of time and the fact that they we are now able to walk upon what remains left John awestruck. There was a photograph of three ladies under a strange ledge like formation of granite taken in 1898, the formation looks the same today a mere 109 years later.

Tomorrow we're off again. Toodle Pip.

Chapter 9

Now for a spot of nonsense

I have just been told by a fellow camper that dogs are no longer welcome at Broome – at least there are no longer any caravan parks that are allowed to have them so it seems our timing was right for once! They will lose a lot of tourists.

John read the words 'iambic pentameter' and said he remembers these words from school days (metrical line in English poetry). I'm darned if I do! I looked up 'iambic' and it is apparently an adjective and a noun. The adjective means 'of or using iambuses' and the noun, usually in plural means 'iambic verse'. Right – I got absolutely nowhere there in my understanding of the first word.

So I look up 'pentameter' and it is a noun meaning either a verse of five feet (work that one out) for example English iambic verse of ten syllables or secondly a form of Greek or Latin dactylic verse composed of two halves each of two feet (pause here because I've been doubled up with laughter) and a long syllable, used in elegiac verse'. So now you know!

What does 'elegiac' mean? This gets worse! Adjectives, (of a metre) used for elegies or secondly 'mournful'. If used as a noun (in plural) means 'verses in an elegiac metre'. An 'elegiac couplet' for example is 'a pair of lines consisting of a dactylic hexameter and a pentameter, especially in Greek and Latin verse'. Next time he can look words up himself because I still have no idea why some writer in the Weekend Australian Review used them unless he wished to seem appear as an academic!

I remember talking to a Jazz critic who wrote for the Courier Mail in Brisbane (not going to tell you how many years ago) and I told him that I read his articles but found it too hard going trying to understand what he was saying and why couldn't he stop using gobbledegook and speak in plain English. At that particular time, the then Labour Federal Government was pushing the civil servants to change their wording, in pamphlets for example, that the general public would receive and indeed right through their own correspondence within their departments and it was common to hear words such as 'Get rid of the gobbledegook' both in the newspapers and within the government departments that I dealt with at that time. I sometimes look up words I read that I would like to include when writing this but then pull myself up and think 'Be fair, I had to look up what it mean so don't use it. I wouldn't use these words when chatting to someone else I'd just met so don't try and seem smart.' I'm used to telling myself off so I don't mind this type of reprimand. I'm pretty nice to myself most of the time so it evens up!

The caravan park here at Victor Harbor is a member of Oz parks so we received our discount and considering the position of the park and the fact that we take up two sites, it is very reasonably priced. It is opposite the foreshore gardens and beach and almost next to the old lighthouse, which conducts tours. It is also within walking distance to town where there are two hotels, three fish outlets (we're going to buy fish and chips tonight from the place that has won two awards), a café, Post Office, a few Real Estate agencies and an IGA store, plus other shops.

The first thing to greet us on our arrival (other than two major garages) was the sight of a giant lobster. It really is enormous and it reminds you that if you go down to the jetty they have lobsters for sale there and even today, a Sunday, the place outlet was open. There is a café there too and of course they sell fish and chips.

If you stop to take a photograph of the lobster, then turn around to the Information booth because there is a delightful park behind with wooden bridges to walk over. On the foreshore there are kilometres of grassland beside the beach. It is really delightful which explains why the park is packed out with caravans and motor homes.

I didn't get to see anything when we arrived yesterday because we had 'the battle of the ants' going on within the van. I have stopped worrying about them everywhere except in our food cupboards and I objected to them being in my cutlery drawer, tea towel and hand towel draw and even all over a drawer that only contains tinned food. I didn't like them scurrying all over our chairs and settee either. They apparently like green tea and loved my Epsom salts which they are welcome to because I only tried using it once but why they had to burrow inside two new dish sponges I have no idea. I did not finish eliminating them until it was time to cook dinner.

It was an interesting journey from Victor Harbour to Kingston S.E. We drove via Goolwa, which we had seen on one of our day trips, but this time the direction took us towards **Goolwa North** and there were more magnificent buildings that we had not seen before. It really is a lovely town with so many beautiful buildings, churches, trees and flowers everywhere. It has

Houseboats On River Murray At Tailem Bend

a beautiful town centre and there is a caravan park there within walking distance to the shops.

Next we went through the Scottish town of **Strathalbyn** which is also a lovely town but did not stop because it was getting hotter and hotter. We went through one small town and as we came out the other end I burst out laughing when I saw a sign that said 'Oops, you've missed us' (it may have been **Belvidere** but I'm not sure).

Next it was **Wellington** and the twenty-four hour free ferry. I had to go before John in the utility as there wasn't room for the bus with the trucks already on it so got the dogs out the other end so that they could go in the water. I wouldn't advise anyone else doing the same though because the water looked horrible and despite the fact that both dogs had already had a long drink each, Jack insisted on drinking the dirty-looking water despite my yanking his chain many times.

We arrived at the small township of **Tailem Bend** where we stayed the night in the caravan park. Just after we arrived there was a cloudburst which took us completely by surprise and it was so surprising that it was on the News that night! Somewhere in South Australia actually had some rain! It was delightful and cooled us down and I became so normal again that I began to do some research and found out that it was not Murray Bridge and inland that I wanted to go to in order to visit a certain stretch of the River Murray. In actual fact I was in the wrong State! Where I want to go is in Victoria, near the New South Wales border called Echuca! It there that the mini-series 'All the Rivers Run' was filmed and I absolutely loved that series and wish they would repeat it on television. There are several paddle steamers to choose from for a trip up the Murray River but I want to go on the PS Pevensey, the 1911 boat which starred as PS Philadelphia in the mini-series.

The Murray River starts in the Snowy Mountains in New South Wales and flows 2530 kilometres before it reaches the Southern Ocean. The length depends on where you are and which guide book you are reading because if you measure it from the Snowy Mountains to Goolwa in South Australia it is apparently 2670 kilometres. It hardly matters; suffice to say that it is a long river! The longest continually navigable stretch is 1986km apparently, but again I guess that depends on whether you have a drought like we have at the moment. The Darling River starts in Queensland and flows into the Murray River in New South Wales and as it helps supply the Murray with water it is of immense importance to the Murray. The Murrumbidgee Rivers in New South Wales and the Goulburn River in Victoria also contribute water. The whole is one of the world's major river networks.

This 'Darling-Murray Basin', which is talked about regularly on the news because it is drying up, therefore involves four State Governments and affects the Australian Capital Territory (ACT) and now the Federal Government (our Federal Parliament is in Canberra in the ACT) is involved in trying to solve the problems of the river as the other States have apparently been squabbling. Let's face it, if one of the States up stream diverts the water the States involved downstream are not too happy!

There is a lot more involved of course and I'm being rather flippant when I really shouldn't be because the situation is really serious with our never-ending drought and the needs of industry and the farmers and the towns who rely on the rivers totally for their water supply. Perhaps one of the T.V stations should rerun the series I was talking about to remind us all of how important the River Murray has always been and still is. In the 1880's several hundred paddle steamers were carrying goods and people along its length. When there was drought it became dangerous though and in 1918 the Federal Government along with New South Wales, South Australia and Victoria formed the Murray River Commission to control development along the river and locks and weirs were built and along the stretch of the Murray inland from Tailem Bend there are six of them and the area is known as the Riverland. Now the Federal and State Governments are revising their agreements and the Darling River has virtually dried up in places.

We were quite comfortable in the park at Tailem Bend until we heard the weather forecast and found out that it was due to be 40C the following day in Adelaide and we thought that the further away from Adelaide we drove the cooler it may well be. Another reason was that John had brought back a tourist booklet on the town of Murray Bridge and it mentioned that it had a variety of places to eat and named three fast food outlets! Why on earth would they advertise that? I had to get to page thirty-five before any attractions were mentioned which included a mini golf course, boat launching ramps, bridges and a cinema. If you read further you find out that you can hire houseboats and that there are some river cruises. The booklet put us right off visiting the place so we set off the following morning for a two hundred kilometre trip along the Limestone Coast to Kingston S.E.

Our first stop was at Meningie on Lake Alexandrina where we pulled into an off-road parking site just before a really nice foreshore motel to have a coffee and so that the dogs could have a swim to cool down as it was already getting very hot. I had dragged John out of bed half an hour earlier than normal and we were out of the park, having hosed the dogs down and had filled up with fuel and were on our way by ten o'clock which is almost a record for us. **Meningie** is quite nice with a Lookout, bowls club, craft shop, jetty a few old buildings and a hotel. It had all the main services such as a Post Office, Police Station and a hospital. As we left town I saw that there is even a golf club on the ocean side of the road but as the terrain is very, very flat around here I wouldn't think it would be that challenging. I'll never know. As I'm driving I hear on the radio that Tailem Bend will be 41C today!

The next stretch along the Princess Highway takes you alongside the narrow but enormously long Coorong National Park which lies between the road and the ocean. With its wetlands it is a paradise for wildlife. At the other end you arrive at Lacepede Bay and Kingston S.E. From this town you can take a sealed road and visit Cape Jaffa, Wright Bay and Boatswain Point (returning each time to the main road to reach the next place).

By the time we had reached here we had had enough of the heat. I cannot cope with dry heat like this. We had the air conditioner on in our bedroom all night. Today I did two loads of washing and guess what? Yep, the sun was covered by clouds, the wind became howling, the van rocked and it rained this afternoon! Callie became quite frightened of the rain (it wasn't heavy rain) which amused me considering that she has been swimming about six times since we arrived here twenty-four hours ago and is constantly being hosed down by us to keep her cool. Fancy being frightened of rain! The other day at Tailem Bend both dogs were so frightened that Callie cowered under the van and Jack wanted to come in. I bodily lifted him into the back of the Ute and shut him in because he was in such a state. The dog's reaction probably illustrates the amount of drought that we have been suffering in the States that we have been visiting over the last forty weeks better than any words can describe. However, whilst we have been away Queensland appears to have been drenched, especially the northern coastal areas and recently in Brisbane.

By four-thirty it was so cold that we were in jumpers, socks and slippers with all the windows shut and thinking about getting the putting the fire on! I'm beginning to appreciate living at the Gold Coast more and more with temperatures that rarely get too high or too low and which do not vary so much on the same day!

The evening before we left Kingston S.E. John did a quick trip to see **Cape Jaffa** which turned out to be a small fishing village with a lighthouse and he returned just as the sun was setting over the ocean. It would have been quite easy to have stayed on a few days longer but we also need time to visit so many places before getting to Portland in Victoria before our friends depart.

ROBE

Just before Robe there is a good off-road parking area by a lake where we stopped for a coffee. We were heading into the township when we saw a signpost to **Beacon Hill Lookout** so went there instead to get an overall view of the area before going into and around the town. From there we could see the town, the beaches and lakes and the coastline in general.

Robe has water on three sides of it and we had a wonderful time there and loved the place. Do not miss the bakery in the main street for superb cakes and coffee and there are so many trees along the main street that there is no problem about parking in the shade, which was handy for us with the dogs. We went to **Cape Dombey** and the **Obelisk** built in 1855 there, **Baudin Rocks**, **West Beach** and around the coastal road seeing **Goat Island**, **Factory Bay** and **Doorway Rock.**

We walked around along the parkland near **Town Beach**, saw the jetty and harbour and the yacht club, the old Customs House which is really quaint and the War Memorial. There is a beach called **Long Beach** (which it is being seventeen kilometres) but there are many other beach areas, a few which you cannot reach as they are down cliff faces and very varied scenery. There are also at least six lakes with **Lake Fellmongery** Ski Lake being the largest. We were very impressed with the town centre and foreshore and the wild seas crashing against the cliffs and rocks along the coastline facing the Southern Ocean. We also enjoyed seeing a lot of old buildings. We had to leave unfortunately because we had booked into a caravan park further along the coast at Beachport.

BEACHPORT

We had booked into a Council Caravan Park which is advertised in a S.A. tourist booklet as having a 'Sewerage Dump Point'. Well, it had two but you are unable to get a vehicle anywhere near them and so they are only suitable for small cassettes. We were rather annoyed at the misrepresentation and only booked in for one night as we needed to empty our black water tank and that is why we had chosen this park rather than the one nearer the seafront. As we were to leave the following morning, it meant that we had to do our sight-seeing as soon as we had parked the bus. First we had a look at the town centre which was small and pretty, with a lovely beach at the end of the shopping street. The lady in the Information Centre was very helpful and gave us a map and a suggested tour route.

It was well worth it as we went on an incredible tourist route called the **Bowman Road** which rivals the Great Ocean Road (although not as long) but this road is pristine and beautiful with not a building in sight. We went the full length, stopping many times to look at amazing coastal scenery as well as the **Pool of Siloam** which is seven times saltier than the sea (good if you are not a strong swimmer) and stayed a long time at the Blowhole. The end of the scenic drive is **Woolley's Rock**. The tourist drive suggests that you return to the Pool of Siloam and return to town via that road but John decided differently and unfortunately we were amongst houses within minutes. We had done so much sight-seeing that day that we were both exhausted but it had been a lovely day.

We were still a bit travel weary the following morning but didn't have much to pack up as we hadn't got much out as we knew it was only a one night stay. We were getting on quite nicely but before 10am some people asked us if we were leaving! Apparently they had booked the site and had turned up early. The guy then started to tell me a long story about his friend who was ill with cancer and I couldn't excuse myself because he was so obviously very upset but I couldn't get anything done. His wife was trying to get him away as she was getting fed up with hanging around and realised my predicament. We eventually got away by 10.15am and set off along the road to Mt Gambier.

MILLICENT

Millicent was a very tidy town with some beautiful rose gardens. We had a cup of coffee there and visited the Information Centre. We noticed the Millicent Swimming Lake and thought what a good idea that is for an inland town but it only 'operates' during the summer months.

One of the main reasons that we went to the Information Centre is because we were not sure that we were on the right road to Mt Gambier. We were not the only ones because another tourist came up to us to say that he was confused. I told him that I had seen a very small sign indicating that he needed to come down the main street for Mt Gambier but he said that the road number that he was supposed to be on for Mt Gambier was the main road bypassing the town, yet the sign indicated that it went to Penola and he certainly did not want to go there.

It is certainly not well sign posted, at least we didn't think so, but if you look at the map that we were given at the Information Centre it is quite straight forward. If you are coming from Beachport or Robe there is a fork and you need to keep right and stay on Williams Road and then go straight on, which avoids the town centre itself and becomes the Mt Gambier Road. We and this other tourist had taken the left fork which is Rendelsham Road. I pondered whether it is intended, so that the town receives more visitors! We purchased coffees whilst there so we contributed to the economy in our own small way. The bonus for us was the roses which we hovered around, smelling each bush individually and all had beautiful perfumes. From Millicent we only had forty-nine kilometres to get to Mt Gambier.

Chapter 10

MT GAMBIER

The town is built on the edge of one of Australia's youngest extinct volcanos and is South Australia's second largest town, with Adelaide being the biggest of course. It has been said that it has one of the longest main streets in Australia and it certainly is very long. We got lost the minute we entered town but did manage to find the Information Centre and get maps. The young girl behind the desk was super friendly and so very efficient and whilst there I even got some information on Nelson (where the Glenelg River meets the sea) and Portland and other places of interest to us such as The Mary MacKillop Penola Centre, which she immediately placed her hands on despite there being endless pull-out drawers to choose from. I asked whether this area is 'dog-friendly' and was immediately given a booklet telling us everything we need to know.

I had phoned a caravan park and found out that they did not have a dump point and were on a septic system and that they did not have town water so our first port of call was the Showground where there is a dump point. The CMCA had held a rally there so we knew that there would be one there and when we arrived we saw some other vans parked. We were immediately welcomed by people staying there and were asked why didn't we book in too as there was a spare place. Apparently the Council is running a trial for a set period of time but only allow a minimum number of sites to be occupied at a time, the reason for which became obvious to us when we set up camp. Anyway, we were told that it only cost eleven dollars a nights and that water and power were included and that there are showers and toilets. We were also told that the caretaker had now left and that we should book in at the garage on the main road and were again struck by the friendliness of the lady who booked us in. She pointed out a tyre company on the corner where John could immediately get a tyre checked as he had hit it on something and the rubber had torn. We booked in for a week and received keys for both the toilets and the dump point with a returnable deposit when we leave. The tyre company told John he could just super glue the rubber which was a great relief as the tyre is fairly new.

Back at the campground we got into position and were amazed that not one of our ramp lights lit up so we had actually parked in a completely level position for the first time on this trip. It was a hot day and I asked John to put the electricity on first as the fridge runs better on it than on gas. When he got his extension lead out, which he was going to need to reach the power post, he realised that he needed new plugs for both ends. I suggested he connect the water and it was then that we found out that there was one tap per five vans! There were hoses running all over the place with double adaptors upon double adaptors. We needed one if we wanted to connect to the water. So John drove off to find a hardware store and spent the rest of the afternoon changing plugs and connecting the water. He spent over forty dollars so the park did not turn out to be as cheap as we had thought! Of course, we may just need that extension lead again and although we have a double adaptor at home a second could come in handy!

Now for some rather startling news - John announced, out of the blue the other night that he's not sure that he wants to travel in a motor home again! This came as a complete shock to me as he is the confirmed gypsy in the family (a trait that one of my sons has adopted) and is always restless and wanting to keep moving and seeing new places. I find this fascinating because we have still have three months to go and have just reached our nine months, which is the length of time that we travelled on our first trip. I was stunned for a couple of moments and then asked him if it is because he'd rather invest money in the share market and get his kicks out trading but he said it's nothing to do with that.

Anyway, back to where we are which is Mt Gambier isn't it? I honestly do not know where I am sometimes and the other night when we were about to go to bed and were enclosed in our van, I thought to myself that I would ask at the reception desk the following morning if there is a K Mart in town. I went outside to talk to the dogs and then realised that there is no reception as we are staying at the Showgrounds. Sometimes when I'm typing this and when I have had to think back to three or four places that we have visited since I last typed, I get up to wherever we are now and have to ask John **where that is!**

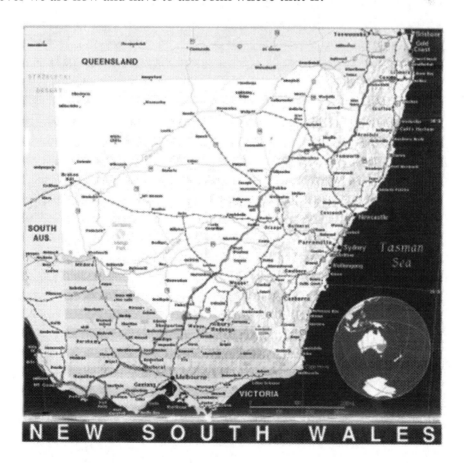

There are so many attractions here that it is hard to know where to start. It is locally called the 'Blue Lake City' and is half way between Adelaide and Melbourne set amidst a unique landscape of volcanic craters, caves, sinkholes, lakes and underground waterways which divers explore beneath the city. There are three Crater Lakes and we visited **Blue Lake** yesterday which changes colour each year in early November (our summer) and changes back to grey in March or April. As it is February it is a brilliant turquoise blue colour. You can walk or drive right around it and there are many lookouts to stop at and your dogs are welcome. At the Blue Lake Reception Centre you can take a glass panelled lift down to near the bottom. **The Valley Lake** is the largest of the three craters and the third is **The Leg of Mutton Lake** which we also saw yesterday from one of the lookouts when touring the Blue Lake. The Valley

Lake is connected to a different underground system to that of Blue Lake and it is a good place for a picnic with a playground for the kids. Of course, you could go to **Brownes Lake** for a picnic too (not sure if I've done all the lakes yet!)

I could start on the caves but suffice to say that the **Engelbrecht Cave** is a huge complex of limestone caves beneath the city and you can do a tour of two of the chambers.

Blue Lake - Our First View

Before giving the dogs a romp around the huge Blue Lake we had parked the Ute and dogs in the under-cover car park opposite the Lakes Shopping Centre and walked around town visiting the **Cave Gardens** in the town centre which has beautiful roses. We went down the steps to look at the cave but you can't actually go into it. We then went to Flannagans Irish Pub where we had lunch and I was given a dinner plate and told that I could help myself to as much salad as I wanted. It cost me four dollars and the salad was exceptionally good.

Very near to the Showgrounds is the **Umpherston Sinkhole** which was once a cave but the roof collapsed and it is now a sunken, terraced garden. We have been told to visit this not only during the day but also at night because if is floodlit at night and that is when the possums come out and are fed. The people here who have been at night have raved about it and have told us we cannot leave until we've been.

The Visitors Centre also incorporates '**The Lady Nelson' Discovery Centre** where there is so much to see and experience that you will just have to go there and find out for yourself. Because there is so much to see here, the Visitors Centre has written up a 'Personal Guide' to help tourists and it includes regional information and map.

There are markets, various gardens to visit, parks, galleries, heritage buildings, antique shops, cheese and wine outlets, theatres, sporting activities such as bowling, Go Karting, two golf courses plus an eighteen hole mini golf course, a skate park and an aquatic centre. Then there are the tours and river cruises or fishing charters and endless nature walks. If you want the beach then **Port Macdonnell** is only twenty-eight kilometres away but that is all I am going to tell you about the regional places as there is just too much information.

Real life intrudes and I've spent the morning washing and typing and John's been shopping for new shoes, a new torch (our large one flew out of the cupboard attacking me in the chest on our arrival here and broke) and a new watch because being unused to rain, he let his old one get soaked the other day and it was not waterproof and it has already gone rusty inside.

We've got the trots. I told you that we're parked at the Showgrounds and tonight's entertainment is the trots. I realised that it is very clever and technical to get horses to race whilst maintaining trotting rather than gallop but I'd rather see a galloping horse any day. John's walked the few metres to join 'the gang' (our fellow travellers who are parked here) who want to know why I'm not there with them but I can see the horses racing from the driver's seat inside our bus and it's cold out there. There seems to be a huge gap in time between each race and John momentarily returned to get a jacket on, to add to his long sleeved shirt. I can hear every word clearly too so it's a little difficult to concentrate on writing this.

Today has been a shopping day, starting at the **Rotary Club's Community Market** where I purchased far too many fruit and vegetables because when I was offered five large zucchinis for a dollar or enough silver beet to last through three meals despite it shrinking when being cooked (like spinach) for only two dollars then I couldn't possibly refuse now could I? Next it was a huge bill at the grocery store as it was time to stock up on fish and meat as well as toiletries and the dog's 'extras' such as new flea and tick collars and worming tablets. I now have bananas, peaches and a huge rock melon that I cannot fit into the fridge so we can't leave until we've eaten some more!

John just returned to say that it's cold outside. I had told him not to take his wallet so I'm now wandering if he really came back to get it because he also said that the horse he fancied just won! Of course it did, that's always the way isn't it? The lady staying next to us has won sixty-seven cents on the last race and is delighted! I've just made a nice cup of coffee. I have to admit that the atmosphere is enticing and as the horses come down the home stretch I feel a touch of excitement. John tells me that I could go over there and talk to the horses but horses have a habit of licking me all over my face and neck and I although I adore them I think I'll give it a miss. (I ended up being invisibly pulled over to the horses but kept my distance, saw a race, walked into the Members Lounge but did not partake of the various food items, met some of our neighbours who were delighted to hear they had won second and third places in the race that I had watched, found and looked at a few market stalls under cover and was well satisfied.)

Yesterday we went sight-seeing. We chose to go down to the beach so off we went to **Port MacDonnell** and our first impression was that we were glad that we hadn't stayed there as we were not particularly impressed. There is a harbour and a jetty and quite a lot of boats were moored there, a very salty aroma and in places there was an unpleasantly pungent seaweed smell. It was the township itself that disappointed us. There is a beachfront path but it is not the sort of beach that you can actually walk along as it's covered in rocks and is rough. Our neighbours here said that they went there and when they saw that their dogs were not allowed on the beach they returned. However, by doing so they missed out on one of the most glorious scenic drives that we have seen.

This is not called the **Limestone Coast** for nothing and the formations of the cliffs, rocks in the sea and the coastal inlets kept us busy for hours with the camera being used continuously. The length of the Limestone Coast is also littered with ship wrecks which is not surprising when you see, from our high advantage point, how many rocks are beneath the surface and hidden reefs. The lighthouse had to be moved because it was too windy! (This might also explain why we have mainly seen only lowset homes (single storey) in the Mount Gambier area but we did notice that people building new homes along the front here in Port MacDonnell were often building a second level with balconies to see the view of the ocean. I do not recall seeing any outdoor furniture on them though. That reminds me, I meant to tell you before that when I get up in the morning I have to put a jumper on, then it comes off and I'm in a summer top (I have to take one out with me in the car if we go out) and then late afternoon I have to put a cardigan on and by evening I'm back in the morning jumper with a thicker one over the top! We have so many clothes out at the moment as the temperature changes so much between morning, noon and night. Now to return to where I was …

We also saw a **Fairy Penguin** colony for the first time and here they are left alone and are not surrounded by tourists who pay for trips to see them. Complete strangers would approach us and it was because of some strangers who called out to us that we saw the penguins and we began returning the favour to other tourists, exclaiming over the beauty of the area and pointing things out to each other.

We had seen a rugged, wild and wonderful coastline and we would have been happy to have left the area but the dogs needed to cool down so we drove along the coast to the other side of town. We had a look at the caravan park that had been suggested to us and at the other end of this park was a 'dog beach'. The dogs had a wonderful time playing and happily got back into the Ute and we stopped in town to buy coffees and ended up eating there. I asked how much a lobster sandwich would cost and when I was told it was over nine dollars I said 'No thanks. How much is a salad sandwich?' That was three dollars and fifty cents and was delicious! I had thought that the cost might be reasonable because Port MacDonnell has been officially named as Australia's Southern Rock Lobster Capital. I thought it might be a case of 'if you've got a lot of something it's cheaper to buy' but that certainly isn't the case here.

On our way back from Port MacDonnell we stopped to look at **Little Blue Lake** where some people were swimming and then stopped at **Mount Schank** which is an extinct volcano. John said that the walk was only 900m and I asked him if that was just to get to the top because there was no way that Jack would make it up to the top and back down. As it turned out he didn't go. It was 1.00pm and nearly 31C and we didn't have much water and when he saw that it would take an hour and I would be stuck at the bottom surrounded by flies he came back.

Have I told you that the flies here have been driving us around the twist? Well they are, especially when I'm cooking dinner and there are swarms of them all over our screens so we have to bang the door to try and frighten them away before making a dash to go outside and do the same before coming in again. John is as handy as I am with the fly swat now.

To get back to **Mount Schank** – the summit is 158 metres above sea level and it appears it must be a very steep track but when you do reach the top you obviously get marvellous views. Once there, there is a steep walk down into the crater, then you've got to get back out again of course. Jack has now reached the point that he cannot manage long walks anymore which is frustrating for us and for Callie at times but I kind of think 'I might well be like that one day and I hope humans don't get too fed up with me and put me down'.

Looking Down Into The Garden

I spotted a garden nursery on our way home called 'Gardenarium' – isn't that sweet?

So it's now Saturday night and we are supposed to be leaving on Monday and we've so much yet to see. Do we have to leave Monday? No, we don't but John is not one who changes his mind so if we booked in for a week he won't want to stay a day longer. I think it's time we had a talk because we just cannot fit it all in – or can we?

We went to **Umpherston Sinkhole** with its beautiful terraced gardens and limestone walls and were very impressed but it is much too cold to go and see it lit up tonight. It's really worth going to and the hydrangeas are glorious and there is some lovely parkland surrounding it.

We returned for lunch and set off again, this time to see the **Laughton Park Gardens** and Tearooms ('a unique tranquil oasis' unless you are a chicken) with great expectations of it as it has won about nine awards. We arrived and duly paid our five dollars each and were asked if we wanted Devonshire Tea, for an extra cost. I told the young girl that I didn't think so but we had no idea as we had only just had lunch and had only just arrived. She replied that she had to know 'Now' and I replied that I wasn't sure. She then told me that she had to know so that they could prepare it and I replied that in that case 'No, we'll go without thank you'. That is not the way to do business in my books. Anyway we had seen it all within fifteen minutes and really didn't think it was worth the visit despite there being some very pretty little spots like fountains and the lake and some statues and so forth, plus a Swiss Cottage cubby house for the children (and me) to admire but I didn't go much on the fake swan on the lake.

Our lasting impression however will be very distasteful because we happened upon the chook pen and I have never seen a bird cage so filthy. It was absolutely putrid and the adult chickens were all up on roosting shelves off the ground but two chicks were finding it hard to find room to move around on the ground and looked so pathetic. The reason they had hardly any room to move was because there was so much thick fruit pulp and droppings on the floor. There was plenty of fruit stacked outside for them and it was obviously chucked inside the door and rotted down into a thick pulp and its accompanying stench. If the chooks had tried to go into this morass they would probably have drowned in it! We felt so angry. We've owned chickens and although some people **may not believe it, they have very distinct characters and can be very good pets for** children because most of them are very friendly. We had one who would come into our house and a few who would knock on the windows wanting our attention. No living being should be kept in these sickening conditions. They certainly wouldn't get too hot because the sun couldn't penetrate where they were and as for running around on lovely green grass, I don't think they would know that they could actually eat it!

Seeking more pleasant surroundings we headed for the **Centenary Tower** at the top of a hill that we had seen before which you access via Davidson Drive near Blue Lake. You cannot drive all the way up so we parked and there was a sign saying that one route was very steep but as we thought it would be the quickest way up we chose that way. We took the dogs and half way up we wondered whether Jack would make it. It was an incredibly steep climb but worth the view when we reached the top. John went up the tower to have a look through the telescope. We were looking over the **Brownes Lake** (which dried up years ago), **Valley Lake** (stunning and a deep green in colour when you are there but when it comes out in photographs you will find it looks blue) and **Leg of** Mutton Lake (also dry) with a glimpse of **Blue Lake** in the distance. We could see the coastline from there without the use of the telescope. We both noticed immediately that a lot of trees had been cut down and asked why and we were told that the area originally did not have trees and it was being returned to its natural state. I commented that we need all the trees we can get on the planet and that we should be planting them rather than knocking them down and was again told that there weren't any there originally and there are so many trees everywhere anyway. I looked at this woman in amazement and pointed out the town and suburban development and asked her if they were going to knock down all the houses and shops and revegetate it so that it becomes like it was originally. She did not answer me as she obviously thought I was nuts. However she did warn me that there was a baby Brown snake around apparently so please keep an eye on the dogs and she provided them with water and wished us a safe journey. I had been looking after John's hat and sunglasses whilst he was in the tower and when we were half way down the steepest part of the path near the top he suddenly asked me where the sun glasses were. I had no idea and said that I had put them in his hat and had placed both of them inside mine so that they wouldn't blow away in the wind. We both thought I had dropped them and he ran part of the way up (I pray I'm that fit at his age) and I carried on walking down very slowly. I am far more worried about walking down steep hills as my right knee is likely to suddenly give way so I was taking small steps and zigzagging back and forth across the path. Glancing down I realised that I had my reading glasses hanging off their chain and my sun glasses hanging off their chain and wondered what I had over my eyes! I started laughing and couldn't stop and sat down further along. In fact I cannot recall the rest of the downward climb as my stomach hurt so much from laughing. I was laughing when John caught up with me and he asked me if I'd found them and I still had them on right in front of him. He had been acting like his father and telling himself off (I'm not the only one who does this apparently) and had been telling himself that if he couldn't look after a pair of sun glasses for a few weeks then he wasn't going to get any more!

We drove down and around the Valley Lake and it's so lovely with the bonus of picnic areas, toilet facilities, an amazing playground for the children down by the lake (including a swing for disabled children), barbecues and plenty of room to play football and so many walking trails to follow, along with wonderful views. The lake had many ducks on it and a couple of black swans and being a Sunday the area was very lively with parties of the elderly and family gatherings and many children but there was little noise and everywhere was spotless with no-one dropping their rubbish on the ground and there is so much room that nowhere was crowded. We were very impressed and all this for the cost of your petrol or pedal power if you have a bike.

We returned around 3.30pm as a few of 'the gang' are leaving tomorrow and I felt I should join the five o'clock get together around whichever caravan or motor home it was to take place at tonight. I managed to stay for about fifteen minutes but I was frozen and returned to our van just as John was going off to join the party so we did a swap! I had a hot bath in our tiny bath, which I can sit in if I cross my legs! Before John returned I was in pyjamas and thick dressing gown and had the fire on. The temperature isn't that extreme but the wind whips around you and the party did break up earlier than usual.

Tomorrow we are going to Penola and John has agreed that we certainly cannot see all the things that we want to see in the time we have left here so we are going to extend our stay. One of the things that he won't have time for is a game of golf and there is a wonderful golf course in the area that we went to today, namely the **Blue Lake Golf Links**. It appears to be very hilly, picturesque and looks quite challenging and interesting.

We didn't get to Penola because by the time the gang head left it was 11.30pm and those who were left felt rather at odds with themselves! I had had two jumpers soaking in a bucket and rather than wring them out I decided to spin the suds out because my wrist has become a bit sore. Big mistake as there must have been too much soap in them and I had water and soap suds leaking all over my wardrobe where I keep the washing machine. It soaked all the paper towels, the soap powder, the tin foil and glad wrap and endless other bits and bobs. Clearing up I noticed that a basket that holds my washing powder and other bits had cracked and needed repairing. Transferring the soap powder to sealable plastic bags, I dropped some on the carpet so swept it out the door and it flew into the dog's bucket of water so their water had to be changed. John was out at the shops so I dried up what I could, sorted out what needed to be dried in our 'hot cupboard' and got a whiskey and lemonade and went outside to calm down. Within a minute a wasp had flown into my face and ice cubes and whiskey flew into the air, down my jeans, over my hands and was dripping off the glass. In the midst of cleaning myself up I walked in some old dog 'poop'. It was not my day and our trip to Penola was called off. John is instead going to trek up, into and around his volcano that he hasn't yet seen and I am going to cut and set my hair so that it looks more reasonable. It's time for 'time out' for me.

John walked up and around the volcano (**Mount Schank**) whilst I cut my hair and set it and felt much better. He tells me that it was a pretty steep climb but well worth it when he got to the top. At the top you immediately find yourself on the rim of the volcano and the wind hits you, surprising you. It is exactly as you would imagine - a rim with a hole and nothing in it. He was surprised that there were no trees growing in it, just low vegetation although there were a few bushes on the rim. The rim was very uneven and very narrow in places and it undulated with steep parts that he had to climb up and down and either side there were steep drops. A sign warned that you that there was no defined path and you go at your own risk.

Tonight we went to see parts of the Mount Gambier night lights drive. **The Lady Nelson** (ship) looked great lit up at night, the Cave Gardens in the city were a bit disappointing and the old Town Hall looked majestic, just as it does during the day. However, we started at the Umpherston Sinkhole at dusk as suggested in our booklet because that is when the possums come out to feed. We met two of them on the steps and fed them some apple which had been left out in a bag on the hedge on the approach to the steps. I stroked one of them and as John seemed surprised and just as I was saying that you have to be aware that they can be aggressive, one of the possums attacked the other and as the one being attacked virtually flew past my head it decided to relieve itself out of fright on my newly washed hair! That was enough for me and the lights were coming on at last in the sinkhole so we admired the sight and left. I wouldn't put myself out to go out at night and do this again nor particularly recommend it unless you really long to see a wild possum.

Tonight we had some new neighbours who were having trouble putting their awning up just as I had started eating my dinner. Knowing how men can be a bit agro if offered help with such things I tried to ignore them but couldn't help noticing the guy losing his cool and yanking one of the arms, which promptly came apart. Dinner finished I wondered over and asked if they needed assistance as they obviously had the similar problems that we are having with our awning (trying to diplomatic) and the wife started by saying 'It's the first time....' When her husband interrupted angrily 'No it isn't, it's broken. Look here, it's broken. It keeps turning around and around and it will have to be replaced'. The wife suggested they contact the motor home company and he retorted that it was nothing to do with them and I smilingly agreed saying 'You may have a leaflet telling you which company you need to contact' and he agreed saying that it was an American awning. Why on earth don't men read instructions? It reminded me of when John and I had trouble when we tried to put our awning up and how apparently people were watching for twenty minutes whilst falling about laughing until one man sauntered over and told us that it happens to all of us the first time we put them up. John had refused to get the instructions out as well and had been telling me to talk quietly so that nobody would notice!

Chapter 11

Penola

When we arrived we parked the car in the shade of the trees near the Information Centre and having picked up a map we had a coffee and gave the dogs a run. We left them in the car with water and went to explore. Penola is such a pretty village with cafes, an old fashioned sweet shop and an absolutely fascinating antique shop with old toys, furniture and even skulls – an endless supply of collectables. There are art galleries and cafes and quaint cottages, particularly down Petticoat Lane.

The Mary MacKillop Interpretive Centre has two exhibitions, one being on the life of Father Julian Tenison Woods, who was to have such a profound effect on Mary's life and the other about Mary. John had thought he was going to be bored and what a surprise he had because we both started with the life story of Father Woods and he was an extraordinary man who had a lifelong interest in science and who questioned Darwin's theory of evolution. There were many exhibits of shells and fossils and other matter that he had collected in throughout Australia and he travelled widely overseas. I think we spent as long in this section as we did in the Mary MacKillop section. As a priest he had to cover a vast area and would take a week in the saddle to get to one town, a month to another, often in terrible weather conditions and still maintain his ministrations to his own congregation in town. On top of all this he managed to find the time to teach poor children.

We were surprised at how many family photographs were available for us to look at and Mary's early days were quite different to Father Woods. He had come out from London and had initially worked for The Times newspaper I believe and she came from Scotland. She was the eldest of seven children in Australia and her father became bankrupt and she had to work, first in a shop and then as a governess. It was whilst she was working as a governess in Penola that she met Father Woods and they would stay linked until his death although they did go their separate ways after a dispute. She visited him before his death though from a paralysis disease.

Before this all happened she worked first for the Cameron family in Portland in late 1862 to help support her family and then in 1863 she gained salaried employment at Common School in Bentinck Street in Portland. At the end of that year Mary set up a boarding school for girls in a stone cottage called 'Seaview'. She left Portland for Penola in 1866. (This information has come from information in Penola and Portland and I'm not absolutely sure of its absolute accuracy but you will get the general drift).

When Mary met Father Woods she was influenced by the help he gave to the poor children when the parents could not afford governesses or school education and she desperately wanted to help him with whatever time she had available after fulfilling her governess duties (I think at that time she was a governess for a family member's children in Penola). They co-founded Australia's first religious order The Institute of the Sisters of St Joseph of the Sacred Heart, initially to provide a Catholic education for poor and isolated children. They dreamed of opening a school, which eventually was built and Mary taught and lived there in 1867. We saw the school as well which is furnished and displayed as a school room of the 1860's with furnishings in the bedroom and the living/kitchen room.

Mary MacKillop has not been canonised but one miracle has been accepted and proven. It will take more than one for her to finally be called a Saint although many think of her as being one now. She had a wonderful disposition and her life was not easy and she had many burdens (as did Father Woods who suffered from frail health) and at one point she was excommunicated from the church along with all of the nuns in her order. Her faith brought love to her heart and she would always be of a forgiving nature and never hold any bitterness in her heart and taught her nuns to be of like mind. Before the Bishop who had excommunicated her died he apologised and they were all re-ordained and the village rejoiced with a party. She left a huge legacy including many schools but I could never do justice in this diary to either of their life stories and I would encourage you to research them yourself.

We returned to the park for a picnic lunch and then drove around the back streets taking photos and admiring some of the buildings. By the time we got back to Mount Gambier it would have been about 3.30pm so we are staying on another day so that we can see the Lady Nelson boat and we have also been told that we mustn't miss the sculptures that are being done at the moment at the Old Gaol House so when I know more about that I'll tell you.

Tonight a couple asked us if we wanted drinks at their place or ours so I suggested ours but before they left our other neighbours turned up so there were six of us and then a new arrival, a coach and out popped four more adults and a small child and our neighbours invited them over too. This had started at 4.30pm and the first couple had long gone home for their dinner so at 7.28pm precisely I called out 'There are no last orders here. Dinners ready'. At last everybody got the message! They hadn't when I had been going in and out the door when I had been preparing potatoes, cutting up and deseeding pumpkin, topping and tailing green beans, peeling and chopping carrots, nor even when the kettle boiled and I made the gravy to have with our lamb chops which surely must have sent a message. It's all good fun though and the new group had just arrived from Tasmania and had picked up the coach they had purchased only three days ago. They asked if we were trying to scare them when we were talking of going up the Adelaide River in Darwin and seeing the crocodiles but we all assured them that we weren't and that it's a really great trip. John and I got a lot of useful information but I'm not sure those from Tasmania left too happy!

It's the following evening and by the time I had got up this morning the first couple to come for drinks last night had disappeared and we went off to see The Lady Nelson only to return to find that everyone else had gone. It's odd this travelling 'meet, greet and do a bunk' type of life, especially when they want to join you for drinks only the night before. I find it odd anyway but it's very Australian to be very friendly on the surface but with little depth behind the overtures. Once you are a friend you become a 'mate' and that's quite a different relationship. At least on the road nobody asks you what you do for a living nor your surname and they know which state you come from by your number plate on your vehicle.

As I've already mentioned, there is a replica of **The Lady Nelson** in town, outside the Discovery Centre and I think, having seen it today, that it does look even better lit up at night. It is and was a small ship and on her maiden voyage to Australia in 1800 she was christened 'Her Majesty's tinderbox' when she was seen sailing down the Thames. Despite her small size, she was the first to sail east through the Bass Strait. At the centre we 'heard and watched' Lieutenant James Grant who told us about his ship. You are not allowed to climb on the full size replica but you see what it was like inside and it certainly was cramped. The ship worked hard covering many voyages until 1824 but calling in at an island named Babar, natives attacked and murdered the crew and the ship ran ashore and was burnt.

The Discovery Centre also has the story of the life of a Christina Smith and we watched the Spectravision where she 'walks out of a photograph' and talks to you. It is quite fascinating watch her 'walk around and sit down'. She came to Australia with her small son when her first husband died and with her second husband established a home and school for Aboriginal people in Mount Gambier. Her second husband died in 1860 and until her death in 1893 she not only looked after her own seven children but continued to care for the sick and needy Aboriginals and part-Aboriginal children. Her great-granddaughter had two books published about her, the first called Twisted Reeds and Reeds in the Wind and a reprint of the facsimile of Christina's diary called 'The Booandik Tribe of South Australian Aborigines' which is a journal of her work amongst the Aboriginals.

There are other sections in the Discovery Centre such as a section about the Wetlands, the region as it was for the early settlers with exhibits, what the marine life was like millions of years ago, a cave walk on a glass floor to see 40,000 year old fossilised bones and rock samples and examples of Aboriginal art on the walls, a Geology Room where you see and hear a neon volcano burst into volcanic activity (made me jump) and numerous other exhibits. It didn't take me long to see everything, mainly because I had read so much yesterday that I didn't feel like reading too much today but I enjoyed the animated exhibitions.

We went into town, took some photos, enjoyed an excellent Italian coffee and went to look at the artists who are presently working on slabs of limestone for the National Limestone

Sculpture Symposium which was at the Old Gaol. The jail is circular with an open area in the middle and school children were trying their hand at sculpting their creations out of small slabs of limestone. I was glad to see that most of them were wearing either protective goggles or sunglasses but very surprised that they were not wearing masks as I can attest that the dust certainly gets in your airways and it cannot do the kids lungs any good. On Saturday the public is invited to purchase the pieces and I noticed that one piece is already sold although there seemed to be none of the pieces actually completed, which is hardly surprising as it is only Wednesday today. However, we will into see them completed as we leave tomorrow for Portland and will be crossing into Victoria and will have to change our clocks and watches yet again

Oh dear, I'm so far behind that I'm not sure if I can recall what's happened. I'll look at my photos to jog my memory.

Our journey to Portland included stopping to look at **Hell's Hole** in the Hells Hole Native Forest Reserve. Hidden inside a couple of men found a 'cenote' (sinkhole) and it is a limestone feature 45m in diameter with a drop to the water of about 30m and the water's depth is about 25m. You have to be a qualified diver and get a permit to dive in it.

Arriving in **Nelson** we pulled up at the Information Centre with the adjacent park by the Glenelg River, had a coffee and went to explore the Estuary and surrounds. It was serene, pristine and beautiful. Nelson itself is pretty where we stopped with huge Cyprus Pine trees forming vast canopies over the parkland providing shade which we appreciated. A Major Mitchell came here in August of 1836 having explored the Glenelg River from Dartmoor and he was disappointed as he had been hoping to find a sea port but the estuary was too shallow.

Picaninnie Ponds in the **Conservation Park** was a beautiful diversion before we arrived at Portland. The water has been filtering slowly through limestone for eons and is crystal clear. We met some snorkelers and divers there and again you must be qualified and obtain permits but I would think that it would be well worth while because the fresh water rising to the surface under pressure has dissolved the limestone to form The Chasm called The Cathedral and it must be quite an amazing sight.

Finally arriving at our caravan park on the other side of **Portland** beside the sea, we chose our own site at the end of the parking areas within metres of a beautiful little beach. We have views from the front of the lounge and all our side windows of the ocean, the seagulls and passing boats. On our other side are some trees where a very plump and healthy looking koala sits in the evening. It would be idyllic if I hadn't read the park rules that we were given. I have never seen anything like it! The whole page is full of thirty-three rules and four warnings and it is assumed that guests are absolute idiots. I took it to our friend's(Sue and Greg) house on the first afternoon we were here so that they could have a good laugh but even Sue was speechless for several moments, which illustrated more than any words could, how stunned she was. She read some of them out to Greg such as one for children being 'Use playground equipment in the proper manner and in accordance with any rules specific to particular apparatus'. Read that out to your kids and see if they understand. Are there specific rules for swings and slides or whatever because if so I've not actually read any? This was a nice one 'Not erect a private clothes' line other than a small temporary line, which is not within obvious view of other park users.' Most of us have little stands we put out under our awnings at times but how do we hide them from view when there are caravans all around you? The idiotic ones were like carrying a torch at night to prevent personal injury and 'Not bring an unregistered or un-road worthy vehicle into the park'. The latter is particularly stupid when they have a vehicle running around this park which the cleaners use and it is so rusty that it looks like the bonnet will fall off at any time and it has no number plates! There is even a special heading called 'Grievances. 1. Use a private, conciliatory approach to the settling of disputes with other occupants, park management, or any employee of the caravan park'. I'm thinking of asking them if it I'm going to be in trouble if I blow my nose in the park as it may cause offence to another person and if so should I draw attention to the above rule!

We also were told that we had to pay a dollar for each dog per day and I asked if that meant the dogs were allowed to use the showers but it's apparently because we use the park bins more often as we have to dispose of the bagged doggy doodles.

We were asked if we had been quoted a figure for a nights stay and when I said we had, we were then asked what we had been quoted per day and I said I couldn't recall but I had it written down in my telephone book. This conversation went around and around and I asked why and didn't they have a set fee? We were told that the owners change it all the time and sometimes give the seventh night free so I immediately said that we'd opt for that. We were also told that sometimes people were quoted only $20 per night so I said we'd have that too. Then we asked for our 10% discount as we are members of the park franchise group. I have no idea whether we have paid for the dogs or not now!

There is one toilet block and laundry for the whole park and we were given a menu and we can order food items if we want. Having read the menu we decided that if we ate there every day our cholesterol would be so high that we'd be dead by the end of the week as everything seemed to be fried and/or fatty so that went straight into the bin.

On our first night we had dinner cooked for us anyway as we were invited to Sue and Greg's and it was absolutely scrumptious and I ate far too much. I think it was the apple pie and lashings of cream that overfilled me but it was so, so good. I didn't eat the next day until dinner time! Sue had also suggested that I do all my washing there as here the water is a mucky brown colour. However, we had so much washing that I did all the coloured stuff in the washing machine here and only took the 'whites'. I had forgotten how clean clothes could appear when washed in a good washing machine, with good water, albeit that she only connects to the cold tap. The next afternoon they arrived here with my basket of washing so neatly folded that we were fascinated by the way she had folded the socks and pants! They also took us out on a tour of the area and we took two vehicles and had the two-way phones running so hot that all the batteries ran out. Sue is a very good tour guide.

Sue had suggested that we leave the dogs in their garden and that they would be quite safe but I demurred at that suggestion as I was worried how they would react. When we did go out, at one point, Sue stayed with the dogs whilst we walked along the cliff tops and she told us afterwards that Jack had not known what to do with himself as he was so stressed out when we left him.

With Sue and Greg we saw **The Blowholes** (which weren't blowing that day), **Bridgewater Lakes, The Petrified Forest** and had a coffee at the café on beautiful **Bridgewater Bay**. The Bay is beautiful and is very popular with the local people. The Petrified Forest is fascinating with what appears to be tree trunks covered in sandstone leaving behind 'petrified trunks' and the walk along the cliff tops is beautiful. It was so nice not to have to look at a map and have a running commentary along the route and the road there and back through the countryside was lovely. Having been offered dinner yet again by Sue and Greg we opted to just have a coffee and come home as it was way past the dogs dinner time again and I wasn't sure how Jack would be.

The night before this trip out with Sue and Greg we had both grieved for Jack as we thought that he was dying. That is what we thought anyway because he could only move his head and front two paws and did not move for hours and hours, which considering he has a pee about every hour is mighty unusual. Lying in bed I was crying from the stomach in heaving sobs and decided that I would be better off outside with him despite the cold and damp. I lay down beside him so that I was facing his eyes which were hazy and I talked to him about getting home with us and stroked him endlessly. He usually likes us to hold his paws but he didn't even want that and I tried to transfer 'energy' to him as he became colder and colder. There was not one part of him that felt warm so I lay outside until 2.30am on a filthy dirty, damp mat with my pyjamas and white terry towelling dressing gown on and slippers. Suddenly I felt him begin to warm up, starting underneath him and gradually all over his body. It was at this point that I finally went to bed. John had a bad night too and saw the sun rise and woke me to tell me that Jack had moved and could stand. When we gave him his morning biscuits which he normally can't be bothered with but he ate them at once so we gave him some more and then more and more and more until he stopped eating. Callie thought it was Christmas as I kept chucking her the odd extra biscuit as she couldn't understand why he was getting more than her. John took them for a walk and Jack was able to run a little.

I realised that when your family or friends die there are often emotional issues such as 'I wish I'd realised that we didn't have much time together' or 'I wish I'd said this or that' or you recall things you wish you hadn't said or done or grieve that you didn't do more but with a pet it is different. I had no emotional hang-ups with Jack because we have given them everything we have been able to and they would both have been dead long ago if we hadn't taken them in so my grief was pure, undiluted love for him. It rather shook me up and two days later I am now feeling rather 'wasted' and have no energy. He's doing quite well although he couldn't use his front leg for a while when we got home yesterday and John had to carry him from the Ute to the mat outside our door. Later in the evening he was able to run again. Tomorrow we have an appointment at the Vet and I'm so hoping we can get him home and it is not decision time.

We did a tour of the town today because I always prefer to do so on a Sunday when traffic does not get in the way of the photographs I may wish to take and after a stroll on a beach we drove to the end of the endless pier and chatted to the fishermen.

Portland is, according to Sue, isolated but it does have advantages. Other than the best vet I have ever come across (different pills for Jack), the house prices are stunningly cheap and apparently if you need to be treated in a major hospital in Melbourne you get priority over people who live nearer! At the moment it has its disadvantages for us because there is a howling wind and we are often frozen and our little fan heater has been on again tonight since we got home. As it is March we have just entered our autumn months but most of the time jumpers and coats are needed and even the locals agree!

We completed the other main tourist drive today and walked through the **Enchanted Forest** (a lot of steps and quite steep in places to reach it) and on to **Flat Rock**, neither of which were very interesting. We went to the **Cape Nelson Lighthouse** which is taller than most lighthouses that we have seen and looked at the views from the vantage points around it and ended up walking down to have a look at **Yellow Rock** and the views from there were worth the short walk and there are ramps for wheelchair access.

I received a text message from Sue telling me that her home phone had been repaired at last so we turned up on her doorstep at teatime and when she answered the door I just stood there and said 'Good'. Obviously she offered us a cup of coffee which we were longing for! As we are seeing Sue and Greg tomorrow afternoon we will have to do our trip to Warrnambool the following day. This is just so that we can say we have completed the round trip of the Australian mainland by coast as we had previously travelled down from Queensland on an earlier trip. We can't say Australia as we have to return to Tasmania because we certainly haven't completed that. Sue and Greg have cancelled their trip away and it seems that we will be extending our stay here - that is if we can hack this cold weather. It is very hot inland at the moment which suddenly seems an attraction but it is also a public holiday on Monday and we feel that the roads will be very busy with people getting away for the long weekend and if they have any sense they will head inland too. Where we are heading is only a couple of hours inland from Melbourne on the River Murray and is a well known holiday destination and camping spot. As we have no idea how long it will take us to get there from here, we cannot book in anywhere.

Sue took us on another tour of the town today showing us the vast amount of land that has been reclaimed from the ocean and pointing out where her husband's family used to live. I have no history like this and I think that he is lucky to be able to point out the places where his ancestors used to live, the land that was owned by family and the fact that there is even a street with named after his family. Sue showed me a charcoal drawing of his great-grandparents and I recall that I only knew one grandmother and that was not a close relationship, let alone beyond that. His ancestors were fishermen as the first settlers in the area were.

Portland Bay was named after the Duke of Portland in 1800 by Lieutenant James Grant when he was charting the coastline in his ship Lady Nelson and the first settlements were by sealers and whalers and from the 1920's to the 1840 the industry thrived. By 1840 the herds of whales were exterminated. In November if 1834 Edward Henty arrived, followed by his brothers and although they were farmers, they also hauled in whales. The Henty's started farming in December of 1834 and they are deemed to be the first settlers in Victoria. Their flocks of sheep and herds of cows flourished and they established various stations although they first lived in a hut. The Government got involved in 1840 and sold town 'lots' and land for cultivation. A building boom followed with hotels, a bank, churches and in 1854 a hospital began to be built and in1856 a school.

An aluminium plant is prominent in the town and we could have done a tour of it but declined the offer. The port is a deep water port and more than a billion dollars worth of cargo is handled by the Port each year. The third main tourist attraction is the **Great South West Walk** which is two hundred and fifty kilometres long, starting and ending at the Visitor Information Centre. We have walked a little of it and covered a fair bit of the coastline by car, stopping at the viewing platforms to photograph the rugged coastline.

In Portland itself there is a large amount of parkland along the beachfront with splendid Norfolk Island Pines and we enjoyed taking the dogs along there and down onto **Nun's Beach** as well as driving to the end of the very long pier where we chatted to a fisherman. We were astounded at how many people were fishing along the pier.

Having shopped today, cooked a chook for the road (so we have something ready to eat whilst travelling) and dinner for Sue and Greg, we said our goodbyes and we are mentally ready to go and physically cannot wait to get away from these cold winds. As the park is fully booked for the long weekend we cannot move sites, so we are leaving tomorrow and have changed our route and are now going to Warrnambool for a one night stay before heading inland. Jack has got used to sleeping in the back of the Ute again which is good because of the cold, moist weather that has been a bonus. He won't stay inside the utility but at least if he sleeps there in cold or wet weather, without getting stressed out being confined, it will be better for his arthritic pain and this morning proved that, as he was much livelier on his feet.

PORT FAIRY

When we flew to Melbourne a few years ago and hired a campervan to drive down the Great Ocean Road (with Helen who then lived in Melbourne) we met a couple at the other end at

Warrnambool who told us that it wasn't worth going to Port Fairy. Our visit there yesterday proved that it is useless asking people what a place is like and you have to find out for yourself, we absolutely loved it.

There is the **Moyne River** which is in such a picturesque setting with boats moored, parkland, restaurant and old buildings alongside and footbridges over to more parkland and you have the sea. You can visit the huge sandy bay of **East Beach** or walk over to the Gannet habitat on **Griffith Island**. A couple we met there told us that in the evening it is an awesome sight watching thousands of these birds returning to their nests on the island.

The town centre has many old and very fine buildings and the surrounding streets are wide and tree lined with giant pine trees that meet overhead in some places and I took far too many photographs of tiny old houses which are beautifully maintained. Some of the gardens are lovely and roses grow prolifically and I delighted in seeing a lavender hedge which was quite high. We toured around and stopped many times and ended up having morning coffee and lunch there and it is only just down the road from Warrnambool and we thought it would be a beautiful place to live. We looked at the house prices and they are very reasonable, although we virtually ignored the modern homes that were for sale further out of the town and concentrated only on the older ones. The residential area around the town is large and it seems to be still growing and I can understand why.

On the day that we were there, people were streaming into the town because they have a huge, four day music festival starting the following day and the place was booked out. There are bands and musicians from all over the world arriving such as a well known Irish band and African music. There will be a mixture of folk roots, blues, jazz, bluegrass, Celtic roots, crossroads country and rock as well as a Folk Circus for the children, markets, buskers and a free Festival of the Streets (whatever that is).

Chapter 12

WARRNAMBOOL

We booked in for our one night stay as arranged and in reception I turned to John and said 'We've made it! We've done the mainland of Australia and we've ended up back in the same park that we came to before!' We hugged each other and kissed each other and the receptionist grinned and another visitor looked totally bemused when I added 'You're never going to ask me to do this again are you?'

The receptionist told us that there is another park where dogs are allowed and I replied that I knew that but it was a few kilometres out of town. When John went back later to enquire, the owner told us that we could stay on over the long weekend despite the dogs. We could stay for five days so that when we leave there won't be so much traffic on the roads. Whilst John was at the reception, I had collapsed on my bed and felt that I would never be able to get off it again. I was overwhelmingly relieved but felt sick with exhaustion so I must have been running on adrenalin for most of this trip which is not the best way to do such a tour but I hadn't realised just how hard it had been for me. I pondered this and thought that perhaps I am just a spoilt brat who doesn't know when she's on to a good thing and that so many people would give their 'eye-teeth' to be able to have done such a trip instead of the daily grind of working and trying to make ends meet or those that are sick, particularly children.

When John returned he told me that for the next five days I didn't have to do anything if I didn't want to and could do what I want. I pondered this too and told him that it was very magnanimous for him to give me permission but I had already decided that is exactly what I am going to do whether he likes it or not anyway! However, when I did get up I told John that had I known that we were going to stay for five nights, instead of driving into the first site that I saw on arrival, which was not a good site as it had pine needles everywhere and we were parked right under the tree next to the road, I would have chosen a different site. I looked around me as everything was set up such as the kettle, toaster, T.V, cups, coffee out, clocks and curtains closed where necessary. The dogs were set up outside as were our normal outdoor furnishings and our bus had been levelled with the hydraulic ramps and blocks placed in front of the wheels. I looked at the site opposite and it was a nice large grassed site which was not under a giant tree and said 'Let's move'. With that I was off in a flurry again as even driving over the road meant that loose cups, jars of coffee and clocks etc could not be left around but it was well worth it.

We had to make that quick decision as apparently there is a huge 'nippers' competition on this weekend here called the 2007 Victorian Junior Life Saving Championships and the place will be teeming with vans and kids. 'Nippers' are the children who are in training to become lifesavers when they are old enough and proficient enough and thirteen to fourteen hundred of them are due to be here so we will probably go down to the beach and watch them. Some will drop out of course as they get older and not become lifesavers but for others it will become a lifelong love and they can continue into their eighties if they are fit enough Not many of them will ever get paid employment as a life saver, with the majority acting as seasonal volunteers. Without them so many people would have died and all Australians value these people for their dedication and the hours they give up willingly to watch over us as we swim and surf. Their biggest frustration is people who do not swim between the flags or who go out in the early morning or in the evening when the life savers have gone. At the Gold Coast some of the life savers got so frustrated that even those who were employed by the Council offered their time for free to extend the hours that they worked.

Warrnambool is also hosting the 33rd Annual Seaside Volleyball Tournament over the weekend and there will be teams from Victoria, South Australia and the ACT (Australian Capital Territory). For those that have well trained dogs there is the Warrnambool Dog Training School Obedience and Agility/Jumping Dog Trials (what a mouthful) being held over the weekend. All will be over by the twelfth of March but the Greyhound Racing is on two days later and a production of Kiss Me, Kate by Cole Porter opens the following night at the **Warrnambool Entertainment Centre**. Two days after that the Gnatanwarr Multicultural Festival starts but I'm going to stop there as you're getting the picture that this is a pretty lively sort of place. I have a three and a half, foolscap page of major events on in March plus one and a half pages of regular activities such as the Go Kart Club Days, Country Music Charity Concerts or Social Croquet.

In the evening I got talking to a young man who has a wife and three young children and he told me that they have rented their house out in Adelaide and are doing what we have done. The older children who are eight and eleven are being home-schooled which means that they have to send their assignments in to be assessed. Sue had given me a load of cards in different colours and I halved my amount and passed it over for the kids to use as folders for their work.

After a bit of chit-chat about different places he looked at me and said 'It's not as easy as you think, is it?' 'What?' I asked. 'Travelling continuously' he added and I looked at him in amazement and told him about the people we had met who had sold everything to live life on the road and that I usually found that it was the men who said it was a great life because they had no lawns to cut or work to go to but their wives usually stay silent.

I told him that very occasionally the wife will say it is a great life but it is very rare in my experience and in those cases the guys are usually silent. I felt like hugging him as we shared our feelings and he told me that he is thinking of getting work again in Western Australia to get back into a normal routine. He hopes that he can earn high wages as he's been working for the Red Cross for years on a paltry income. Again, I laughed and agreed with him, telling him how I'd worked for five years in a legal centre, two of those years without pay to help get it set up and had only left due to becoming ill with sheer exhaustion and had then decided to earn some 'real' money and had gone into the Real Estate industry.

This morning I haven't done anything except for download my photographs of Port Fairy and catch up with this diary. I did watch the gardener 'scalp' the lawns, this always amazes me when we are in drought. We have seen so many caravan park gardeners cut the grass so low that they leave dust and roots behind and the grassed areas become patchy as the sun scorches what is left. What I saw today was so awful that I took photos of the difference as he rode up and down on his ride-on-mower. I haven't seen this done in northern Queensland, nor in northern New South Wales and yet they get far more rain there. I am looking forward to getting back to Northern New South Wales and the hinterland of the Sunshine Coast just to see the green grass again. I am also looking forward to going to North Queensland again and as they seem to have had continual rain since we were last there, as I write this they are experiencing cyclonic conditions and it should be an amazing sight up there. Being a tropical climate it is so green and so dense with growth, it must be magnificent having had so much water the waterfalls will be stunning. When we were last there, there wasn't much water to see at the waterfalls and the dams were low but that has certainly changed.

We're off tomorrow having stayed here for five nights and we have loved it. This afternoon we went into town despite it being the Labour Day public holiday in Victoria and found that the major food stores were open as was a huge camping shop where I found a lovely cream lounge chair, presumably for outdoors but which will look great in our rumpus room and it only cost thirty dollars.

The caravan park is now too quiet with the mass departure of all the children and we miss their vitality and noise! We watched some of their races and were heartened to hear the cheers and see the hugs for the children who came out of the ocean last. One girl returned so far behind the rest of the entrants that she was grinning from ear to ear as she thought it so funny. The mayor turned up to give his speech and the bagpipes played and it was wonderful to see so many happy, fit and friendly kids. The parents were in jumpers and jackets as it was so cold and windy but the children didn't seem to notice as they were running on adrenalin.

We also went to watch the dogs going through their paces and they were having such a ball. I told John that if I had a young dog I would certainly join a group that do these games because it is such great fun for the dogs. The dogs were jumping over hurdles, running through tubes and zigzagging back and forth through poles. One of them got so carried away that he did a few extra! One was so fast that his owner picked him up and hugged him close as he (the owner) danced around.

We have also done the scenic tour around the coastline including the **Hopkins River** mouth and **Wollaston Bridge.** John found the golf club but didn't play, we revisited **Cannon Hill** with its views of **Lady Bay** and **Lake Pertrobe** and we got lost several times in town as it seems to have grown so much since we were last here. We cannot recall there being so many shops and it is certainly a very well serviced town.

Just above the park is **Flagstaff Hill** which is an interactive, 1870's maritime village and museum and we loved it when we visited it the last time we were here. Now they also have a night show called 'Shipwrecked' which includes a sound and laser show and from our lounge we watch the lights at night and can also see the lighthouse which is lit up. We went there again because the Information Centre is also there and I found a present that neither of us could resist for one of my kids and I just hope that next Christmas I remember that I've put it away somewhere! Have you ever done that, bought something for someone and then forgot you put it away? I usually know that I bought something for somebody but cannot recall what it was nor where I've put it and I begin to wonder if I'm imagining it or it was it just a dream that I had had and I turn the house upside down looking for 'whatever it is'. I do find 'it' eventually and sometimes it delights me and at others I'm a bit disappointed and wonder why I bought it in the first place!

I've been reading Bill Clinton's book again and was surprised to find myself thoroughly enjoying it. I am in awe of his intelligence and his thoroughness and his capacity for work. The book gets boring in places because he seems to feel that he has to mention every person he has ever met in his life and include details about everyone who has helped him along his way and I lost count after the first few chapters when he was unknown to the world in the way that most of us are. However, I have just read the section that led up to his deciding to run for President and his journey towards that end and he mentions names of ordinary folk that he met. Now I realise that he probably had someone keeping notes and he kept a journal. When he says that he was shaking hands with the waiters and kitchen workers and had a brief conversation with one of them who became a lifelong friend of his, I feel a warmth creep through my sole. There is so much more to this guy than I had realised, he immortalises in print the names of many ordinary people who approached him with problems and questions about what he would do to make their lives better if they voted for him. He also seems to have the ability to go to bed very late and then get up for an early morning run, anyone who can do that commands my total admiration!

He also talks of his mistake of negatively attacking his opponent in an election and how the public retaliated against him for it, we have seen so much of this in politics in this country and I'm sure that most people in Australia are sick to death of it. He also concentrated on education, responsibility of the individual and other concerns that are very relevant in Australia today and I thought 'Can't we adopt him for our President here?' When I think that he had to battle pre-selections in fifty-seven states in America and that our leaders only have to deal with seven I look at our contenders and wonder how they would cope in America! I don't think we have anyone who could be a President here so we may as well keep our Queen. I've always previously believed that we should become a republican country but I am beginning to change my mind which rather amazes me!

So, I am awed by his intellect, his ability to always listen and learn from any individual and then I looked at the photograph on the front of the book cover. I said to John that with his looks, his brains and his charms I could not imagine working for a man like that on a daily basis because I would be asking if I could massage his feet within three months if you understand my meaning! Still, he hasn't yet become President in this tome and apparently I am in for another thousand names to mentioned according to John and will probably be bored rigid by it. However, at the moment I want every politician in Australia to read his book and learn some lessons from it, particularly regarding the problems we have in this country today as he was certainly very innovative.

GREAT OCEAN ROAD

Although we are not travelling the 240 kilometres of this magnificent coastal road, I have to tell you a little about it. According to one television reporter, The Great Ocean Road has been named the best self-drive road in the world. That might be taking it a bit far and I'm not sure where that statement originated but it is certainly very, very special.

The building of the road commenced in 1918 with three thousand returned servicemen from World War 1 who cut out this road with pick and shovel as they had no mechanical equipment to hand. It was opened on November 26th in 1932. It was one of the very first toll roads and a charge of one shilling and sixpence per car and a shilling for passengers.

As well as driving along the road there is a walking track of ninety-one kilometres and you can do guided walks, accompanied by a ranger, and the walk can be catered to your fitness level. It usually takes about eight days and not only would you see magnificent views and isolated beaches but also forests. Naturally you will see The Twelve Apostles and other major points of interest and the towns along the route.

If walking is not your choice then take the opportunity of flying over The Twelve Apostles in a helicopter for a totally different perspective. Perhaps you would like a cruise into the marine sanctuary to see the fur seals and the trip also includes snorkelling over a wreck. For the adventurous you can go on Argo Buggy rides and climb up obstacles or drive through water. These buggies have eight wheels but they do not have any suspension! However, you will ride through thick bushland and fern forests and gain a spectacular view of Apollo Bay from the lookout.

There are all types of accommodation along the way (including caravan parks) and a lot of ship wrecks to read about on information boards along the cliffs. Pieces of the cliff faces can collapse from time to time but as long as you are sensible, there are some wonderful short walks that you can take from the car parks. Don't rush your trip and read the information because some of the stories of the shipwrecks, the passengers and what happened to them, are so descriptive that you will feel as though you can imagine how they felt. When we went we experienced bitterly cold and strong winds yet still found it an amazing trip but I would advise you do the trip in the warmer months.

Now back to our present trip:

Chapter 13

EN ROUTE

What a day! Before leaving our park we had to empty the black water but I'd already warned John that there was no hose that we could connect to our van to flush the system out. There was only a tiny hose with an attachment that could not be removed, to clean up the area that the waste goes down. There was a kitchen sink next to the area but no tap could be connected to that either. Its Murphy's Law that if things aren't as you expect the unexpected happens – well it was with us anyway this particular morning in trumps.

John was to stay by the van where we attach the wide hose and I was at the waste end to ensure that the hose did not move and this was on the other side of a brick wall. We placed a bucket under the exit attachment to ensure that there were no spillages. Everything commenced beautifully until John popped his head around the corner of the wall to speak to me and the end attached to the van came off spilling our toilet waste all over the grass and path. We tried unsuccessfully not to panic. We spent an hour trying to clean up the area using copious amounts of disinfectant and buckets of water. When we had finished it was already midday.

There was a boom gate to exit and I had the number so went through. I then tried to re-enter the number for John to exit but it wouldn't work so I left John there blocking the traffic and went to the office which was closed, despite a sign saying it was supposed to be open. Another guy approached and I asked him if he'd rung the bell but he was just standing around patiently. In the meantime, John was inching forwards towards the barrier and the guy next to me asked me if he was going to try and crash his way out!

I had intended to tell the park owner or manager (not sure which he is) about our accident with the black water spill but he didn't open the door. Instead lifting a small screen, he had obviously been enjoying his lunch because his mouth was still full and he looked pretty annoyed. I told him that John couldn't get out and he released the gate and we fled!

Whilst all this had been going on the dogs had been in the back of the Ute and Jack was obviously too hot because as we hadn't driven far. I noticed how restless he was and asked John to stop, sooner rather than later. He passed a couple of places he could have stopped, so I overtook him and stopped myself but it was too late. Jack had messed the back of the Ute and it was everywhere. So at the side of the road we had to pull out their leads, dog bed, Ute cover that we fold up and use for Jack to sit on and the fitted rubber mat and use most of our spare water to clean up. The flies told me where I hadn't sprayed with disinfectant. Then Jack started to vomit.

On our way again I was thinking that it was time for Jack to be put down but when we stopped at the next place, for me this time, he was prancing about like a puppy again. We were by a bridge over a river so I thought it a good idea to take the dogs down so that they could have a bath. They walked in, Jack drank a bit and Callie walked out and her feet and legs were absolutely black! I rushed them back to the toilets where there was a water tank and filled a bucket and proceeded to wash Callie's legs and then Jacks and I had to scrub them with a brush. I could not believe the things that had happened in one morning and to think that Jack drank some of that water!

Our next stop was at a town, probably **Mortlake** and we sat at a barbecue table in the shade of trees in a strip of parkland which ran down the centre of town and had a coffee and the dogs cooled off. Well I did anyway because John remained in the bus having some lunch first. I couldn't face food. I think we got from Mortlake to Lismore without incident and then it was across country towards Ballarat.

We are presently camped 25k south of Ballarat and John was disappointed to find that we had driven only about one hundred and fifty kilometres today but with the mornings disasters it doesn't surprise me at all. We think we are at **Scarsdale** but are not sure as we only stopped for John to get gas and for me to let the dogs out. We asked if there were any off-road spots that we could stay at tonight and it was suggested that we come to this park. We had both had enough and this is a lovely area but I'm not sure if it is supposed to be an overnight rest stop. We couldn't have gone on anyway and I grabbed a whiskey and lemonade whilst John fed the dogs. He then got a glass of wine whilst I found the surface spray as the flies also liked the barbecue table outside our van door where John had prepared the dogs dinner.

I was now more than ready to eat and came inside to strip the rest of the chicken carcass and told John that he was on 'fly-swat duty' whilst I did it. John was trying to get a second glass of wine whilst swatting flies and naturally dropped some wine on the floor and grabbed my dish cloth which I grabbed back off him! What's paper towelling for if not for this occasion? Buttering the bread on the wrong side, I piled chicken, stuffing and pineapple into the middle of my sandwich and toasted it in the frying pan with a lid over the sandwich to ensure it heated right through. John went down the steps of the van and spilled his wine on the entry mat and was telling himself off and I told him to 'please just get out of the van and shut the door because the flies are coming in again and I want to eat!' Once he'd washed the rubber mat and grabbed his wine peace reined.

I then raided the fridge for any salad that we had left over and found some diced beetroot and diced tomatoes and leek and added that to my plate, along with half an avocado that was left over. A cup of coffee and a couple of triple chocolate biscuits later and I'm feeling a whole lot better. John came back from exploring with the dogs and couldn't believe I'd eaten 'dinner' because it was so early. I didn't say anything and he looked at his watch and realised that it was well after six o'clock but he didn't get his lunch until about three so he's not hungry. Actually, he's on the bed asleep!

I suppose that finding places to stay for free could be fun but I don't find it so, especially when I'm tired and have two hungry and fed up dogs. Let's hope that everything goes smoothly tomorrow.

I always get confused between Ballarat and Bendigo in Victoria. We went through Ballarat before with my daughter and John, having hired a campervan to tour the Great Ocean Road a few years back. After Warrnambool we came inland and when we reached Ballarat Helen and I both told John to keep on going, as we didn't want to stay there, much to his disgust. Both towns were built around the gold rush and both have some fine buildings but this time as we drove through Ballarat John agreed that he didn't want to stay there either. **Ballarat** is famed not only licence fees for the gold but for the Eureka Stockade in 1854 when the miners refused to pay and fought with the police. They didn't win the physical battle but the government changed its policy and the miners only had to pay one pound a year for a 'Miners Right'. Good on 'em, I say – just the sort of battle that I'd be attracted to!

As before we drove on to **Daylesford** which is such a beautiful place and we toured around the small town centre and admired the old homes and scenery before searching for the lake. We didn't stay the night as we had the previous time but we did find a café by the lake near a second hand bookshop which my daughter had told me about but which I had missed before. We had small, half cold cups of coffee and I baulked at the price of the scones but I did buy a hardback book at the bookshop and found out that they sold coffee and cakes and we wished we had gone there instead as they also have outdoor dining overlooking the lake. The dogs enjoyed a paddle and didn't bother the black swan, the ducks nor the angry goose.

Daylesford was also founded on gold because not all the leases were productive in the major centres such as Bendigo and some leases were sold off to mining companies which were formed and the people came to the twin towns of Daylesford and Hepburn Springs which are only three kilometres from each other, where they were able to find gold much easier.

Mineral springs were also found and appreciated by a group of Italian and Swiss settlers in the post gold rush days and these people realised that their value may be higher than the gold. They were right as the area has eighty percent of Australia's naturally occurring mineral water. It is the spa centre of Victoria but at the moment the spas are closed for refurbishment. As well as immersing yourself in a food and wine tour of the area you can enjoy every type of remedial treatment that your heart desires and that is why it is a top tourist destination for those that know about the area.

We drove on through **Castlemaine** noting that it is quite pretty and has a fairly large suburban area around the largish town centre with masses and masses of trees lining the streets.

When we reached **Bendigo** we decided that we had had enough travelling for the day and we were looking for the Showgrounds. I was in front and stopped every time the lights turned amber so that I wouldn't lose John and we saw the **Sacred Heart Cathedral**, so magnificent and proud up on the hill and the beautiful Alexandra Fountain (c. 1881) with its seahorses and nymphs. The fountain was apparently built from twenty tons of granite. We also saw the Vintage Tram which runs along the main street and apparently out to a place called Emu Point where more than 4000 Chinese people settled during the gold rush. We passed magnificent buildings and every shop imaginable including departmental stores and we realised that we had to stop here longer than we had planned despite the traffic which terrifies me and the fact that we were supposed to be heading straight for Echuca.

This Beautiful Building Also Houses Vintage Clothes

I wrenched my shoulder in the shower a few nights ago and have had three sleepless nights with copious amounts of painkillers and as I am feeling washed out I sent John into town to the Information Centre to find out about the places we have read about since our arrival last night as we have realised that there is a lot to see. There are even six golf clubs for John to choose from!

Meanwhile, I sat out in the sun warming my shoulder and as the pain refused to go away I drank a whiskey and lemonade, which not being the best remedy, worked and the discomfort eased considerably! Half 'pissed' (a very Aussie term) I suddenly found myself in a cloudburst of rain and at present am sitting on the steps under the awning which John had put up to give some protection for Jack from the sun. The ground which is so parched suddenly smells so sweet and I enjoy this moment of complete tranquillity and the perfume of the land. How precious rain is and how much more we appreciate it in these drought stricken areas of Australia. However, Bendigo is noted for its mild climate which gives rise to the amount of outdoor, pavement dining and Mediterranean produce and surrounding the city are many wineries.

Bendigo is a large inland town and certainly much larger than we had expected. Gold was discovered in 1851 by two women who were washing in Bendigo creek and reached its peak in the 1880's when it lost its importance for the economy as the towns in the area were established as was farming and economic activities such as agriculture grew. However, more gold was found here than anywhere else in Victoria and in the 1880's the goldfields were the richest in the world.

One of the tourist leaflet states that 'Bendigo is a city of bold statements and this Central Victorian hotspot lives up to every one of them. The showpiece of Victoria and once the richest city in the world, Bendigo is now Australia's most beautiful regional centres.' That is the impression that we reached when we drove through and talking later to our neighbours camping here, who know Melbourne very well, they agreed with us that it is far better than Melbourne.

John returned from the Information centre with a pile of leaflets and a couple of maps. He tells me that there is an interactive centre there and I must go there and that the whole town is riddled with mine shafts, some of them going down more than a thousand metres. It is time to stop this and look at the leaflets.

Well we paid for three nights stay here at the Showgrounds and will be extending again having been into the city centre today. John dropped me off at the Information Centre whilst he went to park the car and he left the dogs in an underground car park so that they wouldn't get too hot. I wasn't as impressed as he was with the centre but I did tour around it and if you are 'into' mining you may enjoy the films. I was far more interested in the architecture and was continually taking photographs as there are so many beautiful buildings. We went into the **Shamrock Hotel** (renamed in 1855) and this hotel is the third Shamrock Hotel to have been built on the site having been built in 1897. I played Russian roulette with the traffic to get photographs of the Alexandra Fountain, photographed every old building listed in our leaflet, found and went into **The Capital** (Bendigo's Performing Arts Theatre) with its eighteen metre high portico supported by ten metre Corinthian columns and found the vintage clothes shop in View Street and even John was quite fascinated by that! By this time it was time for a great Italian coffee nearby at a pavement café and we were surprised that it was cheap at only three dollars.

Next it was time to find some of the churches and the Cathedral. The building of it commenced in 1897 but it was not finished until 1977 because of a lack of funds. It is Gothic in design and over eighty-seven metres in height and we not only walked all around it but also spent quite a bit of time inside, admiring the paintings which lined both sides of the interior walls which lead you on a journey of Christ's final hours starting with him talking with Pontius Pilate and ending with his body being laid to rest. There was one large painting at the back of the Cathedral of Christ resurrected. John was surprised that there were no stain-glass windows but I think I was more moved by the paintings than I would have been by any windows, however beautiful.

We returned to the car via the Mall where I noticed that the ABC shop had a sale on of books for only five dollars each. It didn't take me long to find one that neither of us could resist. It's a Peter Cook and Dudley Moore book called 'Goodbye Again' and features transcripts of their sketches and I started reading one of them out loud to John. It was about Dudley having a temperature and Peter discussing germs and how God made them first and there were millions of them but He got bored with them and decided to produce people……(something to that effect anyway. I was having difficulty reading because I was convulsed with laughter and we were still laughing when we entered the shop despite the fact that I was only half way through it. Another customer was listening to me and grinning whilst we were trying to pay amidst our howls of laughter but I didn't get the time to finish it all. We've put it aside for now because I must get through Bill Clinton's book and it is difficult enough to find the time to read anyway.

John went and got the dogs out of the car but the noise and traffic confused them so I held on to them whilst he went and fetched the car and we decided to go and book John in for a mine tour for tomorrow morning and return home. I feel that we've only 'touched' the city as we still have so much to see. To start with we have not been into **Rosalind Park** which is in the centre of town and is twenty-seven hectares! There is enough to see there to keep us happy for a whole day and we can take the dogs. We also haven't been to the **Golden Dragon Museum** and I haven't looked at the shops, other than a few antique shops and the ABC shop that I mentioned. There seem to be a fair few shops selling second hand clothes which always interest me as I like to find clothes that you cannot find in the major chain stores. We got slightly lost on the way home and came back past a lagoon and have decided to visit that tomorrow on our way into town. I also noted a sign at the entry to this Showground about the markets which are on every Sunday. I had booked into a park in Echuca on Sunday but we think we'll stay here and leave here on Monday instead.

Finding the time to write this diary is sometimes difficult and I now have to recall our 'Chinese Day' and download the photographs I took on that day despite the fact that I am at our next stop! This time however, I am going to write backwards by telling you about Sunday before Saturday! Sunday was the day that we left to go to Echuca as planned but I awoke at 7.30am to find the market in full swing. We were parked on the top of three levels and had been told that no-one would come up to our level but there were cars driving up to park. This was a bit worrying as John needed room to get out later! I found a red 'witches hat' used at road works and placed it behind our bus to stop people parking!

Having taken the dogs for a walk I walked down the steps to look at the stalls and there were so many of them, both inside the large warehouse buildings as well as outside and by the time I returned I felt absolutely worn out with all the sights, sounds and aromas. I still hadn't done any packing up nor had breakfast which ended up being a banana. I had just finished putting everything away and shutting all the windows and roof vents when a lovely couple came dashing up to ask if we minded them asking us about our van. We ended up talking to them for about an hour and the guy amused me when he told us that his partner had never been outside Sydney and was amazed that people smiled and said 'Good day' and had remarked that if she did that in Sydney the people there would think she was nuts. Anyway, she wanted our telephone number and address as they are interested in purchasing our bus but are not sure that they will have the ready cash when we want to sell. We have just ordered a new windscreen which will have to be fitted so we won't be selling it until we have had that done.

Now for the previous day which started for me with 'very urgent laundry'. When it gets to the stage where I have no clean knickers left and John has two pairs but no socks we have to start counting the days and pulling out the necessary number from the dirty laundry bag to get us through to the day we hope to get it done!

John's day started very differently because he visited the **Central Deborah Gold Mine** in Bendigo. The mine no longer operates as water, contaminated by minerals, has reached the lower levels of the mine. However tours do reach eighty-five metres below the surface. John enjoyed donning a helmet, mining lamp and the accompanying heavy battery pack and went on a tour through a honeycomb of tunnels with a guide to level three, which is sixty-five meters below the surface. The tour group were shown 'fools gold' on the rock surface and then the real gold. They heard about the hardships that the miners suffered and the 'widow-maker' miner's drill which was actually shown in operation. They were warned to cover their ears as the sound of the drill in the confined space was deafening. The term 'widow-makers' arose because so many of the miners died from the dust and conditions by the age of thirty-five.

Originally only two candles per shift were issued to miners, that being their only light and they had to pay for the candles themselves. Originally the miners only had helmets made of cloth and compensation for death or injury was pitiful. The operation of other machinery and a variety of drills of different vintage were shown as well as heavy mine machinery on display.

Management had various methods to stop miners sneaking gold out from the mine for illegal sale, the main one being that the men had to strip off in one room, have a shower in another room and then had to walk past the foreman before dressing to leave the mine. Theft was never fully stopped as some miners swallowed nuggets to be retrieved later!

John returned for a quick lunch and then we started our sight-seeing together by visiting Rosalind Park in the town. We climbed the **Observation Tower**, viewed the Bendigo Heritage Mosaic depicting Bendigo's mining history which was completed in 1987 by hundreds of volunteers from Bendigo and we went to see the **Cascades** which are water fountains.

We spent most of the rest of the day in a different world. We visited the **Chinese Joss House** (place of prayer) which was built in the 1860's with hand made bricks. Apparently the Chinese religion is a combination of Taoism, Buddhism and Confucianism. The God worshipped in this temple is Kuan Kung, a warrior hero.

The first small building where we entered was the Caretaker's residence with information on Chinese beliefs and the gold rush in Bendigo and there were a lot of items to view. In the Front Entrance Chamber there was an altar with a figure of Confucius and an altar cloth depicting The Eight Immortals. There was also an example of the type of altars which was normal in most Chinese homes.

The Temple was where we spent the longest time where there was a figure of Day Fong Sun, the God of filial piety and wealth who symbolises love and respect for parents and who after the death of the father, mourned so long and sincerely that tears turned to blood. There were figurines of the twelve years of the Chinese horoscope cycle which is based on the moon rather than our western horoscope which is based on the sun. I took a photo of the Rat for John and the Horse for me! **The Temple** was rich with colours and again there was much to see.

Th**e Ancestral Hall** is dedicated to the memory of ancestors and there was an altar and a large commemorative tablet to all the Chinese who died on the goldfields. There were two wooden panels which read 'Buddhism brings you luck and eternal good fortune' and 'The Spirits of the dead bring you good omens for ever'. A white Buddha of Yu Loi Fa, the protector of the very poor and pictures above the altar depicting the First Lord of the Heaven, the Queen of Heaven and several others that I do not know of caught our eyes. There was an altar to Kuan Yin, the Goddess of Mercy and apparently she is so popular that her shrine is found in practically all Taoist temples. A banner over the front door means 'Inherit the past and usher in the future' which is sage advice.

From there it was time to find the Dragons so off we went to the **Golden Dragon Museum**. The **Kuan Yin Temple** was more like a history museum starting with the arrival of the Chinese during the gold rush years through to the present day. There were so many pieces of beautifully carved furniture to see, so many wonderful dragons, recreations of street scenes, shops, workshops and homes with models dressed as they would have been many years ago. Then there were the carved screens, beautiful costumes, the jade and the beautiful ornamental pieces to view as well as a lot to read. We had probably spent too long in the **Yi Yuan Classical Chinese Garden** looking at the architecture and admiring the colours and pergolas before we went into the museum because we were the last to leave and they needed to close so we obtained a 'Pass Out' just in case we wanted to return in the morning again without having to pay another entry fee.

It was well after five o'clock by the time we got the dogs out of the Ute for a walk and all they really wanted was their dinner but John suddenly had a wonderful idea. 'Let's go and get the shopping out of the way' he declared and I was too tired and stunned to argue. I did try to put a halt to his idea by saying that the shops would be closed but he asked a passer-by who told him that they were indeed open until quite late on Saturday evenings. I felt like clouting this complete stranger! So we went to do the shopping and I walked around in a daze whilst my head was still swimming in red and gold and all things Chinese. I couldn't seem to quite capture that Buddhist peacefulness somehow as I still had to cook dinner when we did eventually get home.

There are two things I would have liked to have done before leaving Bendigo and the first is that I would have loved to have gone on the **Vintage Talking Tram Tour** and the other would have been a visit to the **Discovery Science and Technology Centre** which is for all ages and is advertised as one hundred percent 'hands-on-fun'. The reasons that I agreed to leave is that someone shouted out of a car that we were 'freeloaders', despite the fact that we were paying money to stay at the showgrounds, the fact that the day before the wind had created a dust storm which had been very unpleasant and the dogs and I got dust in our eyes and I was so covered that I had to strip off my clothes in the shower cubicle and wash my hair as well and the fact that I needed to get the sheets and towels washed and there was nowhere there to do them and it was too dusty to hang them up on our line anyway. **The Showgrounds** were cheap, the amenities clean and it was centrally located but it is not a place that we wanted to stay for too long. We had no plans originally to stop in Bendigo, not even for a coffee break or lunch stop. Had we known that we were going to like the City as much as we do, then we would

A Different View Of Murrumbidgeee River From Our Park

have booked into a caravan park for at least a week. Had I known before what I know now, I would have suggested to John that we book ahead to spend Easter here and enjoy the Chinese Parade at the Bendigo Easter Festival which is an annual event which, from what I've read, seems to be quite spectacular. I believe events are planned over a four day period and details of this year's events were about to be released when we left.

Chapter 14

ECHUCA

In a previous section headed 'Victor Harbour to Kingston SE' I mentioned wanting to go to Echuca on the River Murray and gave information on the length of the river and the boat I want to go on. Well we are now here and although an electrician told us today that it never rains here, it has been since we arrived yesterday which was when our 240 volt power system failed us following a smell of burning wiring! Because I have two weeks worth of washing to do it is also due to pour with rain tomorrow and I may be forced to use a tumble dryer for the first time on our trip.

We have enjoyed our first full day here and have already our electricity supply repaired, John has found a dentist who may be able to fit him in tomorrow to repair a broken tooth, we have thoroughly enjoyed visiting the town centre shops and have found everyone to be very friendly and helpful. The shops are interesting because there are a mixture of antique and second hand bookshops, shops retailing some exquisite home wares and several shops selling variety goods at very cheap prices. I was surprised to see some of the franchise clothes shops here as they seem somewhat out of place in such a historic port town. However, it is a pretty town and there are many places to dine or enjoy coffees with tables both inside and outside.

We have been over the bridge into New South Wales and seen **Moama** on the other side which is much quieter and has a totally different atmosphere. We had picked up our huge parcel of post and have dealt with all it contained and we have also just had a fine roast pork dinner which I rarely have the time to cook. It turned out surprisingly well, cooked in the electric frying pan, despite the fact that I forgot that the electrician would return and turn the power off to do further repairs half way through its cooking period! Even though it's been raining it has been a very good and a very full day.

Today has not been so good! I bathed in Murray River water last night because the water for this park comes from the river and you need to use the water tanks for drinking water. The guy who owns this park has been using the sprinklers all day yet there are pools of water all along the park roads as we have had so much rain! What a wicked waste of the River Murray water! It is still pouring with rain and we arrived two days ago and the dogs are getting a bit fed up. I was fed up today too, as I spent all afternoon getting the three loads of washing done and drying most of it in the one tumble dryer that ate up dollar coins. Then it was ironing, bed making, downloading over one hundred photos which were still on the camera from our trips to the mine, park and Chinese day in Bendigo and also dinner to make. The electricity cut out twice again and the second time we could again smell burning wires so we are pretty worried about it.

The next day I awoke to see dense fog outside the windows which I haven't seen since living in England! I took the dogs for a walk with a waterproof coat on and my 'wellies'. It's a good job I wore them because I came back with them caked in mud having been down to the river. At last the fog lifted and we enjoyed a hot but steamy day and took the dogs to town with us. We explored the river parks, admired the huge trees and investigated the shops along Main Street which we hadn't visited before. There were some really quirky shops there and I came out chuckling from one of them only to hear a passerby say 'Everyone always comes out of that shop laughing'. They had so many gifts with humorous jokes on them as well as others with beautiful words. There were shops with antiques, old books, furniture and household goods, arts of all kinds, a camping shop and a couple of old fashioned sweet shops. We also visited the **Old Port** area which we loved, watching a horse drawn carriage clopping past, looking at the steamers running up and down the river, looking at the shops and we went to investigate the underground sly grog bar in the **Star Hotel** and the escape tunnel. The amazing thing about this underground bar and tunnel is that the property was privately owned for years and it was only when the National Trust took over its ownership that this underground area was discovered.

In a book of hereditary we found my maiden name and apparently, as it had an asterisk next to it, I also have a coat of arms. It is the first time that I have ever seen my name in print in any hereditary information.

I also asked if there was a DVD available of **All The River Run**, the TV series (or even a video tape) and was told that there were none available, but that I could put my name down and the shop would forward it on to my home address. I'm glad that I did not take up the offer because the next day I found out that there was a video. It had been edited and shortened and no more were going to be produced, it was not a financial option to digitise, and that the full version would not sell. I wonder how much postage money this shop is sitting on!. I asked why it is not shown on television again, especially as there are continual reruns of British comedies and other programs and many of our own are continually repeated. I was told that Channel Nine own the company who did the original edited version. Shame on Channel Nine when they re-run so much rubbish and yet they have such a quality Australian series with Sigrid Thornton as the female lead.

It would attract a higher viewing audience with a new generation who are far more aware of the environmental problems than we were when we first saw the series. As the Murray River is mentioned nearly every other night on the T.V news, wouldn't you think that something would click in their heads and that they would cash in on this series by repeating it on prime time television and then releasing DVD's for sale. My daughter, being one of those 'next generation members' has told me that she loves Echuca but she has never heard of the series as she was a toddler when it was televised!

Let's give you some info on the area instead of prattling on like this:

The twin towns of Echuca and Moama were founded by two ex-convicts from Lancashire, England. They were sentenced on the same day in the same court and one them, named James Maiden, started to run a punt in 1846 across the river carrying stock and people from New South Wales to Victoria (on the other side) and he also built Moama's first Hotel called Maiden's Inn. However, in 1953 the other convict arrived, named Henry Hopwood and he suggested a river port be formed and he built a bigger punt on the site which is now Echuca (on the Victorian side) and he went on to build shops and hotels and became known as the 'King of Echuca'. One of the hotels that he built is the Bridge Hotel which we visited. An example of his high self esteem is epitomised by an advertisement that he apparently put in the paper which read '**Hopwood Bridge Hotel**. As this is already known to be the best hotel outside Melbourne no more words are necessary' (I believe I have the wording correct).

It was he who persuaded the Victorian authorities to extend the railway from Bendigo to Echuca and to build the first part of the wharf at Echuca in 1865 so that produce, wool and timber could be transported to Melbourne from here by rail. The goods arrived by boat via the Darling, Murrumbidgee and Murray Rivers. In 1879 an iron bridge was completed which linked Echuca and Moama. However this bridge was just for the railway and people were not allowed to use it and still had to use the punts. The people rebelled one day and swarmed over the bridge so it was decided that the people could use it after all. Henry Hopwood, being such an enterprising fellow, charged three shillings (I believe that's the figure we heard but it seems extraordinary) for each vehicle and a penny for each and every sheep to cross the bridge. Not to be thwarted, people started to use the train instead and eventually the fees for the bridge were stopped, but to this day, the bridge has never been officially opened by either the Victorian or the New South Wales Governments.

There is an odd story about the fact that nobody in authority could agree who would be responsible if, for example, someone died on one side of the river or the other. Would the New South Wales authorities deal with it or the Victorian? The river eventually became part of New South Wales and that solved the problem! Normally the boundary lines were down the middle of the river but now they are officially staked out.

The world's largest fleet of operating riverboats run from here and it always has been and still is a working port and the original, huge red gum wharf has been maintained. Echuca was once the world's largest inland port being 1.2 kilometres long and was apparently a pretty lively place with (about eighty) pubs, breweries and brothels alongside the finest European fashion boutiques! They worked hard and played hard in those days.

The Mary Ann was the first paddle steamer to journey along the river reaching Echuca-Moama in 1853 but she was abandoned and sank at Mannum where she still is today.

The oldest wooden-hulled paddle steamer in the world is the **PS Adelaide** of 1866 which could carry forty-nine passengers and we have watched that paddling up and down the river. The Adelaide was originally used to bring wool to Echuca and later to tow barges loaded with red gum logs for the saw mills. She has been restored and is now one of the fastest paddle steamers capable of sixteen kilometres per hour (twelve miles per hour).

The **PS Pevensey** (which was named 'Philadelphia' in 'All The Rivers Run') is undergoing repairs to its engine but we are hoping it will be well enough to run again by Thursday. She still has her original engine and considering she was built of wood and iron, here in Echuca, in 1910 as a barge and became a paddle steamer in 1911, she is entitled to an overhaul now and again and we are prepared to wait. She has the capacity to carry one hundred passengers and used one ton of wood per hour under steam. However, even today, if they are to run the paddle steamer they have to start preparing the boilers eight hours before departure.

The **PS Canberra** was built in 1912 in South Australia and was a fishing vessel and general cargo steamer before being converted to a tourist vessel in the 1940's. It has been restored and is now powered by a 1923 steam engine.

Ps alexander arbuthnot

Another original boat is the **PS Alexander Arbuthnot** which was also built out of wood in 1923 to carry forty-seven passengers. It was the last paddle steamer built for the riverboat trade (the first time we saw that coming up the river we could not make out its name!)

Then came the **Pride of the Murray** in 1924 and it was built in Echuca and carries ninety-nine passengers and can be used for functions as well as daily tours.

The last I will mention is the **PS Emmylou**, the prettiest and although she was built between 1980 and 1982 she is powered by a hundred year old engine. She is the only wood-fired paddle steamer in the world offering regular overnight cruises or two and three night cruises. She is fully licensed providing a local wine list and morning and afternoon teas, lunches and dinners are available.

So you can choose a paddle steamer cruise on, get married on, stay overnight on or perhaps choose to dine on such as the floating restaurant called the **M.V. Mary Ann** where you can enjoy authentic Italian food. Of course you could also go DIY and hire a houseboat or just a speedboat for a few hours.

The paddle steamers towed barges which carried the cargo and there is one here called **Ada Barge** which was built in 1898 and which carried up to four hundred tons of wool bales at a time but it requires extensive restoration. The **D26 Barge** which was built in 1926 has been restored and is at the wharf.

There is a lot to do here, you should come here and find out for yourselves. So I won't tell you about the wineries, nor the fishing, the wetlands, the red gum forests, the National Holden Museum, the Jazz, Food and Wine Festival, the Blues….no, this must stop. Did I say fishing? Well you need to know about the **Murray Cod** because it's Australia's largest freshwater fish and can grow to 1.8 metres in length and weigh up to 113kg – catch that and eat it! It would make one heck of a burger.

A new day and our second very hot day greeted us this morning and we were due to go out on the PS Pevensey. Our neighbours and the park owner suggested that we leave the dogs under the awning and our neighbours offered to come and visit them as soon as we had gone. The Manager of the boats that run from this one particular company had told us that we could take the dogs on board but I wouldn't have been able to relax. When we arrived we found that the boat wasn't running! We were offered a cruise on a different paddle steamer, but as we were very annoyed the Manager told us to follow him whilst he tried to find out what was going on as it was scheduled to run. To cut a long story short, he offered us a two day pass so that we could go and visit all the historical exhibits, join the guided tour and told us that we could go aboard the PS Pevensey on our own and have a look around. This turned out to be very advantageous for us because it took us well over two hours to see everything with the guided tour being an hour long on its own. The only part of the tour that we had missed was a visit to the Star Hotel which we had been to yesterday anyway.

There is so much to see and so much to learn about the old port days, not only about how the town was first settled, the paddle steamers and the trading but also about the arrival of the railway and the bridges. Then there were all the personal stories to listen to, for example inside the rail carriages, films to watch, displays to look at and a vast amount of machinery to look at. We saw engines for various industries, farm machinery, logging machinery, steam engines, photographs, old newspaper displays, rules for employees who worked for the railway and of course the paddle steamers and thoroughly enjoyed our quiet tour of the PS Pevensey. When we left the museum area and old wharf we went to the Bridge Hotel and viewed the 1800's hotel rooms and squatters suite. Then we rushed home for the dogs, both of whom were fast asleep! Tomorrow we actually get to go down the river on the paddle steamer at last.

We are now staying on until Sunday as we have to stay here anyway tomorrow night as we don't want to pack up and rush off after a morning on the river and the seventh night is free (in our case the Saturday night) and the electrician is returning that morning to check the wires in our transformer at the back of the bus. I believe it is causing the problem so we are going to get all the wiring checked.

What a busy morning! The Fishing Classic is on this weekend and as there is a boat and five thousand dollars worth of prizes up for grabs and it is for all age groups, our park has been busy as we have a boat ramp here. I wondered why so many policemen were around on an intersection towards town this morning and then it became obvious that there is a cycling race on today too. Returning from the shops I saw a gathering of motor bike riders who had arranged to meet here at a hotel. In the meantime, whilst I was in town, the electrician found not only a burnt out wire but also a badly burnt plastic bracket exactly where I had told him the problem area was and that was repaired with no extra charge. Just after he left, John went to put the awning down because the wind was so gusty that the metal bars almost toppled him over and swung over the top of the bus and broke! He's been running around since I've been back trying to arrange repairs, so it seems we will be here longer than we thought. It is certainly a lovely town to get 'stuck' in though so I'm not complaining.

We were driving around town yesterday and found another shopping section in town with a large Safeway/Woolworths store, butchers, chemists and other shops. I spent most of my morning, enjoying an extremely hot and good cup of coffee at the café and reading the free newspapers provided. I also bought a lot of hormone free meat at the butchers and was amazed at how cheap the bill was. We are amazed that we had been here nearly a week and hadn't known that the shopping area existed. (Excuse me, a metal bar just blew off the roof. Oh no, another one…….)

The dogs were not killed nor was I, as I clambered up the ladder and over the roof. I found a metal mallet that John had left up there on the awning – just over our entrance door! Jack Nicholson may have enjoyed sitting in a chair on top of a motor home the same as this one of his film(About Shultz) but I'm not into it, especially with wild winds like this. Yesterday was 37C and I didn't know what to do with myself. There is a pool here but it wasn't cold enough so I resorted to the hosepipe several times. Then overnight it rained, was very cold first thing and I needed a blouse, jumper and anorak on to take the dogs for a walk, plus my boots which got muddy again. By late morning it was bright and sunny and it would be burning hot if it wasn't for these winds. This place is advertised as having more sunny days than the Gold Coast and a Mediterranean climate. Sorry, I think it's typical Melbourne weather and it drives me nuts as we need so many different types of clothes out for the same day. The Gold Coast has been hot this year but at least it is more consistent and I don't think that it's got as high as 37C.

We have just been told that the house next door to us in Currumbin has sold for an amazing amount of money and it is a third of the size of our house on a much smaller piece of land.

That's nice news. Thank goodness we had a lousy agent and took it off the market last year! We now know that we can expect at least seventy-five thousand dollars more than we thought for our house, I have to work my butt off for a year to earn that in the area that I worked in Real Estate. I don't feel so bad about not working now!!

Yesterday we at last went on our river trip and I just loved being on that boat. I stood beside the captain, watching him manoeuvring the paddle steamer which was not as easy as I'd thought because of the river currents, the bends, other boats coming past and the fact that some parts are deep and others very shallow. Paddle steamers don't need much depth of course, only about a metre and loaded as a cargo boat it apparently only drops about four feet according to the captain. However, the river can still be too shallow in places and I was surprised to see the captain turn the wheel left, seemingly veering the vessel towards another paddle steamer but then realised that the current was driving us the other way – anyway it was interesting for me to watch. I asked him whether it was true that the Murray is eighty percent full in this area. He showed me the natural river height and added that this year they had stopped the flow (the river has several lochs and weirs to regulate the flow) a month earlier than usual and that the water comes from the Snowy Mountains here and is pretty good. We have already noticed that the river water is so much clearer than the tank water, the latter which is supposed to be the drinking water, so we are now giving the dogs the river water to drink and they have stopped getting upset stomachs.

We then had a coffee and I asked what temperature the milk had been heated to as it was perfect and was told that they didn't use a thermometer but that most cafés heat it to sixty degrees and they prefer to heat theirs to about seventy. I approve because coffees are too often served not quite hot enough for me and I cannot drink anything really hot because it causes me to have hiccups so I'm sure that other people must find the same problem.

Sunday was a lazy day. It was a good day. The shops are open seven days a week though if you must stir yourself on a Sunday.

Chapter 15

26ᵗʰ March 2007

Would have been my Dad's Birthday if he hadn't died, I was twenty-six. It also meant that it was our Wedding Anniversary and we think it was our 24ᵗʰ – we're hoping it was because if it wasn't it would have been our 25ᵗʰ! We've been trying to work it out but have failed so when we get home we'll check our marriage certificate and if it was our 25ᵗʰ then we'll just pretend that it's next year and celebrate then!

It was a good day and we decided to have lunch out rather than dinner (our normal routine). We had planned where to go but I spotted a restaurant near the Amcal chemist which advertised that their food was all home cooked and the menu looked enticing. We had seen the pavement dining area but it turned out that there was a very pleasant small rear courtyard which is where we chose to sit. John got impatient waiting but we had the most succulent, thick steak (I had mushroom sauce with mine and John had the pepper sauce), excellent salad mixture and chips and it was certainly worth the wait. I found it very relaxing looking at their herbs growing in pots and their Grecian fresco on the garden wall with music playing in the background and we didn't get home until 3 o'clock so I guess we were there for a quite a while.

It is a fully licensed restaurant but we were too full for any drinks. I asked where they bought their meat and was told where their supplier is and also told that there is a farm gate shop. I could go and buy the meat and cut it up myself as they do and that because this meat has never failed them they are afraid to try any other supplier. I haven't the room in my freezer to purchase such a large piece of meat and am no expert at cutting it up. It is an art in itself and can make a lot of difference to how the meat cooks.

Today John has gone to golf and I have been trying to catch up on some hard copies of photographs of our trip for our album. I have spent the last two nights doing it and am still behind by fifty files! It is quite tiring trying to be very selective and choosing only four or eight photographs for example, out of perhaps thirty of a particular place. I have not yet got to Mount Gambia and that one will be a nightmare as we did so much there. I have only just finished Margaret River in W.A and I shouldn't have put it off for so long. We enjoy our albums though and I kept the last one on our coffee table and we looked at it so often so it is worth maintaining. Having done some hand washing and the vacuuming it's time to get back to the photos. Talk to you later.

Saturday 31st March

We were at last able to leave Echuca today having waited for parts to arrive for the awning and for the repairer to find the time to fix it. We did not travel that far today, stopping off along the way to visit **Cobram** where we found a bakery opposite the Old Court House which served the most beautiful pastries and perfect coffee. We also went down to the river there, in several places as it turned out because the first two places that we tried would not allow dogs.

When we arrived at our destination, **Tocumwal,** we were told by the lady at the Information Office that everyone stays down by the river for five dollars a night so we went to investigate in the Ute. A friend of ours had advised us not to park under the red gums as they are not called 'widow-makers' for nothing and can drop huge branches very suddenly. John told me that when he had been at the repairers the other day there were a couple there getting a quote on their caravan because a tree branch had damaged their van badly. When we were at the site we thought that we could park next to the river, away from the trees but I was concerned because there were so many dogs off leads and so many vans and tents there (it is the Easter school holidays now so there were a lot of children too) and there was even a horse having a swim! I started to move the Ute only to find that I was getting bogged, I had to reverse four times and try different routes to get out of the sand. I told John that I wouldn't want the motor home being parked there which only left the areas under the trees, so we went off to find the caravan park we had intended staying at originally. When we got there the manager asked us if it was the school holidays! I didn't answer and he replied answering his own question and then told us how much he would charge us, we told him the price was ridiculous and walked out. We tried the other caravan park (we are members of both the parks anyway) and although the lovely lady, Joy, seemed a bit concerned about our two large dogs which they do not usually accept, we ended up with a beautiful site with thick, lush, springy grass. We enjoyed lazing around after arriving but will leave tomorrow and have another look around the pretty town on our way out.

When we were in Tocumwal this morning I looked at the 'Specials' board at a hotel which usually signifies what on the menu is cheap that day and often on Sundays it is a roast. The blackboard read 'Cooks Playing Golf at St Andrews' which made me laugh. I've seen many signs saying 'Gone Fishing' but not that one. Now I'm wondering if it was because it is April Fool's Day! When I get home and I'm sick of housework again I'm going to make up a sign saying 'Pretty Woman's gone looking for Richard Gere'.

NARRANDERA

I've been experiencing one of those sublime moments that seem to occur far too infrequently. Our park is by **Lake Talbot** at Narrandera (we are now in New South Wales having crossed the border at Tocumwal). John was in the shower and I moved to the front of the motor home and we are overlooking the lake and boat ramp. The view across the river is of trees and some look like weeping willows and they cast their shadows over the water as it is now 5pm. It is totally peaceful as I watch the wide arc of ripples running across the water formed by a boat that has just pulled in. There is only the sound of the ripples, the water sprinklers and the birds calling their evening songs. Another lady sits under a tree further up reading her book. An elderly man stands and just looks at the view and feels the tranquillity like me and we do not speak for it would spoil the moment. Although this part is called a 'lake' it is part of the Murrumbidgee River and it looks very full and very healthy and the weather is perfect being sunny and brilliantly bright but not too hot.

Beside the park is a water park with two enormous swimming pools and a super enormous children's pool and the cost of entry is only two dollars! There are also some water slides, one quite big but you have to pay extra to go on them – a whole twenty cents extra. On our first afternoon I went through the park gate and across the narrow road and wondered why a couple were standing beside their car just looking at it as if perplexed. I soon found out why – the place was closed! Our park had many visitors from Victoria because the school holidays had already started there but the New South Wales children were not due to break up for Easter until later in the week. John asked the park owner why it wasn't open and was told that it depended on how many people were there. Well we would have been, the couple outside would have been and another couple who recognised us from a previous park had been heading there when we arrived! Perhaps if they had been open they would have found that they had plenty of visitors as it was hot that day.

I sat on the river bank and watched two families with their young children and a boat. The older members of the families had been water skiing and between their turns they had pulled the small children along behind on boards. The little ones wanted to learn to ski but were also afraid to learn. The adults put them on skis in turn, showed them how to bend and how to hold on to the bar and the boat set off with an adult holding the child against the boat so that they were safe. One young child was asking to go but was also crying with fright but when he returned he was euphoric. It was wonderful to watch. We have a view that is so beautiful and the town and suburbs are so pretty that we have booked in for two nights and are wondering whether to stay longer. We are at the stage of weighing up how long to stay in a place against how long it is going to take us to get home without pushing the journey too hard.

We are well into Autumn and I can highly recommend this Riverina area (which is inland) at this time of the year. Back in Portland, on the coast of Victoria, they have been having bitterly cold and windy weather and I can now well understand why there is a mass exodus at this time of the year, with people seeking warmer places to spend their winters. Two days ago I had two jumpers on at this time of the evening and I now sit here in a summer top.

We spent three nights at Narrandera as we loved our site and surroundings so much and I spent one morning looking around the town on my own and taking some photos whilst John looked after the dogs because it was too hot to take them anywhere. That last day John noticed that the river had algae along the foreshore and wondered why it had changed. The morning we left I had the radio on and one of the local townspeople were enquiring as to why their water had turned brown since water had been released into the Murrumbidgee River a few days before. One of the outcomes of this bad water was that both the dogs initially got bad stomachs again on our second morning. We changed their water and gave them some out of our reserve containers which we knew was good water and I went down with the same problem that same afternoon. Three days later and I am still suffering and feel absolutely wiped out with exhaustion.

Upon leaving the site John forgot to lower the TV aerial and it was badly damaged by overhanging trees, another thing to fix! Always go through your check list before leaving the site, just as an aircraft pilot does before takeoff.

PEAK HILL

Peak Hill - Gold Mine - One Of Several Craters

We are trying to stay at different towns than we did on our last trip and the caravan park that we are in was recommended to us. It is very cheap and even cheaper for the first night because we are CMCA members. It costs $19 ($17 for CMCA members) the first night, $16 the second and $13 per night thereafter. It is a small park but has a good amenities block and lovely owners.

So yesterday we travelled three hundred and twenty-five kilometres which, for Jack, is good. The dogs were so well behaved all the way and it was me who kept asking John to stop every time we saw a public toilet! We travelled through **Finley**, **Narrandera**, **West Wyalong**, **Forbes** and **Parkes** before arriving here. At Forbes I lost John! He had been looking at the prices of gas at the petrol stations and decided to turn around and go back to a previous gas station. I carried on and pulled over on the road to Parkes. I kept getting these frantic calls on the two-way radio asking me where I was and that he was on the right road and he couldn't find me. Then the two-way kept fading out and I knew that he must be going in the wrong direction, but tell him? Oh no, that would have caused a row. He suddenly contacted me again and said he had been on the wrong road by which time I had walked and watered the dogs, had a sit down on a wall with them in the shade and had got them back in the Ute! With all the stops for me, a lunch stop and stops for the dogs it took us a lot longer than most people to get here.

We had originally planned to get to Dubbo by Thursday to get the remainder of our awning fixed but then I realised that it is John's Birthday on Thursday and didn't think that rushing through Dubbo and getting repairs done was a great way to celebrate! So we are staying here for three nights and will leave on Good Friday, hopefully a quiet day on the roads, the seventy odd kilometres to Dubbo where we have booked into the same caravan park that we stayed at last time as we liked it so much. On Tuesday, when everything opens again, we will get the awning fixed and continue on our journey towards home. At least this time we will be at Dubbo when it is warmer as the cold nights drove us away much quicker than we wanted last time and I always said that I'd like to go back one day.

Peak Hill is described in the tourist book as 'the little town with a big heart of gold...' and indeed it was founded on the discovery of gold in 1889 and there is a tourist gold mine here including scenic views from the hill and you can try gold panning. There is also a golf club and it get to it you drive via the Fauna and Flora Park noted for its orchids in the cooler months. There is also the **Goobang National Park** which is about 42,600 hectares (forty species or orchids have been identified there) and there is a lookout with superb views but we will not be able to go because of the dogs.

I've read that Peak Hill is rich in arts and crafts so that will keep me happy today and we are also going to check out the hotel and clubs and decide where we will enjoy John's Birthday dinner tomorrow night.

In the morning we are going to return towards Parkes to visit **The Dish** made famous more recently by the film of that name. The film was about the story of the part this telescope played in the 1969 Apollo 11 Moon Landing and it was also an amusing and moving film and one that you could watch more than once. The Dish is a sophisticated CSIRO radio telescope (as opposed to an optical telescope) in the middle of a sheep paddock. We expect to stay for several hours as there is a **Discovery Centre** with experienced staff to talk to and displays, hands-on There is a film called 'The Invisible Universe' which sounds interesting and another where you have to wear glasses to see the 3-D vision of an imaginary future space flight to Mars where you can stay in a hotel.

There is also a café and free BBQ and picnic facilities. We have to turn off the highway twenty kilometres this side of Parkes and go another six kilometres. If you are passing by there is apparently plenty of room for caravans and coaches to park. Entry to the Discovery Centre is free so if you are interested in buying lunch or coffee or want to browse the books and just look at The Dish then it will cost you nothing. There are modest charges to see the shows. When the dish is tilted is being used for Astronomy but if upright it is undergoing maintenance and it will continue to probe for radio emissions from deepest space until well into the twenty-first century. It can be used day or night because radio energy has no colour.

Well the day turned out to be cool enough for us to take the dogs which meant that I could go too. I had phoned the centre first to ask about shade and we parked them under trees with water and they were fine. Unless you have children I wouldn't bother with the 'space trip' film as it was pretty daft and showed the rocket going straight up to the moon without showing its orbital path and it was a bit disappointing. However, everything else was fascinating and as we were leaving John spotted a dish at one side of the picnic area and read that you should stand facing into it and whisper and get someone else to do the same at the other dish way over the other side nearer the entrance to the centre so we did this. It was amazing as the clarity of sound was better than when we are sitting in the van together! I am seriously thinking about getting them installed all around our house and garden so I don't have to raise my voice all the time for John to hear me. When he had a hearing test before we left he was told that he was a 'borderline case' and whoever did the test has no idea what they are talking about – they should try living with him for a day!

The previous day John had visited the **Peak Hill Gold Mine** where, between April 1996 and approximately 2002, three million tonnes of ore were sent for treatment. Two and a half million tons were discarded but ninety-five thousand ounces of gold was extracted, worth fifty-five million dollars. There were five open cuts (craters) only two hundred metres from part of the towns residential area.

There were photographs of historical mining times as well as modern processes and John said that he walked a fair way as there is a pathway over the old workings and he walked around the two open cuts.

GOOD FRIDAY – DUBBO

A sign greets you reading 'Welcome to the Mighty Tidy Town of Dubbo' which it is but when we booked into our caravan park and settled onto our large site, we discovered too late that there is Bindi everywhere. Bindi flowers form spiky thorns (there are actually two kinds) or spiky balls and we are treading them into the van and as they are blowing around outside we cannot keep our ground mat clear of them. They are getting caught in Jacks fur and have to be cut out and whenever we take the dogs for a walk they invariably start limping or stop altogether and lift their legs to ask us for help. We have paid for four nights so are stuck. We are also stuck because we have to get the awning fixed on Tuesday. On the other side of the park there are sites but it would take us so long to put everything away and move that John doesn't want to bother. I wanted to jump at the chance of moving to a beautifully grassed site where the neighbour told me he was walking around bare footed. We are digging Bindi thorns out of our shoes every time we come in the door! We have been to this park before but I certainly did not have this problem then or we wouldn't have returned to it. But I suppose it depends on the Season of the year.

We are back to the question that we asked ourselves the last time that we were here and that is 'Do we go to Dubbo Zoo'. It is one of Dubbo's biggest tourist attractions and I have found out that there is free accommodation for your dogs. **Dubbo's Western Plains Zoo** brings thousands of visitors to Dubbo every year to experience the African Savannah. You can drive around the six kilometres in your own car (or use an electric cart or bike) as it is an open range zoo of three hundred hectares with over one thousand five hundred animals. The animals are separated from you by hidden moats and barriers. We feel we should go but have to admit that neither of us is a bit interested in going to see rhinoceros, tigers and lions in a zoo. However, if you do like these animals then this is a superb zoo with personal encounters where you can feed animals or go behind-the-scenes on the 'Early Morning Walk' to get close to the animals. There is a successful breeding program of endangered species including Australian native wildlife. The admittance ticket lasts for two days so it seems that there is a lot to see, experience and learn.

Bill Clinton's Book and I have been together in bed a lot these last few evenings because my stomach complaint has continued until today (hopefully it's gone anyway) and I am still overawed by the machinations of government in America and can now understand why any Presidential aspirant needs so much money to be able to campaign. I was talking to John about the size of Australia versus the size of America, the amount of states that America has being disproportionate to Australia versus the population and how much of the Australian land is unpopulated. It made for an interesting discussion. I now have a very high regard for anyone who has become a President in the United States, even those in my lifetime that I haven't liked!

Dubbo city centre has a very long main street with masses of trees so parking in the shade is not a problem. There are a large variety of shops including a Meyers departmental store and it was heartening to see that there seems to be an enormous amount of boutique shops thriving as well as the usual franchise chain shops.

On Easter Sunday John set off to enjoy an ultra-light aeroplane gathering whilst I watched and listened to a choir singing in a cathedral on the television. I needed to be reminded and enjoy the true meaning of this public holiday. I didn't enjoy being away from my kids yet again during an important part of my year. We had bought chocolate eggs but my stomach was too bad for me to eat it until late afternoon. On Monday we spent the morning visiting the **Old Dubbo Gaol** and I spent the afternoon in the Dubbo Hospital! It was therefore a day of confinement, the former which was very interesting and the latter boring although also informative!

The doctor asked me when I'd last had a particular examination and I thought about it for a while and said 'I think I had one of those done about fifteen years ago'. 'No, no, no. You would have had one done before your gall bladder was taken out wouldn't you'.

'No'.

'No!' 'So you had a xxx test done instead?'

'No. I had no tests done at all. The surgeon said I needed it our because of my symptoms'. By this time he had his head sort of bowed with one hand on his forehead'

'Tell me you had a zzz test done at least.'

'No. I told you, absolutely nothing. After I'd had the operation I started coughing blood and he found two duodenal ulcers so I got treated for that with the tablets'. By this time his head was on the desk with his face in both hands. I tried to cheer him up by telling him that I was given something – a card which stated that he was a Barrister of Law and the comment that he charges so much because people like me sue him and his insurance costs are high. He looked at me without speaking and his eyes seemed as though they were looking in two different directions.

Later he asked me, or rather told me that I must have had dietary advice and I said 'Yes. That I could eat whatever I want to within a week.' He looked away and groaned. He wanted me to stay so he could sort me out and I rather liked him, particularly when he yawned whilst listening to my chest with his stethoscope and I told him he shouldn't do that and that I was the only one entitled. He told me that it's boring listening to people breathing which made me laugh and then added that his eighteen month old son keeps waking up at 4am every morning. I suggested that he might just want to play and is sick to death of teddy bears and try giving him some books to read because it sorted my eldest son out when he was not much younger than that. He grimaced and assured me he didn't want to play and I retorted that he was the doctor so either work it out or stop getting up every night and he'd soon get the message. That's the best tip I can give any new Mother – be a really heavy sleeper like me and you won't hear them anyway so they'll sleep through the night from around ten days old which is when you will become immune to their noise. All mine did except for the week when my eldest started to wake up as I've said but he made the fatal mistake of grinning at me and clapping his chubby hands with glee and that was the last time I got up! We had angry screams the first night after that at the same time, a shorter period of angry screams the second night; a whimper on the third and then all was peace again. I was told to feed my babies every four hours which meant waking them up – absolutely ridiculous. I had a foster child that needed spoon feeding with milk almost continuously and another that had to have half strength formula every two hours because of lactose intolerance and then my last daughter wouldn't wake up! I'd give her a feed at eleven o'clock at night and she wouldn't wake up until the same time the next morning! I was so worried that I took her to the doctor but she was so plump that I was told to stop worrying.

Anyway, the last thing the doctor said to me whilst I was trying to get out the door was 'Don't eat any big meals and get that test done as soon as you get home'. I then knew why the roast pork dinner I had had the night before had felt like a lead weight inside me. I wish Dubbo was nearer home.

10ᵗʰ April, 2007.

We didn't leave Dubbo until around midday as we had to get petrol (the bill was astronomical as both vehicles were running on empty), get the awning mended and go into the city. We have only seen the town centre over Easter and mainly when the majority of the shops were shut for Easter and it was interesting to see what a hive of activity it usually is. Dubbo has a very long town centre road with most of the chain store shops and a great many independent boutique stores. Trees line the roads and there is also a mall and with all the outdoor dining and some interesting old buildings the overall effect is that it is a very attractive town. There is also a great deal of parkland around the main centre within easy walking distance.

We had been told by a previous caravan park owner that we could avoid using the main road out of Dubbo when heading to Coonabarabran and that it is straighter, less hilly and has less bends and that 'all the people using caravans use this road'. An added bonus is that you travel less kilometres. We took his advice and turned right at **Brocklehurst** to go via **Mendooran**. A second right turn found us on a quiet back road travelling through forest reserve and it was very pretty. It was also very bumpy in parts so it is a road that you amble along and hope that you have no screws loose in your vehicle.

We stopped not long after taking this road as Jack obviously needed to stop and he had a very upset stomach from being bumped about. John found the oven door open, the cupboard door beneath it open and one of our flasks on the floor along with a slab of cheese out of the fridge! By the time we reached the other end of this road where we rejoined the highway the contents of some of our cupboards were all over the place. I'm not sure it's such a good idea after all and the main road would have been much quicker. We were previously told that you do not travel on the roads on Tuesdays either side of town because of the trucks which load up on Mondays. Because it was Easter, we were told that Tuesday would probably be quiet on the roads but Wednesday the trucks would be nose to tail along the highways and as long as you avoid Tuesdays I would advise you to steer clear of our 'short cut'!

Chapter 16

COONABARABRAN

We are now happily ensconced in the caravan park that we stayed at during our first trip to Coonabarabran.

We had to get our winter quilts (doonas) out and put them on our beds the first night we arrived and in the morning I got out of bed and started shivering. I later found out that John had left the windows open in the lounge and kitchen along with the roof vents. Then I found out that the hot water tank took ages to heat up and wondered what the temperature had been over night. Luckily we had put the dogs in the back of the Ute. The days are glorious though with clear skies and temperatures in the mid to high twenties. However, first thing in the morning required two jumpers, Ugg boots and jeans and I saw some children with jumpers and anoraks on like me. On the other side of the road was a cabin which had been occupied for the one night and the lady came out in the morning in a sleeveless summer dress, bare legs and sandals. I pointed her out to John and he said 'From Melbourne'. 'No, from Eastern Europe I reckon or else she's come from Mars' I answered. I'm into all this astronomy stuff now as you can tell!

I sit outside in the evening now and can easily spot twin stars and have regularly seen orange ones and a red one. I didn't know you could see red stars but apparently it is not the whiskey and you can see them with the naked eye.

I watched a sensible man back his car up to his caravan today. He has an outdoor aerial with extension poles and he puts one in a holder on the back of his four wheel drive and another where he normally put his aerial and puts a red tag on top of some sort. Anyway, he uses these visual posts to back up to an exact position and the red tag tilts over! His wife was inside the van and he didn't need her to say 'Right, no left, back a bit, a bit more, no, no, no go forwards again…' which is what we usually hear and which has put us right off towing anything.

We've seen some wonderful letter boxes on this trip and we were to see many when doing a circular tour from Coonabarabran when we went to the Siding Spring Observatory. We have also seen a lot of amusing names on the front of motor homes. One which we saw recently had me confused for a second because I wondered why anyone would want to let people know their name. It read 'Miss B. Having'.

The Siding Spring Observatory is a collection of ten telescopes including the Anglo-Australian telescope which is one of the world's largest on Mt Woorut, I have pages of information which I am not going to relate here because you'll have to go yourself. We were told at the Information Centre that the short trip was about seventy kilometres but don't believe it because we did fifty kilometres on the main road returning to town having been through the National Park. In all we reckon that the short trip was about a hundred and forty kilometres. **The National Park** is about thirty six kilometres west of town being about nine kilometres past the Observatory. Siding Spring Observatory is Australia's largest Optical Astronomy Research Centre. The work that is going on there is extraordinary and one of the basic facts that I learnt is that today's Astronomers do not often look through telescopes but take their data from computerised readings.

Anyway, when we got there John went into an Exhibition area where you have to pay to go in and I decided that I'd prefer a coffee and cake and I had a ball. A coach load of pensioners had just arrived and some of them were looking at some wind chimes that were on sale with a sign stating a forty percent reduction in price. 'How much is that?' asked a lady to no-one in particular. Well it's just over half the price so add a couple of dollars I told her. 'How much is the wind chime?'

'Twenty-four, ninety five' she answered.

'Twenty five dollars so halve it, making it twelve dollars, fifty cents and add two dollars fifty I said. She looked at me absolutely baffled so I told her to go to the counter and get the lady to tell her!

Anyway, I have a copy of one of the mobiles on offer so I touched it and told everyone to look at how pretty it is when it moves and I had them hooked. I suggested hanging it under a patio or near an open window and that I find it so relaxing to watch. The upshot was that I sold all but one in stock and one of the ladies asked me if I worked there!

I decided that because I had sold so many wind chimes I deserved to go into the Exhibition section without paying the fee and have a look around. I picked up one litre milk bottles to feel how heavy they would be if you were trying to pick them up whilst on various different planets which varied in weight enormously. On the walls there was so much written information that everyone there, including John, felt totally overwhelmed and didn't bother to read it. In the meantime John had walked up the hill to look at the telescope which was obviously not working because it was daytime whilst I chatted to the receptionist/coffee bar attendant/information officer. This amazing young woman had managed to serve a coach load of pensioners, give advice to the coach driver as to how he could handle driving up the hill so that those who could not walk up it could get to the telescope. She made me and several others coffee, cleared tables, given out information, taken the entry fees to the Exhibition. If that wasn't enough she was suddenly flying out of the door to ensure that the coach driver had taken the right road and had stopped in the right place and all whilst continually smiling and being pleasant!

Closer to Coonabarabran is the **Skywatch Observatory** and **Astro Mini-Golf!** John went to the Observatory on our earlier trip but had always regretted not getting to Siding Springs on our previous trip because we were in such a hurry to get to north Queensland as it was so cold in mid winter.

In the **Visitors Centre** in town there is a skeleton of a Diprotodon optatum, the largest marsupial that ever lived. John saw it and told me about it unfortunately I forgot to go back to the Centre to have a look.

We saw the movie 'Japanese Story' on television whilst we were there and it was one of those movies that I will never forget, mainly because the story was so surprising, amusing and so moving. It starred Toni Collette and Gotaro Tsunashima and they were superb in their respective roles. If you want to know what the Outback is like then watch this film.

We also watched another program about how over sixty volunteer engineers rescued and restored the first Qantas Boeing 707 which was discovered at Southend in the U.K. We watched as they repaired and replaced so much of the plane over many months and then finally the pilots arriving to fly the plane back to Australia. At this point John Travolta joined the program and we found out that he has been flying since he was a teenager, which surprised us. He owns and flies an old Qantas Boeing 707 so he was ecstatic on being included and at one airport met them in his plane. Later that evening there was a newsflash that John had just made an emergency landing in his own Boeing 707 plane and could have lost his life. It seemed an extraordinary coincidence.

GUNNEDAH

On route to Tamworth we stopped at Gunnedah and what we saw of it was pretty although we didn't see the main shopping street as we were sticking to the main road but there were flowers and trees everywhere and even the hospital had vines growing over it and a lovely waterfall in the front gardens. We stopped by the **Agricultural Museum** to give the dogs a break and have a coffee. Should you ever stop there do smell the roses climbing up the wire fence to the left of the museum. The creamy/yellow colour ones smell divine and I was oh so tempted to pinch one but made do with taking a close-up photograph.

We had thought about staying at Gunnedah for the night but decided to see how far the dogs could travel comfortably and as the only caravan park we saw was on a major junction and seemed very empty but we decided that it was probably a bit noisy there and we kept going.

As we were leaving we passed a police car in a sixty zone (I was doing about sixty-two kph) and John was shouting into his two-way phone 'Where are you? I can't see you, where are you?'

'Did you see that cop car?'

'What cop car?'

'The one on the left, very prominently positioned, just on the side of the road. You passed him.'

'No. What was he doing?'

'Taking photos of the number plates of people speeding!' (What did he think he was doing, his nails?)

Actually I was talking into my tape recorder when I passed the cop and he probably thought I was talking on my mobile phone. With two mobiles and a two-way sitting beside me as well as the tape recorder, I wonder if he would have believed me!

TAMWORTH – THE COUNTRY MUSIC CAPITAL OF AUSTRALIA

I'm not really 'into' country music although I used to like John Denver's music but I had never heard of Slim Dusty or any other Australian country music artist until I had lived here for a while. We have been to Tamworth twice previously, the first time when we stayed in a motel for the night when travelling to Canberra and on to Thredbo in the Snowy Mountains and the last time when we just drove straight through when driving north. When we stayed at the motel there was a spa bath and I emptied out the miniature bottle of bath foam only to find it frothed so much that the bubbles quite literally went up to the ceiling and I panicked and didn't know what to do or how to get rid of them. A friend was telling me that she stopped at a motel a few years later and I asked her if it had a spa bath and she had done exactly the same!

I told John that it was about time we actually stopped there and had a look at the place. I was tying up my Ugg boots at the time and had jeans on and a roll-neck jumper on and grinned as I said to John 'I should fit right in'. I also have a suede cowboy hat – a pink one!

I was listening to The Country Hour on the radio whilst travelling and to cut a long story short, one of the subjects was Border Collies and about the four thousand dogs being exhibited at the annual Royal Easter Show in Sydney at the moment. Apparently the Border Collies have a tendency to yap and if they do so it is apparently because they are bored so get them moving by giving commands such as "Sit. Stand. Get the Newspaper" as they get so bored being idle!

It was a very pretty, hilly journey with a lot of blue wildflowers growing among the roadside grass. We were doing the maximum speed limit and everyone was overtaking us despite many double white lines down the centre of the road.

Tamworth has reverse parking along the sides of the roads and I hate reverse angle parking with a passion as it hold up the traffic so much. There are also a lot of small roundabouts with pedestrian crossings within metres of them so if you start going around a roundabout you may get stuck trying to turn off it because people are walking across the crossing or parking. It is absolutely nuts and a woman suddenly stopped dead in front of me the other day as she spotted someone getting into his car as parking space is at a premium in the main shopping street. It is a lovely tree-lined street and again another very, very long one with so many shops. A little out of town there is another shopping centre with Woolworths and Big W and variety shops and cafes and that has under cover parking which is great if you have dogs like us. We couldn't find anywhere to park in the morning in Tamworth so went to the other centre and shopped and returned to town in the afternoon when it was quieter. We left the dogs in the shade of the tree and despite there being an hour limit on parking we returned before our time limit and the dogs were in the full sun and were far too hot. We took them to the lovely **Kable Avenue Bicentennial Park** which is only one block from the action in the city centre and sat

Tamworth From Oxley Lookout - Large Town

under a tree with them for a while to cool them down and watched the ducks on the pond. Have a wander around there if you are in town as there are a few things to look at.

We are not that impressed with our caravan park as it is too expensive per night and the washing machines cost more than any other park we have been to in Australia and John tells me that there are only two of them for such a large park! There is a swimming pool but it is adjacent to the main road, well away from where we are. We'd need to drive there! Actually, we are paying more per night than we did over the Easter holiday period which is ridiculous and that is with our discount for being members of this park franchise. I'm thinking of avoiding this franchise in future.

We went up to the **Oxley Lookout** and you certainly get a good overall view of the area and Tamworth has a very large suburban area that we were not aware of but our visit was marred by the amount of rubbish about and so much broken glass everywhere which was lousy for the dogs.

We haven't really given the town enough time as we haven't been to see the **Big Golden Guitar Tourist Centre** nor the **Gallery of Stars Wax Museum** nor even the **Australian Country Music Foundation Museum**. Considering that Tamworth has the largest annual country music festival in the Southern Hemisphere we haven't done it justice.

John would have enjoyed the **Powerhouse Motorcycle Museum** and I would have enjoyed some of the arts and crafts and galleries and in particular the **Coffee Bean Roasting House** in the city because at last I would have learnt the art of roasting and processing coffee beans and would have loved to have taste-tested the Australian macadamia flavour.

There is a place called **Manilla** about thirty minutes drive west of Tamworth and it has really captured my attention and there is a caravan park there but it is the wrong direction for us and we are leaving to head north east tomorrow. Had the price of the park been cheaper we would have stayed longer and had planned to stay for a week. However, we will be stopping off at Moonbi which is about twenty minutes along the highway we are taking, to visit Claycraft Productions to see the unique porcelain figurines and traditional Australian bush buildings. From the photograph in a magazine that I have seen the figurines are really very unusual.

Moonbi - Claycraft Productions - More Amzing Models

MOONBI

We found **Claycraft Productions** a few kilometres off the main road and it was amazing. I'm not going to tell you what amazed us for it is for you to find out but we did admire the porcelain figures, as well as the building they were housed in plus other models that are for sale. There was a book of photographs which fascinated John and the inscriptions that visitors had written in them were pertinent and sometimes quite moving and the photographs wonderful. It costs nothing to go there and it's well worth the visit.

URALLA & ARMIDALE

Uralla was a lovely small town and we should have stayed there. The journey itself was pretty because of the time of year that we are travelling along this New England Highway. The journey was hilly as we were driving over the Great Dividing Range (well part of it anyway as we still have more to cross further north) and it provides some glorious views. The trees provided a full palette of autumnal colours ranging from deep red through to copper and orange, bright golden and very light green trees along with the normal array of deeper greens and browns set against the backdrop of the ranges and the clear blue skies, it was stunning. Uralla had plenty of trees parading their beautiful colours and many fine buildings. Old fashioned street lights, antique shops, heritage buildings including the **Thunderbolt Inn Hotel** which is a fine looking building it is really beautiful. There was a second hotel further along and again in was a fine building, an **Information Centre** and a Caravan Park and the rural scenes around it were lovely. It is only about twenty kilometres or so to Armidale from there and I was later to wish that we had stopped here and by-passed Armidale. We have stayed there before and it is certainly worth a visit but I just wanted to be out of town. John is worried about how I will cope when we get home and have to face so much traffic and I told him 'Just the same as last time. I'll hide in the house until I'm forced to go out'.

We arrived in Armidale and drove in the Ute to the two caravan parks which were, unfortunately at opposite ends of the city. We called into the **Information Centre** and came out loaded with information none of which we used because by the time we had gone from one end to another I had had enough of being in a town again and John agreed with me that we would travel on to Glen Innes. Should anyone be interested Armidale is a sister city with Reading in the England. I find it vaguely interesting as in Reading I went to college, had my first employment and got married there. Actually I did a lot of things for the first time there as it was the sixties after all when I was a teenager.

The journey to **Guyra** from Armidale was again so pretty and we were gradually climbing as Guyra is at the top of a ridge. The road teases you because you do one long slow and seemingly endless climb only to suddenly drop down again and then you face the next hill and you think 'Why did you bother dropping down. You know we've got to get up anyway?' We were seeing a lot of Liquid Amber trees which are beautifully yellow at present but it was the vivid golden colour of the poplar trees that we found so glorious and as we drove through stands of them on either side of the road, they showered us with a halo of golden leaves – quite magical. If only they were permanently that colour because they would make such stunning Christmas Trees! So this Ben Lomond range area of north-western New South Wales is certainly a beautiful place to be in autumn.

Do not fly through **Glencoe** like we did – stop and look at the **Red Lion Hotel** on the left and there is a rest area nearly opposite.

Chapter 17

GLEN INNES

We stopped as planned in the first caravan park that we came across and it is such a lovely small park with very friendly owners who have only recently purchased the park. You can fossick in the park and apparently someone found a black stone yesterday which is worth a fair bit of money and this morning someone found a clear, light blue sapphire of over 4 carats. We're going to have a go!! We are right in the heart of fossicking country after all. There is an annual festival called **Minerama** here and it's the biggest in New South Wales where gem, mineral and fossil dealers display specimens, jewellery and there are gem cutting displays and fossicking field trips. There is also a **Gemfest and Swap Meet** where you can buy gems and minerals and again go on fossicking field trips. Check with the Information Centre for dates. You can also buy sapphires here of course or online at www.AussieSapphire.com.au

As this is a 'Celtic' town you can also buy Celtic designs featuring local gemstones here at the jewellers and at the Information Centre including the rich royal blue Reddestone Creek sapphires. I spent time at the **Information Centre** reading Druid Astrology cards and that meant that despite John and I both being Arians, we did not have the same cards for the Druid calendar and I was so astonished at how accurate the descriptions of our personality traits were that I read those of my kids too and they were spot on. I was quite staggered by it. You can buy the cards for three dollars.

Having done two lots of washing and toured part of the town, we are now inundated with information again. Tomorrow we have to go and see the **Australian Standing Stones** (granite monoliths) which is where the annual **Australian Celtic Festival** is held. It is also the venue for the summer and winter solstices. There are twenty four stones in a circle for the twenty four hours in the day, three stones in the middle for Scotland, Ireland, the Isle of Man; Wales, Cornwall, Brittany; and the Australia Stone for the Australians. Then there are the four cardinal stones for true north, south, east and west and seven stones marking the summer and winter solstices (longest and shortest days in the year). It's being held in here next month. A lone piper at dawn signals non-stop entertainment at the Standing Stones, street parade, mass pipe bands, re-enactments of ceremonial roles, Celtic strongman events, kirking of the tartan (whatever that is), Celtic foods and last year the Spanish 9th Roman Legion and 42nd Royal Highland Regiment but I am not sure whether they are here every year. I feel sorry for the piper at dawn, presumably dressed in a kilt.

I read that there are four distinct seasons here, unlike Queensland and it states 'occasional snow'. On our last trip through here we hit a snow storm which I wrote about in my first diary which is why we did not stop here then! We are 1062m above sea level and although we have enjoyed fine sunny days yesterday and today, this morning I awoke at seven o'clock to fog (or a heavy mist) and watched it rise quite rapidly. I was so fascinated that I took a photo because of the beautiful clear vision ahead and the density of the fog/mist in the valley below. Two jumpers on plus a pair of Wellies and I was off in the bracing fresh air to walk the dogs. The thought of wearing a kilt at dawn made me shiver. I mean, if you are standing there using bagpipes you can hardly jump up and down to try and keep warm (with or without knickers on) or rub your hands together can you? Being a 'lone piper' you can't even have a whinge about the wind up your kilt to a mate can you? Well of course you couldn't anyway with that pipe in your mouth but you know what I mean. Perhaps they send someone out from Scotland who is used to the cold. Do you think that's why pipes sort of sound so high pitched? Is it because of the bitter cold wind blowing up the man's kilt?

There are two World Heritage-listed National Parks within driving distance here with the **Washpool National Park** being noted for its lush rainforest and rare birds and the **Gibraltar Range National Park** for weird granite formations, heaths and swamps. There are three more National Parks much closer to Glen Innes and four more in surrounding areas. If that is not enough then there is the **Torrington State Conservation Area** covering over 30,000 hectares and enough things to look at to keep everyone happy! Have dogs, can't travel to the above but hope you enjoy some of it!

(Just watching the news – a girl was being towed out on her surf board to a wave by her father today and got attacked by a sea lion in Western Australia. Apparently there are three known cases of this happening but it has amazed people. The poor thirteen year old girl had her throat bitten; her jaw bone badly damaged and has lost three teeth! She is obviously lucky to be alive.)

Skip a day because we hardly did anything yesterday except for washing bedding! However today we went to see the Standing Stones and to the lookout above them for a good overall view of the town and surrounding scenery and this afternoon we bought a bucket of mud and rocks and learnt how to fossick. It was good to have the park owner teach us how to do it as he did the first three baskets for us and we found a sapphire in the second basket of washed rocks. I later found another one and a few other stones that we liked. For example there was a 'party diamond' (I think that's what he told me) which isn't really worth anything but I was told that if I sent the first sapphire off to Thailand to the American company there who cuts and polishes them it would be worth about sixty dollars. Hardly worth the trouble! He had to get back to work so he didn't see the second one John found but it was about the same size. Anyway, we were glad we hadn't bought the three buckets for twenty dollars because it took us long enough to get through one bucket and we'd both had enough.

You can make a living at it if you do it a lot and, of course, occasionally people have that 'lucky find' and that must be very gratifying and well deserved too because it is an awful lot of work for very little most of the time. John asked how the stones could be identified if they were being sent away and apparently they are weighed by the carat and recorded this end first with an email being sent in advance. Another guy here told me that he'd had no trouble and even the stones that weren't worth cutting and polishing were returned with explanatory notes. Now we have this little bag of stones and no idea what to do with them and the bag will get put into the back of a cupboard and gather dust. I suppose I could stick them in my photograph album on top of a photo I took of the fossicking area so at least we look at them now and again and see the reward for our effort.

Tomorrow we leave for Tenterfield and then across the **Great Dividing Range** and **Blackall Range** to Casino to check out whether it is worth keeping our few shares in the Casino Village development. It combines permanent residents in their own homes as well as motor home sites for casual travellers such as us, or permanent motor home sites for people that want to stop travelling and live in their motor home in the park. There has been so much development since we were last there that it will be interesting see the place and to learn about all the activities that they now have in place for people to enjoy on a daily, weekly and monthly basis. For example they have a film night once a week, aqua aerobics daily I believe; a market once a month and dinner dances and so forth – too much to list here.

WARDELL 23rd April 2007.

Well, I've aged another year since I last wrote in this diary and my special day was spent at the **Casino Village Motor Home Village** and now I have to backdate my thoughts to when we left Glen Innes.

The journey to **Tenterfield** was pretty and we stopped in town by a park and watched an Aboriginal family with extended family or friends having a wonderful time playing with all the children that were around the front garden and a couple of adults playing tag! They all wandered back and forth between the park and the house which was in a cul-de-sac and I enjoyed their laughter and happiness. There were cars coming and going as more people arrived and left and they didn't seem to have a care in the world. Tenterfield is quite a nice town but as it was still so early in the day we decided to continue on down to Casino. The journey over the Great Dividing Range was a drive that required two hands on the steering wheel (I know you are supposed to drive like that but in this case it was imperative!) The road is very steep in places with continual bends which makes it extremely difficult for anyone to overtake and most of the time I was only comfortable at driving at around 55kph which frustrate the drivers who knew the road better than I. The dogs didn't like it much particularly Jack and we had to stop at one point because he was starting to be sick. It's a lovely journey if you haven't got a string of drivers behind you! We came to a straight section at long last and then began the climb over the **Richmond Range** and I wrote about that in my first diary but this is what I said when I was using the tape recorder in the car this time….

'This part of the journey is so very beautiful and I don't want it to end. It's very steep in places and the road is narrow but it is…..oh my! Oh, that is so beautiful, so, so beautiful'. I switched my tape recorder off as we came over the brow of a hill as I was too moved to speak into it any longer and thought 'This is what I want and where I want to live. If only it was in Queensland instead of New South Wales'. Below us were green hills, valleys and farmland and it was such a beautiful vista and in the distance I could see the sea. John suddenly spoke on the two-way radio and he was saying 'This is what I want' and I was so glad that he feels the same way as me.

When we arrived at the **Casino Village** we were stopped at the entry point by gates which had sprung up since we last visited and they weren't working so we had a queue of vans in front of us. Someone came out and manually worked the gates and we were told to all go through. Just as that happened John, who had got out of the bus and was talking to some people in a four wheel drive vehicles said to me 'You borrowed their radio' and I looked at him as though he was nuts. I thought he was talking about a radio/CD player and I have never borrowed one from anyone. I approached the vehicle and recognised the lady in the back and indeed we had borrowed her radio – the radio she used to contact my son when we were stranded before Esperance in Western Australia by the cyclone. As we were suddenly told to get moving we did not have time to continue talking to them. In reception we were told that they might not have a place for us and I answered 'You will find a place because I booked a site'. I was told that seventeen vans had come in during the day that hadn't booked and I reiterated that I hadn't taken it for granted that they would have space and that is why I'd booked. Some bookings were juggled and we had a site which didn't impress us much as we had the sun on us all day and it was very, very hot. I couldn't sit outside the van and it was appalling for Jack who was struggling to breathe.

I was awed by the development there and although I knew that a lot of houses had been built and that there were people on long term sites who now call the park their home, I was more impressed that the tiny sapling plants were now large hedges surrounding individual sites and the size of the trees. As a share holder I was impressed with the facilities too and the free activities provided. The following morning I went to talk to people at a group craft gathering and was pleased that some of them lived there permanently and some were visitors as I had heard that there was some segregation going on which annoyed the visitors. One of the ladies visiting reminded me that we had met at Albany and that she had been desperately trying to find a dentist to get a tooth out.

What I hated about the park is that it is now like a housing estate and it has lost its magic. I never did find the lady who had helped us out with her radio because there were just too many vans and buses there to be able to find her. All we could see from our van were more vans, a house and our Ute which we were using to try and give Jack some shade so it was almost parked in front of our door! There were lots of things we didn't like including the prices charged although we did not pay the price for the drive-through site that we had which was probably because I made such a fuss at reception. Previously, as shareholders, we had paid eight dollars a night and this time we paid fifteen and when she told me that I remarked 'That is nearly a one hundred percent increase in two years which is ridiculous.' Little did I know that we should have been paying twenty dollars! We had paid for three nights believing that we would extend and stay for at least a week but left on our third day.

WARDELL

At last we are back in the park I love at Wardell, near Ballina and we have glorious rural views which includes three horses and a foal who likes to play football, the dogs are so happy as are we and it is only costing us twelve dollars a night! We have oodles of space and the dogs can romp around off leash in the large grassed area between us and the paddocks. We are about five kilometres from the beach and about sixteen from the town of Ballina. I have found out what has happened in the last three years to the people who had encouraged us to stay on the last time we were here and have met us with three people who are still here. We intend to stay here until we have to move to Tweed Heads just prior to arriving home. It is also cooler and even the bit of rain we had last night was welcome and today is a glorious day again, not too hot and not too cold. We are off this afternoon to collect our mail in Ballina. I didn't want to go because I am just so happy right here in the park with the horses in front and the pool behind us but changed my mind as I was curious to find out if the town had changed much. I ended up buying myself a new garden chair and an umbrella as we now have three broken umbrellas yet I cannot recall when we've actually used any of them!

Ballina has changed and it's better with more shops and services and it development along the riverfront which is quite attractive. It seems tidier and more prosperous but is still fairly laid back.

When we started our first trip in this motor home the size caused interest and comment but that has changed dramatically quickly in the last couple of years. There has been such a rapid growth of large vehicles in the parks that we go to that I start to wander about the future.

I'm not just thinking about environmental concerns but the fact that so many people that we have met do not seem to mind that they don't see their children or grandchildren for many months of the year. In a couple of generations we have gone from a time when the whole family grew up in the same town or village and children knew their extended families. Now so many families are split and living in different cities or countries and kids living alone in units/flats and sharing more of their hopes, dreams, failures and fears with their friends rather than with their families.

Now we are seeing my generation 'running away' reversing the roles, instead of the defiant teenager who runs away and everyone agrees needs parental guidance! Parents like me aren't around anymore to give advice unless it is from the end of a mobile phone or email. It's not the same as sitting down together and talking about life in general until you get down to the core issue of why your adult child really came to see you. I'm one of those parents so I know that I haven't been there for my kids when needed and I'm the one that still preaches to them 'Family comes first'.

Australia is not like Europe and you cannot get, for example, from Broome to the Gold Coast in the same day. Well, you'd have extreme difficulty unless you hired a private aircraft and pilot to get you to Perth or Darwin with an interconnecting flight directly to the Gold Coast or alternatively Brisbane and then hire a car to get you to the Gold Coast! Australia is just too vast. Now that so many parents are running off for six months of the year or for a year like us this time or else permanently on the road. What will the next generation be like? Are we being selfish or are we right in doing whatever we want to do, when we want. How many parents have said to their kids in the past that they are not thinking of others or that they are being selfish or accuse them of only thinking of themselves, especially to their teenage kids? I'm sure I must have said one or all three of those things over the years.

Are our kids really happy for us or deep down do they resent our abandonment of them? I don't think I would have liked my parents doing what I have done as I always knew that if I needed them they would be with me within twenty-four hours and would drop whatever they were doing to be with me. There were times when they had to do just that and my mother-in-law also got on a train and arrived to help when I fell ill and needed help to look after the children when they were little. I always knew I could call on them, that they were reliable and that they would do whatever they could to help me.

You can tell that I am having the time to relax and think about things at last in this beautifully peaceful place. Our neighbours here have sold their home to buy their American fifth-wheeler and enormous, seven litre American four wheel drive which cost ninety thousand dollars alone. They have two children, one son whom they haven't seen for several years and the other with grandchildren. We have met so many people now who have sold their homes to fund a lifestyle like this and wonder how they could be so brave and so sure that they would like the lifestyle because many of them haven't done any touring like this before. We have had a motor home before and have hired them to tour but the motor homes were used for holidays and did not replace our home.

A common comment I hear is that they couldn't stand the thought of renting their homes out in case the home was damaged but in many cases the rent they would get would fund any mortgage repayments if they had drawn back on their equity to try this lifestyle out first. Prices of properties are continually going up all over Australia, albeit slowly in some places and despite the drop in certain areas around Sydney. Staying in the market is insurance as you can always sell at a later date and buy something cheaper if you don't like the life on the road.

In England we used to call travellers Gypsies and that is literally the lifestyle that so many are choosing here in Australia. I wonder if the growth rate will continue and what that will mean in the future for our towns and roads and will families be able to book into a caravan park for a holiday with their children because they may be always full, having been pre-booked by these permanent travellers. Already many town councils have had to open showgrounds to house caravans and motor home travellers because all the parks are booked out and people are still pouring into their town. In Broome in W.A and Bowen in Queensland this has already happened and we were forced to use the showground in Bowen for one night ourselves and that was when we first travelled.

With most travellers escaping the cold winter months, most of Queensland will be inundated in winter as Broome is now. What with trucks, four-wheel drives towing caravans, motor homes as large as ours which are becoming quite common and fifth wheelers, the normal car driver is going to feel quite intimidated or at the very least very frustrated if held up by a combination of the aforementioned. We have already experienced being held up by a string of vehicles ourselves.

Apparently the companies who make caravans and motor homes cannot produce them quickly enough. In many cases the quality of the finished product is falling which is not surprising but disappointing for new owners. We have heard so many complaints and know some of the companies which have had a good name which we now would not deal with. The demand is enormous so what will next year be like and the year after that.

Another phenomenon is that the people we are meeting on the road now as opposed to two to three years ago are getting younger and no, it is not because we are getting older! Our neighbours both took redundancy packages and they are nowhere near retirement age and there are many more people who are in their forties and fifties doing this and there also seems to be a lot more young couples who are home schooling their children and young couples without children so it's not just retirees in their sixties and above that are becoming gypsies. I use that term because in England gypsies were frowned upon (and many still are I believe) and yet here people want to be them!

There is a huge black market between travellers that the tax office will never discover. It's amazing what people make or the skills that they have and the things that they sell and then there is the sly grog! Yes, people even make and sell alcohol whilst travelling. It's all part of the fun I guess and people make so much stuff that they even have stalls at markets to get rid of stock from time to time. We met one couple who reckoned they had a million dollars worth of jewellery and I was amazed at how many markets they had suddenly dropped in on and managed to get a spot for the day. I bought a beautiful necklace fairly recently from a lady who wanted me to look at her 'pretty things' and when I later went to her van she had a table set up with a variety of pieces that she had imported. Need some artwork of your choice on your van, not a problem. Need a plumber, just ask around the park you are in. Many people will help you just because they want something to do and it will cost you nothing but you'll likely find a skilled tradesperson anyway who you may pay with a 'slab' of beer or with cash. Some travellers work for a few days fruit-picking to supplement their income, in which case they will have to pay tax of course or get jobs for a few weeks packing at a supermarket or whatever. It's a new lifestyle of choice with no particular destination in the minds of many people we have met. We have heard so often people say that they don't know which way they will go next and may toss a coin or 'It depends on the weather'.

Just to change the subject, it's raining and for the last few nights we have had storms but it has been dry, hot and sunny during the day, a bit like November used to be but this is April! Our autumn is therefore more like what our spring used to be like but our Prime Minister thinks that economic matters are more important than global warming and we wonder about that statement as there won't be an much of an economy if we have more and more natural disasters like tsunamis, floods, droughts and cyclones like we have been seeing in recent years! I was astonished to hear that the Gold Coast had a tsunami warning recently. Is that why we are running around Australia leaving all responsibilities behind – are we running away to enjoy life whilst we still can?

Bill Clinton and I have just parted company as I finally came to the end of his book and I will miss him but not to the point that I will start reading the book again! We had a few hours of sunshine this afternoon and took the dogs for a walk in the tiny hamlet of Wardell and I was about to go into the café opposite the hotel when I spotted an 'Op Shop in an arcade beside it. An Op Shop is a charity shop that sells second hand clothes and in many cases, such as this one, crockery, books and ornaments. I immediately saw what appeared to be a new pair of trousers and a super cheesecloth shirt hanging together, being displayed and as they both fitted me I bought them and then found a matching fancy belt which all up cost me eight dollars fifty cents. All the belts cost fifty cents, even the leather ones. The other two items cost four dollars apiece! All I had to do was to cut off about a metre from the legs of the trousers as I have such short legs! Well perhaps not that much but the lady behind the counter was most concerned and said that so many people can't sew that she wondered if I was able to do the alterations! Perhaps she's right but is it so hard to get a pair of scissors out and thread a needle? What do they teach kids in school today? I recall being first taught to sew at school when I was six by which time I could do adding and subtracting of sums which were then in pounds, shillings and pence (quite complicated in comparison to metric sums). By seven we were being taught how to write stories which had to have 'a beginning, a middle and an end' and were being taught ballroom dancing of all things as well as percussion musical instruments. The latter two have been of no use to me whatsoever but some of my friends may still play the triangle, tambourine or use castanets!

Now on the subject of 'black water' I am not alone and many other people have told me that they have problems too with because I have mentioned so often in this diary having stomach problems on this tri the water. Today John and I have read an article about people who empty their cassette toilets into the toilets at caravan parks. We cannot do that because we have a tank and need to find a specialised 'Dump Point'. The article mentioned that someone was seen using a tap outside the toilet to rinse out their cassette and it is the same tap that some people use to fill their drinking water tanks or kids sometimes grab a drink out of. As the tap had touched the inside of the cassette it was obviously left in a condition that nobody would wish to touch. The article went on to mention that infections such as Giardia Lamblia, a very nasty parasite that affects the small intestine can be caught and apparently doctors in Queensland and interstate are very concerned at the prevalence of it amongst travellers. It can be fatal in the very young and elderly. You can also contract Hepatitis B. Doctors have found that many travellers are obtaining water from near the toilets whilst touring so do not obtain water from taps near any toilets! Dogs can be infected and become carriers.

If you obtain water from rivers, creeks and dams, boiling the water will kill Giardia. Water purifying tablets may or may not but will certainly not kill Cryptosporidium that causes similar problems, being diarrhoea, bloating and nausea, stomach cramps, loose pale stools, weight loss and fatigue. If you are having problems then you have to have laboratory tests and Giardia Lamblia is a notifiable disease. So many people have the wrong belief that boiling water makes it pure – it doesn't, not even if you boil it for six minutes or longer. I believe if you are an expert traveller you learn how to filter it through charcoal afterwards or something. Whatever, there are several stages to ensure water is pure that only a minority even know about.

Guess what I'm going to do when I get home? Yep, I'll get tested for the lot because despite only drinking bottled water I am still feeling really rough at times and the pain can be so sharp that it shoots up through my chest and sometimes into my shoulder or arm and I'm sure other people would think that they were having a heart attack. The dogs will be tested too. If my tests are positive in some ways it will be a relief as I will know what I have to take to get some relief but on the other hand the tablets I had before for Giardia gave me so much grief that I had to stop taking the second packet.

Please take this seriously because bad hygiene practices are not just a problem in Australia and it must be a common problem all over the world so if, for example, you have been camping in Spain or Canada or South America and you have had similar problems then get yourself to a doctor and get samples tested for these problems. It may not be 'traveller's tummy' or 'irritable bowel syndrome' and your doctor may not even think to test you for these other things.

Some young children in Australia have never experienced rain – isn't that amazing? Well, this will be an exciting and perplexing week for some of them because farms that have become dust bowls are about to receive a downpour for the first time for years. One old man on the television tonight said he had heard that before and doesn't believe the forecasters but this time they are right. We have had a lot of rain here but there is a huge mass crossing slowly and hopefully drenching, some of the inland parts of Australia and they may be able to grow some crops for the first time in years. There are advertisements on television now directed at farmers advising them that help is available if they are depressed and it is not 'unmanly' to seek help because so many have committed suicide from despair.

This morning we could smell a foul cabbage smell again which we have experienced before from water so we first decided that we would not fill the dog's bucket up from the tap as there was obviously some run-off from the land into the dam that provides water for this property and that the water couldn't be very good. Then, when we closed the windows before going out, we noticed that the smell appeared to be in the van. 'It's a dead mouse!' I exclaimed 'Why didn't I check the mouse traps just in case because it smells the same'.

An extensive search of the van found no dead mice but two traps that had rolled over and had snapped shut so were useless so we reset them. By this time I was starting to feel somewhat nauseous and had the torch on and was pulling out bottom drawers to check under cabinets and in all nooks and crannies but couldn't find a thing and the smell was getting worse by the minute. There was nothing for it but to use my nose and sniff around the van. There was nothing in the bedroom or bathroom so those doors were shut off and then a crawled along the floor smelling all corners of the van until I reached the front. Beside John's driving seat there is a floor vent and when my nose reached it I heaved and ran out of the van! I told John that there must be a dead mouse under the vent but that it was in a very awkward position because of the chairs almost covering it and perhaps we could open the outside storage areas to find access to that area. The first large one holds the gas fuel tank and we shone the torch into all corners but couldn't see a dead mouse.

Next to that is a small storage area that houses the house batteries for our 12 volt system. When we took the knobs off the front battery I got a funnel and put it into each cell and sniffed and that battery seemed okay. When we got to the back battery it was a different story. The cells were almost dry and I was sniffing acid. I don't advise you to ever do what I did because I felt cross eyed and sick for a long time! I was slightly edgy with John in the kind of way where you have this strong urge to decapitate someone for not having maintained a basic maintenance job. He told me that he was going to get around to it and had done the front battery the other day but they are heavy to pull out and he hadn't got around to it!!! Perhaps I won't get around to cooking any more dinners or won't get around to washing his clothes for the next few months. In just over a week he'll be able to get away from me when I'm angry because we'll be playing skittles across our empty floors in our huge house but he can't get away from me here so I only have one week to retaliate. Pity. There is my final lesson on rotten cabbage smells – it's usually bad water, dead mice or rats but now add dry battery cells. It's time for a shower as it's after 11pm.

It's still raining and everything outside is soggy and I must do a machine load of washing so will be forced to use a dryer for the second time in a year which is not too bad is it? Of course, it is my fault because the other day I was so fed up with moving my garden chair to try and find some shade and with having to move the car to provide shade for the dogs that I suddenly exclaimed 'I'm sick of this sun' and as soon as I said it I knew we'd get rain. I didn't realise that it would continue for so many days though!

We went to buy the Saturday paper and went to the local Wardell market and that was fun. I saw that the two dollar bags of tomatoes had all gone which is not surprising as tomatoes are six dollars fifty cents for a kilo in the shops at the moment. Then I saw some jars of pickles and jams and as I arrived at the store I overheard a guy say 'Which is the Rosella jam that is famous around Australia and is made here by an old lady?' I too had heard about this jam when we were last here but we were not here when the monthly market was on.

The guy behind the counter pointed out the various sized jars (which cost the same whichever size you purchase) and said 'That lady over there with the walking stick is my grandmother and she still makes the jam'. The man who was enquiring said 'It's always cheaper to buy in bulk so how much would two jars cost?' and he was told that he could have two jars for six dollars instead of the three dollars fifty cents apiece. The jars had pretty little fabric caps on and I found two jars that I liked and then swapped some caps around so that I had two caps that I liked and bought my two jars for six dollars too. I hope we like the jam! The ingredients are simply rosellas, sugar and water and I do so love food that has no other additional and usually quite unnecessary additives in it but celebrates its own simple perfection.

John then saw a garden lounge chair which we both really liked but we have absolutely nowhere to put it so decided against getting it. A lady with children asked how much a tray of toys would cost and was told 'Take them away for two dollars' and she was so delighted. Then I spotted some pictures stacked against a wall under plastic sheeting. I liked both of them and John asked me if I needed any more and I said certainly not because I have an art gallery already and have many pictures in storage but I looked at the frame and asked how much I could buy it for and was told three dollars. As it is a proper frame, by which I mean it has glass to the front and a removable back I realised that the frame was worth buying without a picture even being in it and I loved the picture anyway. It was a bit difficult to look at the items for sale properly because all the store holders were desperately trying to keep their goods dry under plastic sheeting but I decided to leave anyway before I saw any other bargains.

Having returned to our van we made coffee and I was sitting reading the paper outside when a voice behind me said 'Hello Mum' and it was my son Colin. However, he gave me such a fright as we weren't expecting him that I jumped and exclaimed 'Oh s…t' which is not very nice and after a hug and my hasty words of welcome and how surprised I was I didn't know what to say to him. I didn't know what to say to my own son who I hadn't seen for a year! I felt confused, disorientated and sad at this weird phenomenon. We have kept in contact by phone of course so I am up to date on his everyday life but it was odd and difficult for a while. I haven't seen him for forty-nine weeks and yet I had no conversation.

We got over that of course but it worried me and as I said to him 'It's like I saw you yesterday but it isn't yesterday, it's nearly a year and it feels so odd and I am going through such confusion in my mind about our return home. For example, normally if it is raining we take off to a place where it isn't raining but this time we can't leave because this is the end of the journey and I cannot get my head to agree with my body and have been feeling listless, odd, a bit depressed one day and raring to get on with things another but I can't until we actually get home and we haven't even done all the things that we've said we would do whilst here, like sightseeing and cleaning the van and bus before we return to the severe water restrictions and can no longer use hoses at home'.

When I was raring to get on with things I was high with adrenalin but had no way to express it so I internalised it – the flight and fight syndrome. I should have gone for a long, long walk to get rid of it out my muscles. I didn't sleep well last night and felt like I had flu first thing this morning but I haven't. I'm also having difficulty in eating and digesting food properly and all I could stomach tonight was about half a lettuce in a sandwich! It has made me realise that if we did this travelling all the time then my relationship with my children would surely change and I did not like the feeling one bit.

My daughter had phoned the other day and said 'When will you be in Tweed Heads?' and I told her Friday and she said that she would come around at night and I said 'What for?' Now how daft is that? She answered that she wanted to see her 'doggies' and I said that as Jack has his tablet in the evenings he would probably be half asleep but she said that she didn't care because she just wanted to see them. I was so matter of fact instead of saying 'How lovely, I can't wait to see you again'. What's happened to me on this trip? I was thinking that it would be inconvenient as I was hoping to go out to dinner with friends as I don't want to cook the night before we return home but I could have suggested to her that we go out for a meal! I'm not sure I like me much at the moment! I daren't ask Colin and Helen how they view my reception of them! Last weekend I was hoping Colin would come and was disappointed when he didn't and then when he does I'm confused so I really am a basket case. We've decided that we must get out tomorrow and do a trip into the country villages and get ourselves motivated again as we only have a few days left here.

Chapter 18

NIMBIN & THE CHANNON

We drove through **Alstonville** to **Lismore** and then turned off to Nimbin as I have wanted to do this trip from this direction for so many years. When I last did it, I was overawed by the beauty of the scenery and it was no different this time. The green gentle hills looked as soft as velvet and I felt that I could get out and stroke them. Every turn in the road and over the brow of every hill we exclaimed at the beauty of the scenery. Colin had suggested that as we wanted to go to "The Channon" we should go there first as the scenery is breathtaking that way but we kept that in mind and stopped many times on our return journey to look back.

Nimbin Markets - Colourful

As I said to John this was a case of 'It's the journey, not the destination' that was important to us. However, on arriving at Nimbin we noticed immediately that things had changed since we were last there but we felt that the changes were good. I had been a bit worried having read about there being many cafes there and thought that Nimbin may have lost its magic but it hasn't. We had a problem finding a parking place though as the market was on. We went there first and it was not too crowded yet interesting and I almost immediately purchased a gift for my daughter. The dogs came with us and were very good and we loved the atmosphere.

I went to look at what was once the only café in town and that had changed for the worse as it looked like an American milk bar which was the only disappointment we felt about the town. Whilst waiting for our coffee we listened to a saxophonist who was inside the café playing. We were outside and I spotted a shop that sold organic products and found some organic Cos lettuce and tomato seeds and also the organic breakfast cereal that I like so much and which I haven't seen since we first started our trip. We wandered into a building that had an art exhibition and then around the village and John and I both agreed that we would like to live there. We checked out the caravan park but they do not take large vans or dogs.

We left with regret to head for **The Channon** although I had wanted to see the area for a couple of years which was prompted because we were offered a house there. We looked at it on the internet, loved it and the price but thought it too far away from everything. There is very little there other than a few houses, a shop and a very good hotel where we had lunch. Again we sat outside to enjoy the view but the inside was very inviting too, sort of like the English pubs used to be years ago but larger!

I decided I'd treat myself to some 'wedgies' which are chunky chips really with sour cream and sweet chilli sauce. I do love junk food sometimes! What arrived was a basket of chips that was so huge that even John could not finish up for me and they ended up being shared out equally between four of us, the other two being Jack and Callie! The sour cream and sweet chilli sauce came in separate bowls.

When we did finally leave we decided to visit **Dunoon**, another village not too far out of our way but that was much larger than The Channon and had a mass of residential housing. We had seen something that interested us in the window of a Real Estate Agency in Nimbin but both of us were quiet with our thoughts for a couple of days. We then both sort of mumbled about Nimbin perhaps not being what we need at the moment but then we saw the photos that I downloaded and stopped talking again!

Eventually we had to leave Wardell and we wondered what had happened to the days as they disappear so fast there although John had cleaned the bus and the Ute and I had managed to thoroughly clean our bedroom. It took me all day to do the walls, ceiling and blinds properly! I also scrubbed our outdoor floor mat which is large and the side awning shade cloth and I also used some special cleaner to clean the underside of our large awning one day and the top side on another. We had thought that we would have cleaned the whole van before we left but it will just have to wait.

We had one last visit to Ballina and this time took the dogs to the surf beach which they loved. When we were leaving, Colin (the park owner) said he'd noticed how lively Jack had been and we both agreed that Jack simply loves it there and eats much more and plays more. This is no doubt due to the fact that he is not tied up all the time, only at night and there is such a vast amount of soft grass to play on with Callie. It could also be because John and I are always so happy there. We should just sell up and move into the park in our bus!

TWEED HEADS

The journey was fairly uneventful and would have been fabulous if it weren't for the major road works and the traffic as the scenery in some places is breathtaking. We stopped at the top of a steep hill and saw **Byron Bay** in the distance and the stunning coastline and we were surrounded by the same beautiful rural scenery that had enfolded us when we went to Nimbin.

Poor Jack, poor us because we do not like where we are nor the owner of the park who is rude and a control freak. Poor Jack because instead of trucks at night which frighten him because he thinks that their headlights are the eyes of giant monsters, he now has flying monsters overhead. The aircraft fly so low and so close to us that at night with all the cabin lights on we can almost see the passengers and he is really upset.

Our poor neighbours, who are in a tent, are so close to us that had we backed in as the owner wanted us to do we could have walked straight down our steps and into their tent. In fact, we wouldn't have been able to avoid doing so. They have a little dog who barked today and the girl was told off by the owner who said 'Your dog can see the two dogs next door by looking under their van.' What do you answer to a statement like that? Of course their dog can see ours and we can't hide our dogs.

We are sited about one and a half metres from a wire fence which is around a private property. They have two dogs, one being a Labrador with a testicle swollen to the size of a tennis ball and another dog that has such wild eyes that it looks rabid and they both barked crazily and ran up and down their fence when we arrived. We feel like the filling in a sandwich as we have no room around us. To our front end there is a house which is higher than us and hanging in their back doorway is a long dress with long sleeves and tonight with the light behind it, it looked like a ghost in the doorway.

We are so far away from the water tap and the electricity point that we have had to join two extension leads for the electricity and two hoses for the water and although John has tried all the fittings that he has, he cannot stop the hoses leaking at one end or the other or in the middle where they are joined and we have ended up turning the tap off and will use our water pump until it's daylight again. We also have a massive tree with low branches right over our engine and front windows and the road to our rear. The tree stops us from receiving any decent television reception. Thank goodness we are only here for two nights! There are also far too many dogs in this park and we had only been here for about an hour when I stepped in some doggy-doodle.

Tomorrow we are having an easy day because we are meeting friends at the Bowling Club (outdoor and indoor bowls) at 11am and will have lunch there and Helen is visiting with a friend around dinner time. I think we will go elsewhere for the rest of the afternoon to avoid being at this park. There are many pretty walks along the river here which winds its way back and forth all over the place Tweed Heads and there are also the beautiful beaches of course. We could go back to the headland where you can stand with one leg on either side of the Queensland and New South Wales at the border which is almost a novelty for us because we rarely play tourist here as it is so close to home.

We could walk back and forth across one of the main shopping streets and be in Coolangatta, Queensland on one side or Tweed Heads, New South Wales on the other. When New South Wales has daylight saving and changes the time by an hour, it causes chaos for parents with children, with school and work hours not being synchronised if you do not work on the same side of the border as the children's schools. It's good fun on New Year's Eve though with two midnight celebrations. Most towns in Australia celebrate New Year's Eve by having fireworks and music and other events as well as people having their own parties at home. In Brisbane and at the Gold Coast there are fireworks at nine o'clock for the children and the fireworks at midnight. Many people come here just so that they can celebrate the New Year celebrations twice!

The next day will be home and that will be weird yet wonderful, I think!

5/4/2007

Chapter 19

A U S T R A L I A

`15/5/2009

As per usual when we set off from home to go travelling around Australia, our leaving is preceded by incredible tension and immediately after leaving we find ourselves in a ridiculous situation. We are in a caravan park **(Tallebudgera Cree**k) a few kilometres from our home surrounded on three sides by water for the purpose of relaxation to recover from our stress and the weather warnings tell us that we are about to experience an extreme weather 'front' which will include severe gales and 'cold water' tornados, the latter which had to be explained to us on the news as nobody knows what they are as this is a very rare occurrence for us apparently.

On the floor of the back seat of the ute are Callie's (the dog's) ashes, in a bag and I have yet to have the guts to even look inside the bag, let alone accept that she's gone. Jack left us a few months after our last return and is passing was horrendously hideous – a wild dog originally with a wild death and Callie who calmly walked into our life, just as calmly left us. She seemed resigned, tired and died in utter peace. I have not been without a pet since I was a small child but at this present time I can only be thankful that Callie won't have to experience the coming storms as she would have been so terrified. A loud noise terrified her and without Jack to protect her she would not have enjoyed this trip.

It's funny how you can get a sense of satisfaction from small things when on the road. In this caravan park we are not allowed to have washing around on site and must use the washing lines provided in an enclosed area some way away. Well, tonight is much warmer than it has been recently and breezy so I did some washing and put it on the rack and put the rack outside. I have been sitting outside with the smug satisfaction that I am bucking the system and getting away with it! It gives me a kick – quite pathetic really but very relaxing just sitting outside watching it blow around!

We have little idea where we are going this time. We were going to Cairns but they've had and continue to have a dengue fever outbreak up north, mainly in Cairns and Townsville and areas in between although larvae have been found as far south as Brisbane apparently. Those people struck down with the dengue fever have been in the north though. As everything that can fly and bite always finds me, we've decided to give it a miss. I have lived up the road in our house since we've got back from the last trip and haven't suffered a bite once but since coming to this park a couple of days ago I have already attracted five bites, even one in my armpit and another on the end of my finger. However, we have to go north to take the opportunity to catch up with friend's who live in Victoria but who are staying at present on the coast near Rockhampton. So we will start by going north and when it warms up we will do an about turn and go south to wherever the road takes us – with two vehicles and no dogs! I wonder why everyone we know is so fascinated by the fact that we take two vehicles but it has been a constant question this week since Callie left us. To be honest, we have nowhere to leave the ute anywhere as there are tenants in our house and we didn't know that we wouldn't have Callie with us until this last week – so be it – we take two vehicles and no doubt we will benefit from having them separate just as we have before. We can stop at a moments notice and John, (Restless Legs who is my other half) can jump into the ute so we can do an immediate, spur of the moment detour en route and we have a bit of space from each other and I can let loose with my music!

OCTOBER 2009 - email to friend

Be Good When Done

"Dear R"

So much has happened so I don't know what you know. I think you know that having finally left the Gold Coast we stayed two weeks at our usual park in **Rockhampton** but there were so many people there that we knew that it was exhausting - none of them 'friends' - just people we know. Ended up going out to lunch with them and 12 came. Anyway, we joined Sue and Greg for a week at **Yepoon** and then headed north, staying at **Armstrong Beach** near **Sarina** for a week where we met a smashing couple who were passing through. They stayed and bought some land! We went up **to Bowen** (beautiful beaches but not so good in town), stayed at two different caravan parks over two

Possum Bundaberg

weeks at **Airlie Beach**, went down to **Cape Hillsborough, Seaforth, Midge Point, Mackay** (still dislike intensely so only stayed 2 nights to visit Bunnings and Spotlight and camping stores etc) and then back to Armstrong Beach where Sue and Greg had arrived and stayed there 3 weeks. Our 'new friends 'Coral and her partner found out we were there and came back up from Maroochydore which is no mean feat as Coral works for the Federal Government and had to take more holiday time off. We didn't want to ever leave but we all had to eventually and Sue and Greg made the first move as they had been there a month by that time and we followed a couple of days later."

Now I'll have to get the map out because I can't recall where next! Oh yes, one night off road by the beach **at Clairview** and then back to our park near **Rockhampton** where there were only two couples left that we knew so it was more relaxing! From Rocky we went to **Bundaberg**, to a park recommended by a friend by the river in town. I had told the park owners that I didn't know how long we were going to stay as it all depended on whether we were happy or not. So he made damned sure we were! He gave us a double drive-through site which means we took up 4 caravan places! Right in front of us was the pool gate, the river, a barbeque and covered dining area and behind us were the showers and toilets. There are beautiful walks along the river there and a free zoo and John became enamoured with an emu that he used to go and talk to every day. They have the most amazing peacocks and every kind of water bird and are allowed to fly free so we often had to stop to let a peacock walk across the road when we drove along that road to town. Just near our park was the most beautiful lawned club and it turned out to be a croquet club which was established 70 odd years ago.

Two French Tourists Brave The Water

Whilst we were there Carmen and Arthur came to join us and stayed a week so we caught up with them too and caught the free bus to and from the local RSL for dinner. That overlooks the

Now Three Stuck

river and yachts so are beautifully sited. Also whilst there we decided to get some stuff done to the bus. The T.V aerial had never worked properly so we got that fixed (had relied on the internal aerial). The ramps had suddenly broken and we needed a new solenoid for them so that was an expensive job but we need them. They level the van hydraulically for us. Then Arthur noticed something else and so it went on and we spent too much money!

However, whilst lolling around for 3 weeks, we became very friendly with a woman in the next van and her partner who is Irish and I believe much younger than her (did not like to ask but I call him 'muscle man' and he's good looking). She has a house in Toowoomba, had recently sold her restaurant in Mooloolaba (which is where she met her partner) and her name is also Coral (now known as Coral from Bundaberg!) She has 3 daughters, all highly skilled, one owns a hotel near Kingaroy, and two are in New Zealand at present although one is doing a second degree. (A great example of a single parent who gets on well with her x-husband and who has excelled at educating her kids). Anyway, they had set off to travel with a four wheel drive vehicle and a tent and then she met a guy when buying her fish from a huge fresh fish outlet who wanted to start selling fish and chips and he asked her if she would help him set up the kitchen and employ people and train them. So she bought a van for $1,000, completely gutted it and they refitted it and she's working again! She was going to leave as she has to get to Cairns for a wedding but has decided to stay on until she can find somebody who is suitably trained to take over from her and will fly up for the wedding instead. Then they will be continuing their travels around Australia as his parents are coming over from Ireland in March and they want to see Darwin, the red centre and Perth. However, she is insistent that we keep in touch.

Hook Island Flotsam

In the meantime the other Coral is insisting that we move to Armstrong Beach with them! That's a whole other story. Because of an initial comment of mine, Brendan (Coral's partner) is now designing and building 6 houses, all in a row along the sea front and they insist we buy a block too! I told her I should have stayed in Real Estate and collected the commission on the sale of 6 land blocks at $180-200 grand each!

Jack And Callie Loved It Here

Whilst in **Bundaberg** we booked to go to Tasmania from beginning of November to end of January so my best friend Barbara who lives in Launceston is ecstatic. Kids now know we won't be around for Christmas! We're taking both vehicles and having a cabin overnight. Discovered afterwards that we could have got a hefty discount with our CMCA card if we had used certain words initially when booking! Frustrating!. I had to go to CES to have an interview and lucky for me a woman had changed shifts and I got her because she was in the medical profession for years and has explained more to me about my condition than any of the doctors or specialists and I at last understand! I have just received mail enclosing a Pensioner Card!

Having left Bundy (I didn't want to) we drove to **Gin Gin** and stayed there free for one night and managed to see the Memorial to those backpackers in **Childers** who died in that hostel fire (it was closed the last time we were there) and then went inland to B.P Dam. That's where we ran into the first dust storm so couldn't see a thing. We had a quick tour around Kingaroy area etc as we'd never been there and then on to Toowoomba. On the way down the range the bus burst the front tyre and to cut a long story short, it flayed out when coming apart and cut so many wires we were horrified! The bus wouldn't drive properly and John was losing the power steering and hydraulic brakes and it would conk out when stopping at lights and we had to get through about 6 sets of lights in about 300m in one road in **Toowoomba** itself - nightmare. By the time we got to the van park I opened the door, grabbed the whiskey and lemonade and tried to stop shaking. How John did not have an accident I will never know. The damage was not that apparent until we hit the centre of Toowoomba or we wouldn't have gone on, the motor kept cutting out in rush hour traffic. The ramps wouldn't work of course – the wiring harness had been severed. We ended up staying a week I think because of repairs. Brent and Helen insisted we come down to the Gold Coast for a couple of nights. We spent it very quietly with them, only catching up with Colin briefly and never did catch up with Kevin! On Monday we had two new different and very large truck tyres fitted at a cost of $600 each!!

We have since been through **Goondiwindi** - what a beautiful town that turned out to be. Next time we travel this route we will stop there for a few weeks and do it justice. We did stop for a coffee in town and found the most delightful 'tea shop'. I call it that because it was like going back in time in England and finding a tea shop in delightful surroundings. Lace curtains draped the full window and the bottom of the window was covered with a half lace curtain. Sitting around a circular table in the window we noticed four elderly ladies, beautifully dressed with perfect makeup and hairstyles and they looked more like they should have been lunching at the Savoy Hotel in London or at the Champs -Elysees in Paris but here we were out west in Australia and they presented such a beautiful photo opportunity that I rued the fact that I had left my camera back in the van. However, when we entered to order our coffees I immediately went up and spoke to them and told them how struck I was and how beautiful they looked – I had been outside the window staring at them so thought they deserved an explanation! It was charming inside as it was furnished to match the picture the ladies painted. The name of the café is also delightful 'Tittle Tattle and Tea'.

We are now at **Moree** where I am about to get into one of the free thermal baths which apparently are in the high 30's. That should do the trick before we leave tomorrow on our journey to the River Murray and then to Melbourne for the ferry.

So there you have it - all in a nutshell!

October 2009 - email to brother

"Dear Paul (from Toowoomba, couple of hours drive west of Brisbane)

Dust picked up by winds from central Australia has blanketed us twice, covering Sydney to the northern tip and has blown on to New Zealand etc. Everything covered in a fine red dust which is so fine that even mouth masked cannot stop it from getting into your lungs. We've had 2 instances about a week apart. One wit from New Zealand said on T.V last night "In New Zealand we do things differently. If we want to move top soil, we get a big truck, dig it up and move it by road to where we want it'."

This morning I was about to go out of the screen door of the van when I saw a Magpie walking by so I spoke to it as I often do - I especially like talking to seagulls cause they sit and listen and sometimes sit down next to me if I keep the talking up. Anyway, this was a young Magpie - I knew that as it was so big, bigger than its parents. It suddenly burst into song and John came to watch when he heard. I was telling it that it did not want bread and should go and look for some worms - normal sort of conversation one has with wild birds - when it started singing and I caved in and chucked a crust of bread out for it. I then went outside and sat down beside it as it 'killed' the bread and then ate it. The bird then walked up to me, looked at me and started singing a beautiful song again and then flew off! It was quite a beautiful moment.

Having finally arranged for an auto mechanic who was also an auto electrician he turned up, had a look under the bus and then decided he couldn't do the job! Then a guy, who we had not met and who was leaving with his wife today (they have a caravan), turned up and started to see if he could help with our wiring problems! Then his wife came around and she and I had a long talk whilst John tried to look supportive for Keith who had started to sort the wiring out for us. Turns out that they come from Beechworth in Victoria where the fires started last summer and he is in the volunteer fire service (had a tree fall across his car and he was lucky to live) and she mans the telephones to organise volunteers for the rural fire service. Actually that is not quite right - she uses her own phone to do it and normally pays the bill but Telstra did wave her $300 phone bill that amounted for the duration of the fires. We got on so well with both of them and they have asked us to call in and see them if we are around their way! It turned out that despite him having been a mechanic, he couldn't repair the wires as neither of us had the correct tools for the job. John had just finished reading a book I had bought some time ago about the bush fire and it individualised families and told their personal stories. John offered it to Margaret but she refused and said she'd certainly buy a copy. I told her that she had to have it because this was only one print run done and she won't be able to find a copy - the Salvation Army did it as a fundraiser. They wouldn't accept money for their time but at least she has the book and half my organic celery!

At 1.30 another auto electrician turned up and now we are mobile again. Well we hope so anyway. We haven't actually moved the bus yet. He didn't reconnect the reversing camera though - told us he sold them! We declined to buy one of his and will get it fixed later. Apparently its 6 years old which is ancient? On Friday when we leave we will go to get the new front tyres fitted and they will be twice the width of the ones we have on now which will be far better for our Australian road conditions. We will then have 2 spares for the 4 tyres at the back - which is good as they don't make them any more.

Hopefully things will now resume in a calmer fashion and we will continue our roll down to Melbourne. Funny life this, being on the road, meeting lovely strangers, talking to birds and fretting over engines and electrics instead of being near our kids and doing the gardening! What do people mean when they say 'getting away from it all?'

Chapter 20

October 2009

I am going to admit that I am an environmental hazard – well not me – it's just that I am a serious knicker polluter. Every now and again I decide that I need new knickers as I have

Mount Kaputar N.p. Another Lookout

somehow changed shape or the knickers have. I have hundreds of pairs but none seem to fit or they leave lines around my stomach or whatever. So I go out and buy some and throw the labels away and chuck them in my drawer. Then I wear a pair and decide they aren't comfortable after all or that they are the wrong size. Sizes drive me batty because I never know if I am a size 10,

12 or 14 when I try clothes on yet I have bought size 14 knickers before only to find that they are too small so I guess they were made in Thailand because those girls there are so frighteningly beautifully petite. That's why I've never been there yet. I only have to glance at one and I feel like an elephant. Anyway I've bought some new knickers and this time I tried a pair on but that doesn't always work because you obviously have to try them on over the top of your

baggy old knickers in the shop and they just do not fit the same way when you get home. This time they do fit. I only bought two pairs because I still did not trust that they would be comfortable whereas usually I buy about six of them at a time because I am frightened to death that the next time I go to look for the same ones that they have disappeared off the shelves. What do you do with old knickers, especially if you've worn them once? It matters not how much I have spent on them, I'm stuck with defunct knickers. I wash them even though I know I won't wear them again and they get chucked into the back of the cupboard. Every so often I grab a heap and chuck them in the bin – what a waste! Some of them are too pretty to chuck away so I chuck them back in the cupboard although I'll never wear them again. So, back to my new knickers – I don't trust them. I put them on, pulled my jeans on top of them and started walking around the van and I didn't feel as though I had any on! I checked and they were there but they are so comfortable I cannot be sure without looking. These knickers were cheap and had 20% off! What if I get used to feeling as though I haven't got knickers on and can't find them in the shops again? This is causing me to lose sleep, along with the fifty new/worn-once knickers that I am now carrying around in my limited space, motor home drawer.

NARRABRI (Mount Kaputar National Park)

We have a wonderful site in a wonderful park and are going to stay for a week. We are surrounded by beautiful green grass, flowers and birds. Wild budgies dance around us and we feel like we've landed in the Garden of Eden. Other than lounging around in our wonderful surrounds all we have done is explore the Kaputar National Park which has been wonderful.

Our first walk and climb was to find Sawn Rocks which is an amazing rock formation. Imagine thousands of organ pipes. Actually that is how it is described 'The organ-piped cliff is the remnant of a lava flow'. It was a fabulous walk with lovely views and the destination perfect. We spent a fair bit of time exploring a dried out creek bed with fallen rocks all around us, unearthed by vegetation. Mt Kaputar is 1510 metres high and we went up to the summit during our time exploring the park. We didn't see it all as there's 51,000 hectares of it! We loved the area and loved exploring it.

DUBBO ZOO

We spent two days at the Western Plains Zoo at Dubbo. We saw all sorts – zebra, elephants, gibbon, African elephants, rhinos, giraffes and on and on I could go. We nearly trod on one wild rodent – a mouse running across the path which I promptly got a photo of! Oh yes, there were also those animals we all know so well, such as the Addax and the Guanaco

White Rhinos

and the Onagers and if you don't know what they are then you'll have to get a dictionary out or better still, go to the zoo because there are a lot of creatures whose names I cannot even recall! The common elands were pretty (yes they are called 'Common'. John's favourites were the hippos and for me if was the otters. I could have quite happily sat and watched them all day. A lady standing next to me from Sydney (New South Wales) was discussing her pet ferret and didn't know that we are not allowed to keep them in Queensland. We're not allowed to keep pet rabbits either. Anybody who lives at either Cooloongatta (Queensland) or Tweed Heads (New South Wales) must find it all a nonsense seeing as one side of the street is one State and the other – well the other! So how do you tell your pet rabbit or ferret that they must not cross the road?

26 October in Seymour, Victoria – email to friend re Victorian bush fire February 7th 2009

I had a long talk with a young man from Kinglake called Dean a couple of days ago. He and his family were not able to escape their home - the fire wasn't supposed to be coming their way anyway so they didn't know they were in danger. He, his parents and his sister and her daughter had bought 3 properties on the one piece of land only a year before. He had decided to take his first holiday since the fire and is using an old caravan that was donated for his parents to live in. The insurance company is paying his parent's rental on a house so he can use it. Rebuilding has only just started so his sister and niece are in a purpose-built emergency home in town and his parents in another village and he has stayed on the property living in a brick shed that saved their lives. He couldn't move into a purpose built home because he has his dog. He told me that the community village that was purpose-built has only just started to feel like a community. Many homes in his street are now up for sale. His niece had started to nag them earlier in the day (she's 10 I think he said) that she had the feeling they were going to die but they really didn't believe they were in danger where they were. (Note: I have read in a newspaper report that the there were no warnings on ABC radio – the radio we are supposed to have on in such emergencies - about any fires within 20ks of Kinglake when the fire hit.) She put all her precious things into the car - the car was destroyed. He told me that some people went to the rural fire office to find out the latest advice only to find nobody there and then they were told by someone who worked in the fire service to go home so that's what they did.

They heard a noise (very, very loud), the sky went black, smelt the smoke and the ground started to shake. When the fire arrived it tore up the mountain in 4 seconds!! He had got the neighbours into his parent's home - they were all there but that caught fire even though it was brick. He was the only one running around with buckets of water but he said with the adrenalin rushing through his body, by the time he got the bucket of water to the place he wanted to dump it, he had lost half of it. All around him, all the time and new fires were sprouting. When everyone got to the brick shed, away from the house, his father told him he needed glasses for them to drink out of - tank water beside the shed. Dean realises in retrospect how stupid it was but he actually went back to the burning house to get two glasses! However, when he was crawling into the kitchen door (he said you couldn't see anything because it was pitch dark so you did everything by touch) he heard their cat who came crawling over to him so he was able to rescue it. His beautiful German shepherd survived and they only lost one dog (the little one he called it). The main fire lasted about 4 hours because it ended up in coming up three sides of the mountain.

He was telling me how many metres under ground the fire was - I cannot recall - years of accumulated leaf litter etc - which was why it was so impossible to put it out. Even if the ground was soaked the fires would come up again from underneath and they have been told that the force of the fire rushing up the mountain in 4 seconds was the equivalent to three atomic bombs going off. Some people ran to the Kinglake Hotel but the owner had locked the door so they broke it open to get into the cold room and the owner called the police! This was in the midst of it! People had been hit by flying embers, their eyes were burnt, they couldn't breathe etc. Dean had all of that and couldn't see properly for a week. He said that the flying embers didn't worry him when they hit him after the fire front had gone through - they were nothing to what they had been through. No locals go to the Kinglake Hotel any more - can you imagine not giving sanctuary in that kind of situation!

He told us lots of stories but I won't go on. He hasn't exactly got 'survivors'-guilt' but he feels guilty that they have been offered so much by so many organisations and people and because they will be better off than they were before, he feels he is 'profiting' from the demise of those who died and he hates that. I told him that those who died would tell him to take whatever is offered as it's only money and 'things' and rebuild the community that they all loved living in so much in memory of them. He is still having counselling and talks to his case worker.

He's left the following morning before we got up so I didn't get to see him again. He was off to Byron Bay to try and escape it all for a while whilst their houses are being rebuilt. I'll never forget him, or his story. At one time I asked him if there were people still in hospital and he said 'Yes. Oh, there's one man - what he went through - well, it was hell.....oh the kids.....no....I don't think I should tell you after all. You'll not be able to get to sleep....' His voice had gone from eager to tell me this guy's story to faltering as his face changed and then got quieter and quieter and that told me just how much he is still suffering inside. I've read the book on the survivor's stories but not story I read has affected me as much as hearing and seeing Dean tell me his. A beautiful guy in his mid to late 30's I would think. Let's hope he has a ball in Byron.

We travelled to and stopped at **Whittlesea, Kinglake, Healsville and Marysville** today – Healsville was not touched by the Black Saturday fires and is a beautiful town. The scenery we saw has to be some of the most beautiful rural scenery in Australia and I no longer wander why some people wish to rebuild in the Kinglake area (which includes Kinglake West, Kinglake Central, Kinglake East and Kinglake). I have so much that I want to tell you but my writing is stilted. I don't even come from there, I have no idea what it is like for so those that survived – their memories, their experiences, their losses but mixed with a feeling of sorrow and sympathy and helplessness is the sight of the trees with new growth sprouting up their trunks so that, in R.L's words 'They look furry'. Houses are being rebuilt, council workers are busy all along the roads felling trees - upsetting some local residents in the process as they feel that too many trees are being felled and in some cases the wrong trees are being felled - the grass is so green and lush it looks like velvet s and there is a feeling of 'things moving forward' when we spoke to the locals. Well, so it was until we reached Marysville. It was different there and we felt shocked. We did talk to one local who appeared to have adopted the 'stiff upper-lip' approach the tragedy. I asked her if they had support like in the other areas and she replied that they could get it if they wanted it. I reckon those that have accepted all the help that is available when it comes to counselling and talking to their case workers are going to fare a lot better in the long run. There were so many people lost in Marysville and it took a while for anything to be done for the future there I believe because of the conditions there. How on earth can I know about anything there! I can't write rationally so I'll leave it for another day. I will add though that the whole area is so beautiful that at one point R.L was considering living there!!! He who believes that he cannot live away from the ocean at the Gold Coast!

Vic - They Must Have Thought They Lived In Heaven

The night we returned from visiting a few of the fire ravaged areas, we were watching a science program on television and they were talking about the Victorian bush fires and we learnt that being surrounded by grass rather than trees is only safer depending on where your house is sited. On flat ground grass burns slower but as the ground rises grass fires gather speed apparently so if you are on a hill you can be in severe danger. We had once seen a house we wanted to buy that was surrounded by grass, up on a hill and I had said to John that I liked it because the area around had been cleared of trees which would protect it from bush fires.

Chapter 21

TASMANIA-Devonport

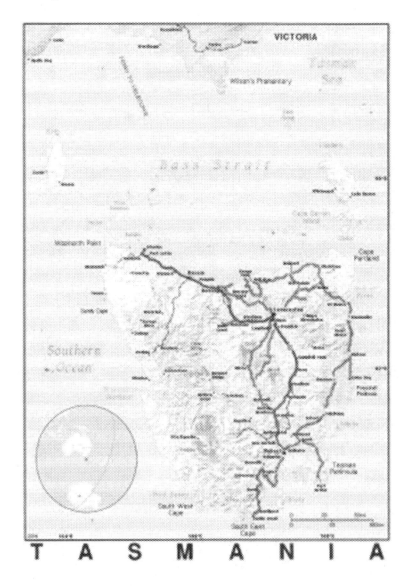

We arrived yesterday after a nightmare trip on the motorway from our park to the ferry terminal and a nightmare time for John getting to his site for the bus to be parked inside the ferry. We arrived at about 5.05pm and he did not park the vehicle until 7pm! He said it was stop/start every few metres and he was sent around and around outside. It had taken me an hour of waiting in the queue and they gave me both tickets so John had no idea of the number of our cabin. When one of the attendants asked us to go in different directions I asked him to pass John his tickets but he refused! At one point I was stopped and I had to get out of the vehicle and walk around to the other side to find out why I had been stopped as the attendant in his warm little office said he was not allowed to come outside! Very unhelpful lot so it was not surprising it took so long to board with vehicles. When I got upstairs I realised that I had no idea what floor I had parked on (there is a good reason for that which I won't bother going into now) so I asked if I could go back down and check what floor I had to get out of the life in order that I wouldn't hold anyone up the following morning but I wasn't allowed to go back down. This despite the fact that the rules state that there is no access to your car after the ferry leaves the dock and we were not due to depart for an hour and a half. Luckily, the following morning I did find the car and then we had the reverse problem with John driving off almost first and me an a long time after him but luckily in Devonport there is room to pull over and wait for someone unlike Melbourne. I don't know how we'll manage on our return journey as parking anywhere near the terminal is frowned upon. We hadn't slept very well and felt jet-lagged all morning but did get out in the afternoon to go into town for a walk around, have a cup of coffee at a lovely Italian Restaurant and to drive the streets and beautiful foreshore to familiarise ourselves with the area. It has changed so much since we were last here when we disliked the area – now it is lovely and the Council still has work to complete along the foreshore apparently. When we came here before there were a lot of closed shops and the town had a dismal air about it but not any more. It's a really nice town with all the major clothes shops that you would hope to see in a coastal town, restaurants and cafes and very helpful staff at the prominent Information Centre!

Today we went to **Port Sorrell** and drove and walked all around the coastal inlet and on our way back we stopped for pancakes with blackberries, strawberries, blueberries (all grown on premises and could have had cherries too) and together with the ice-cream on top it became brunch! We also stopped at the Potato Shop where I was delighted to find that they had the 'carbon footprint' labels beneath the products so I bought some broccoli that had travelled two kilometres! It is so very, very good to have such beautiful fresh vegetables and local fruit around, including the beautiful berry fruits which are now in season. Tasmania is like a large 'Devon' with so much to see and so many beautiful local fresh products and they include wines and cheeses as well as nuts. Today we saw a sign for a bag or walnuts for two dollars outside an acreage property.

A mobile auto mechanic is here at the moment and we only phoned him mid morning. We seem to keep developing the oddest problems, or old ones not repaired such as the reversing camera which the previous auto electrician failed to complete. We are still trying to find the cause of a leak which everyone says is the power steering fluid yet we never have to top it up. None of this worries me one iota because I am so happy to be in Tasmania amongst friendly, relaxed people who seem to love to help. In Melbourne we couldn't get anyone to do anything and we never even had a phone call from the gas water heater technician despite our phoning him twice and waiting two weeks! This guy is so good that John has given him our whole list of odds and end we want checking and I have just found that he has found the cause of the leak and it is not the power steering which is obviously a relief!

Spoke to soon – still got something leaking! Also a caravan repair shop did not have the gas man at his centre at noon when we got there and I had to keep reminding him to phone him. As it turns out the gas man was not authorised to repair our water heater and sixty-five dollars later there is absolutely no difference – the darned thing still won't stay on and heat the water. The owner of the business then sold us some damaged awning clips for forty-five dollars – not a good introduction to the outskirts of Launceston. However, **Longford** where we are now staying is lovely. It is a village with the caravan park sited beside the river. A bonus is the superb meat retail/wholesale depot just out of the centre which I had been told about and the meat is so cheap and, apparently very good.

When we were based in **Devonport** we did the usual tourist drives around and one day included an exhibition of sea shells and a studio where they make stunning glass marbles which were both at **Sheffield** and Looking Glass Cottage at **Railton** which showcases fibre optic spheres and lights and is described as a 'wonderland of fairies, dragons and fantasia' is the guide book. Then there was the shop called Reliquaire at **Latrobe** which 'did my head in' and I couldn't get out of there fast enough! It is extraordinary and it is so difficult to describe the goods for sale because there are too many. There are a series of small rooms and you need a map to get around, plus corridors and dead ends with a small paved court yard with at least three doors off it at one end. So

Another Pretty Picture At Gorge

really it is a maze. There are hundreds of dolls, marionettes, puppets, teddy bears and games plus masks that would look in place at a Venetian ball, creepy things to frighten the children, dressing-up clothes and clothes and countless other items. One room has perfumed soaps etc in it but I was way past the point of looking closer by that stage. There were extraordinary 'faces' looking at you from every nook and cranny, walls, ceiling and floor. Some of the figures were large – bigger than many children. I sat on a bench outside whilst waiting for John and stared at a green lawn just to attempt to clear my head. I wondered how long a two year old would last without throwing a tantrum because I had sensory overload. I also wondered and John thought it was" just surreal and spooky" when he came out, if children would have nightmares after being 'watched' by so many weird faces. Older children would like it because there really is something for everyone albeit that I cannot recall what! Within easy reach of

Devonport there is so much for children to see on a wet or cold day and we did not get to a place called **Promised Land** where you can find the miniature Village of Lower Crackpot and the world's largest maze complex which is a family attraction called Tasmazia, nor Aunty Iris's[Doll Museum with over 2000 dolls, the chocolate factory, Platypus Encounters let alone the **Imaginarium Science Centre in Devonport**! Everyone would enjoy the Don River Railway in a vintage steam train because at least you can stop and let somebody else drive you around! We were in and out of our car all day what with taking photographs and buying coffee and lunch or browsing through book stalls and shops.

We had driven to **Spreyton** before going on to Sheffield and the scenery was stunning, much better than when we returned to Devonport via Latrobe. Or perhaps I just didn't see anything as I was still too stunned by that shop!

LAUNCESTON

We are staying by the river at **Longford** and we are so glad that we chose this park rather than one in Launceston. It is on the junction of the South Esk and Macquarie rivers and it is a pretty village but what has surprised us is how much there is to see so near to us. The last time we came here we stuck mainly to the coast and we missed so much but then we only had ten days and this time we have three months and we are already beginning to wonder if we are going to have enough time to see what we have been told to see! The surrounding countryside reminds us of Devon, with rolling green fields, flowers and the towering mountains in the distance (something Devon doesn't have). Anyway we filled a whole day up just touring locally thanks to the Archer family who used to own two places which are on the 'must see' list of things to do. **Woolmers**, a private mansion, has recently been nominated for World Heritage listing and was home to six generations of the family from the early 1800's through to 1994 and it still contains all the original possessions. The village of Brickendon is still owned by members of the 7th generation and is still farmed by them. There is a convict-built farm village and heritage gardens, the latter which are on the other side of the road where their private house still stands. They also showcase a **National Rose Garden** with nearly 4,000 roses from all the rose families and the roses have in their first bloom of the season at the moment. We went to another homestead called **Clarendon** and looked around the grounds as well.

Evandale, which an absolutely stunning Georgian village dating back to the 1820's, is also not far from here and we have been back since our first visit for the weekly Sunday morning markets. They hold the National Penny Farthing championships in February! The Tasmanian Honey Company is nearby with the best (to my mind) honey in the world – Leatherwood honey. If you like honey, I have been advised that I should have stopped at the Mole Creek Honey Garden when driving to Launceston from Devonport, turning off at Deloraine.

We spent another day at the **Cataract Gorge** and cliff surrounds in Launceston and walked our socks off uphill, coming back via the **Basin Chairlift** for a bird's eye view. I have far too many photographs and none of them do the place justice because with our peripheral vision we can see so much more of a scene at one glance than with an ordinary camera. There is a beautiful large swimming pool, plus wading pool for visitors to enjoy for free and it was well used when we were there as it was a very hot day. The swimming pool with lake behind, the gorge and the stunning trees and plants, the green lush grass and blue sky – just breathtaking! There are walking tracks everywhere – through 192 hectares - and you can see where the South Esk and Tamar Rivers meet. If you don't want to walk far, at least walk up to the suspension bridge for the chance to see the stunning views in reverse. It provides such stimulation for artists and photographers that they the **Kings Bridge Gorge Cottage** is available for Artists in Residence.

Cataract Gorge is only fifteen minutes walk from Launceston city centre but as the Gorge took up all of one day we spent another day just walking around the city. Many of the buildings have had their facades restored and if you remember to look up and around instead of at the shops, you will see some wonderful old architecture. I was delighted with the city as soon as I saw my favourite coffee franchise but fine dining, cafes and restaurants, bars, bistros are everywhere.

On that subject I have to add that we love the real milk we buy here with the cream on top! Just realise that when you do come here, unless you walk a lot, you are going to put on weight but the upside is that your immune system should get a huge boost with all the fresh berries everywhere and bags of apples for a song straight from the trees etc. Tasmania boasts many wineries, fine cheeses and fresh whole foods. I don't think I want to leave. The only downside I have found so far is that I cannot by my vegetarian eggs (no offal etc in the chicken feed) and they are the only eggs that do not upset my stomach for some reason. I am going to have to question people selling eggs privately to find out if they feed them pellets or just vegetables. I am also finding it impossible to find organic meat and having got used to a good steak which melts in the mouth, we were disappointed with steak we had bought from a butcher back near Devonport. Just outside Longford village there is a retail/wholesalers butchers, part of the meat-processing plant and I have stocked up again today with all manner of meats and am hoping to have better luck with this supplier.

We spent two separate days touring along the **Tamar River**. Our first trip started along North-East Trail as far as **Bridpor**t and we returned via **Scottsdale**. We covered over 500ks that day but as the sun doesn't set until well after 8pm we were able to enjoy a dinner tout at Perth, a small town very close to Longford on our return. There is too much to tell you about that trip but it is worth visiting **Windemere** and **Hillwood** on your way to **George Town** which was settled in 1804 and was the third settlement in Australia and has a lot of heritage buildings. Avoid Bell Bay en route because you can't get to see it because of the aluminium smelter and factories. It is purely industrial and you are not allowed to go through to the bay.

We travelled every road we could, bought vegetables and fruit, did not go on the wine trail or to the **Lavender Farm** or any other attractions like that and it was a long enough day as it was! We stopped at **Low Head** at lunchtime but shouldn't have passed the small beach area because there was nowhere to sit at the lighthouse. We took the dirt road to Beechford which was fine for our two-wheel drive and went to **Weymouth** and **Lulworth** before arriving at Bridport. The biggest highlight of our day was the trip back from Scottsdale to Launceston on the A3 road and I think that is a day trip well worth doing. The scenery is awe-inspiring. Take yourselves up to Scottsdale for lunch and come back the same way because you will be so glad you saw the scenery from both directions. The trip stunned us the last time we were here and it was even more beautiful this time in the soft light of the late afternoon sun.

Another day we travelled along the length of the Tamar River on the other side. We stopped at **Beaconsfield** (now renowned for the miraculous escape of two men in a mine disaster) and bought lunch at the **Tamar Valley Wholefoods and Coffee Shop**. I mention that because just remembering our lunch makes my mouth water. We wisely chose the venison and mushroom pies, served with a delicious small salad and really well-made hot coffees. There was so much meat in those pies and it was so tender that even R.L ate slowly, savouring every mouthful. We drove on to **Greens Beach** to look at a house that we once considered buying, stopped at the **Yorktown** monument and then on to **Beauty Point**. On our return journey back to Launceston we turned off to **Gravelly Beach** and drove as far as we could and enjoyed the change of scenery because this is a residential area alongside the river. We turned off again after that and drove along every road we could get to that skirts the river. There are so many lovely areas to live in and around Launceston. There are also too many other things that we haven't seen or done that I haven't mentioned but they are for you to discover.

It is so very different travelling around this island to the way we tend to travel on the mainland where, in so many places, you can drive for hours and see very little change in the scenery. My school friend who lives not far from Longford will be coming here for a weekend in her new caravan soon. A distance of 17.4ks with a travelling time of around twenty minutes by car! It will be a complete change of scenery for her. So, try not to come here for only ten days as we did the first time because we went back to Queensland exhausted and had missed huge areas

Tasmania - Ross River Bridge - Daytime

of coastline and the Huon Valley and all of the hinterland other than the main highways.

ROSS

We headed off to the east coast and parked the bus at **Campbell Town.** John jumped into the ute and after a look around the town, we headed to Ross as two lovely young women we met whilst having coffee in Launceston had suggested that we not miss it. After a quick look and a coffee at the bakery, we headed back to Campbell Town so John could collect the bus and here we are ensconced at Ross for at least two days. It is beautiful and we are so glad we did not pass by. The caravan park is beside the river almost beside the beautiful Ross Bridge with its intricate carvings completed by a convict and for which he won his freedom. The town centre has not changed much since it was built and the beautiful Georgian buildings are proudly maintained and the avenues of trees add shade and beauty. Needing a walk, we started at the bridge and followed the designated path to the Ross Female Factory site which was originally a male prison, later converted to a prison for females who were pregnant or who had children. If an unmarried woman became pregnant it warranted a six month jail term in this type of prison. As soon as the babies were weaned they were taken away from their mothers and they were swaddled for up to three years. Once the children were three, they were sent to a Children's Home if the mother hadn't been released. Apparently it was not a happy place for the staff, let alone the inmates. Semi-detached superintendant's and assistant superintendants homes were open for us to walk in and look at and it was here that we read some of the stories of the inmates and staff. Even the two police guards asked to be transferred because of arguments amongst the staff!

From there we walked across the railway line and up the hill to the distant original graveyard. I nearly got blown over on the way back because the wind is very gusty today and the forecast is for 100k+ winds and to be prepared for power lines to be blown down and trees. The sky has been grey all day but it is not cold and the only reason I wore a light jacket was because the pockets could house my camera, water bottle and mobile phone.

Eventually we walked back to the top end of the village and went into **Classwood** – which sells all manner of items made from several different types of tree. Next it we stoped at the Tasmanian Wool Centre which also houses the Information Centre and we were grateful to finally sit down and watch a superb film about the history of Ross. There is no charge to enter the museum and there are enough artefacts to interest almost everyone. We stopped to take a photo of the village from the other side of the war memorial, which is apparently what nearly every visitor does when they come to Ross! We had also passed several very beautiful churches by this time but unfortunately they were closed. Tomorrow, we will check out the shops and find out when we can see inside the churches and also take another look at the junction in town which has inspired it to be called 'Temptation, Salvation, Damnation & Recreation'. Incidentally, once parked here you do not need a vehicle as the town is two minutes walk from the park.

We had a lovely day walking around the town and talking to people and we actually got in the car to drive around the other side of the railway line and to find what we thought was a village about 3ks down the road but it appears it must have been a private estate as we went a lot further and never found it! Having talked to the locals we were not sure whether to feel enchanted, intrigued or horrified by the rich complexities of living in a very small village. We heard about things that I'm sure we should not have heard about and as they were told to us in confidence, purely as an aid to describe village life, I will not repeat them! In retrospect, as I am writing this a couple of days later, I think I feel intrigued and bemused. Nothing is as it seems and John has decided that the English program on television called Midsummer Murders is actually filmed here! We left Ross having purchased fresh bread from the bakery and fresh vegetables from the market, just as the Harley Davidson motor bikes started to roar into town for a meeting – we are being followed.

Chapter 22

BICHENO, COLES BAY, SCAMANDER, ST HELENS (Freycinet Peninsula and Bay of Fires)

Tasmania - Bicheno - Coles Bay - Stunning

We arrived at Bicheno and were surprised at how small the town centre still is. Actually you could hardly call it a town really. However, it is the gateway to the Freycinet Pensinsula (correct spelling) which is why you come here and we explored the area to and including Coles Bay endlessly ending up at the Freycinet Lodge for a much needed cup of coffee and the coffee was so good that I immediately bought a second cup!

Today we drove to St Helens and to see the **Bay of Fires** in the sunshine because the last time we were there it was raining. Bathed in all its glory it is a sight you could never forget. We took our photos from **Binalong Bay** as you can get the whole bay in one camera shot. It was an easy journey although we stopped many times en route, first at **Lagoons Beach**, then at **Four Mile Creek** before exploring **Falmouth** which is a very quiet hamlet but with lots of new houses being built and plenty of house blocks for sale. Scamander R.L described as 'scrabbly and untidy' so now I have a new word to add to the Oxford English Dictionary. We

Tasmania - Bicheno To St Helens - Bay Of Fires From Binalong Bay

again stopped at **Cockle Cove Bay** rest area and ate half our lunch and had a coffee. We returned later to St Helens to look at the town. I went into the Information Centre and asked where people went for their groceries. Having established that the girl working there then said to me 'You have just arrived?' so I told her that we had arrived before and were staying for about three months in Tasmania. 'When did you arrive?' I told her I wasn't sure of the date. 'You are staying in Swansea?' 'No, along the coast'. 'Are you in a caravan or motorhome?' 'A motorhome'. 'Are you staying at Bicheno?' 'I expect so because we came over the range and landed about there' (as you can tell I was getting somewhat irritated! 'Where are you staying there?'…..The questions came thick and fast and as John walked in the door and said he was with me I heard her mumble 'Two of them'. However, before he arrived, I had begun to feel really angry at her rudeness and was expecting her to ask how much I weighed along with my date of birth and I said 'Will you stop questioning me please. Isn't it I who should be asking you questions as I'm here for information?' As John walked in I saw a pad of maps of St Helens on the table and trying to remind her that she was there to enthuse about all the places we should visit and glorious vistas I said out loud 'Ah, a map'. No such luck as she turned away so we walked out. If you ever encounter this then ask a local and I was lucky enough to strike up a conversation with a council worker (well I think he was) who was working on a rest area near the beach at Binalong Bay and he was a great guy who loves the area and who told us to go to **Dora Point**, how to get there and that the dirt roads were smooth and fine for a two wheel drive and also to go to **Humbug Point lookout**. He should have been paid that girl's wages on top of his own as he was friendly, helpful and suggested places for us to visit. He also added local knowledge and all this when he was supposed to be taking his lunch break as his co-worker was doing. I drove one way today and John drove back and it is a good compromise as we both have the luxury of looking out of the side window whilst travelling and enjoying the glorious views. Next stop Swansea – well that is if there is a caravan park with more than about 6 sites like the one we are in now, if they will accept a large motorhome because one park here won't despite allowing a large fifth wheeler into their park (overall length with tow vehicle being longer than ours) and we will only stay for more than absolutely necessary if it is a decent park and they seem few and far between here in Tasmania as a Tasmanian resident told me today! It really is becoming a headache. One of the major park franchises here has got rid of all their sites and now has only cabins and that seems to be becoming the trend as they can ask for so much money to rent them out for the night. It is also happening on the mainland but not to the same extent.

On a completely different note – we are amused at the weather reports here. When they give information about sea swells for those that have boats they often tell the views that the waters are 'confused'. I haven't actually heard them mention the height of the swells yet but I guess 'confused' means not to take your fishing boat out! Apparently some trawlers set off this morning from here and had to return to the harbour almost immediately.

SWANSEA

We stayed at a caravan park there for a couple of nights and this time it was to our advantage that we had a 'big rig' because they couldn't fit us into the caravan park and told us to go to their cabin park along the road and we were given a fabulous site overlooking the bay. We probably should have stayed their longer but I was suffering withdrawal symptoms for a major shopping centre which was causing me some concern as to my state of mind as I usually hate them. Anyway, after sightseeing the first day there wasn't much left for us to see so I spent a lazy day luxuriating in the view and reading a superb book that someone had left in the laundry. I was determined to leave it behind for someone else to read so reading was virtually all I did all day.

John was active and played golf, enjoying himself immensely as he played better than he had done for months, scored some pars and found some golf balls! He ended up playing nineteen holes.

Swansea is an extremely pretty town and beautifully maintained. They proudly claim to have the only black Wattyl bark mill in Australia and the timber is beautiful and we would have bought something made out of it if we could have afforded anything! They also have a walking track which, having lived in Wales with its unpronounceable place names (unless you speak Welsh), greatly amused me. Try saying this – Loontitetermairrelehoiner Track, which is a walking track around a headland by the beach.

TRIABUNNA & ORFORD

What we noted on our journey from Swansea to Triabunna is how unbelievably undeveloped the coastline is. I had thought that over the years, since we were last here, developments of houses would have sprung up but no, it is as pristine as ever – looks almost untouched by mankind. When you reach Orford though, it is very built-up with a large amount of houses.

We had totally forgotten how small a place Triabunna is and after a drive around, decided to continue on to Cambridge (Hobart suburb) as we knew we would be flat out trying to explore Hobart and surrounds before getting the ferry back to the mainland. Orford is just after Triabunna and is very pretty. The journey became interesting with hairpin bends roads again, up and down the ranges and at one point we were following the river on one side of us and forested cliffs on the other and the scenery was spectacular. It is a lovely journey between Triabunna and Hobart with some very beautiful spots to stop and look at the scenery. One of the hills we went up and over was '**Break-Me-Neck Hill**' which is fairly explicit! Then we went down '**Break Me Gall Hill**' and I'm a little confused about the meaning of that!

HOBART

Mt Wellington - Hobart From Summit

So here we are, parked up and it is teeming with rain. I did get my dose of shops yesterday at **Eastlands at Rosny Park** which is not far from here and just before you go over the river into Hobart. It is a perfect place to settle in as it is so easy to go in all the directions you need to explore and despite being so central it is rural. It turned out that this local undercover shopping mall is the largest in Tasmania although by Brisbane (Qld) standards it is not that large at all for which I was grateful as I get claustrophobic in shopping centres that are so large you can easily get lost and where you have to mark which door you came in by so you have some idea as to how to find your car afterwards, that is if you can remember what floor in the parking areas and which way to go when you get out of the lift! No such problem at this shopping centre with Coles and Kmart downstairs and Woolworths and Big W upstairs and street level parking outside. I applaud the fact that on each of the two levels they have my favourite coffee bar franchise so to me it is a civilised shopping centre overall!

We have been reading tourist information leaflets and have been on the internet and are rather overwhelmed at the distances we have to cover to see the places we want to see around Hobart and have even discussed changing our ferry tickets so we have more time in Tasmania. As for now, we have managed to book probably the worst van site in the park as we have a mini-flood outside our door. We took it as we were told that we could probably stay on this site for three weeks if we needed to whereas other sites had bookings on them. If the rain gets worse as is forecasted, we may have to even evacuate the site! Since we left in May (it is now the end of November) we have been so lucky with the weather and when we first encountered rain during the day the other week I had to reassure John that we could go out in it. When I said we were going out he had looked at me in horror and said 'But it's raining' and I told him that other people do manage to go outside when it rains. It was only sprinkling on that day and I must admit that today I don't think it's a good idea to go out unless absolutely necessary as there are warnings of localised flooding throughout Tasmania and many roads could be affected along with fog on higher ground. There is a very scenic hill opposite our site, alongside this park and the top of it has been covered in cloud all day.

Thank goodness I have forgotten to take my camera out with me at times because Tasmania has a scenic shot at every turn. On Sunday we explored Hobart, mainly in the car as it was teeming with rain and a wind was howling. We usually choose a Sunday to explore large towns and cities because it is quieter on the roads and we can decide where we want to come back to. We passed the **Hobart Royal Botanic Gardens** on the way back so went in there. We've been there before but I particularly wanted to see '**Pete's Veggie Patch**' which has become well known for T.V viewers in Australia. The wind had died down and as we were suitably dressed, we thoroughly enjoyed our wander around and the coffee we bought at the café there!

Another day we went to explore **Cambridge**, where we are staying but other than the general store and pub there is only Cambridge Aerodrome and Cambridge Park which consists of a newish group of buildings housing retail sales of beds, camping and fishing stores, a Hervey Norman electrical store etc (which we went in as I must buy a new laptop) and which we came out of more confused than ever as to what we actually need! We went to **Sorell** that day too and did detours looking at local districts. We also went to **Seven Mile Beach** which was deserted except for dog owners with their dogs, the latter who were having a ball.

We have also driven around quite a bit of the Hobart suburbs, particularly surrounding **Rosny Park** and **Rokeby** but are finding that we have to use many tourist leaflets to find the places we want as we haven't been given any detailed map which includes the suburbs and it is quite frustrating. One place will be on one map and then you get another map out to find a neighbouring suburb and so-on. Actually, we have found this throughout Tasmania – it is frustrating being a tourist here. The caravan parks are not as plentiful as we had expected and they are not as good as on the mainland yet some are dearer than those at some of the best rated parks in the top tourist areas of Queensland.

The roads are absolutely superb here though and the only odd potholes we have seen were somewhere around St Helens. Because the roads are so smooth and the scenery simply stunning around every corner that you travel, it is very easy to drive around Tasmania so long as you do not mind climbing up and descending steep hills, navigating hair-pin bends and can keep your eyes on the road. It is much better to be a passenger so that you can see all the views where you cannot possibly stop.

We have also done a day trip from Hobart along the **Huon Trail** but as we wanted to see the area properly we chose to only go via **Margate** around to **Huonville** and back in the one day. That turned out to be a wise decision as we would otherwise have missed so much.

We first got stuck at **Kingston** which is a pretty suburb with good shopping facilities. We drove along **Kingston Beach** towards the blow hole and it was so pretty, even on a very dull day which it was. Even the suburban streets were pretty and congratulations are due to all the home owners who present their houses and gardens so beautifully. Hills surround part of Kingston Beach and from there on to **Electrona** and **Snug** you get wonderful rural views plus view of the boats on the bay below. It must be a lovely place to live if you work takes you into Hobart and surrounds as it is quite near the city. At **Kettering** we stopped to enquire how much it costs to go over to **Bruny Island** and picked up their timetable for the ferry. Next stop was **Woodbridge** – a delightful village with beautiful surrounds. We drove up a long, steep hill just so we could look down on it! We passed **Flowerpot** after that – what a wonderful name! At **Verona Sands** there were beach houses and it was in that area that I noticed an almost hidden entryway off the road leading to a hidden parking area. The rock steps leading down to the beach were also overgrown but I found them and sat on a rock to look at the view. It was so stunning that John and I just sat there in silence marvelling at the deserted beach, the island out to sea – too difficult to express how moving it was. Just after the turn off to **Eggs and Bacon Bay** there was a lookout and it was there that we met a couple from Bath in the U.K. I told them that I had doubted that I would find anywhere prettier than some parts of England, particularly Devon or the Cotswolds yet I had to admit that it is probably more beautiful here because it is so untouched and there isn't the traffic and let's face it – the weather is kinder! This is their sixth trip to Australia but their first time in Tasmania and they are as impressed as we are. There are so many Georgian villages here and the same stonework on houses as in the Cotswolds – beautiful sandstone look homes. Actually, you find examples of all the English style of homes including Tudor-style and Victorian along with the Australian Colonial homesteads and the Queensland-style (off the ground) homes with verandas all around. Most villages tend to be themed though to one style of home with the others being outside the village centres where you all find the huge manor houses surrounded by acres of land, many of which are heritage listed now.

17 - Launceston - Historic Military Buildings - This Park Closed For Renovation - Look At Timber Roof Tiles Falling Off

But it is the endless farmland, the soft rolling paddocks that roll down to deserted beaches with the blue sea beyond, the myriad of islands off shore, the endless huge trees, the profusion of flowers with vines trailing down from house rooves and walls and the hedges that we see little of in Queensland. To be honest, we'd be crazy to have them growing over our houses on the mainland because the termites would get in and our rooves would cave in – but here, no such problem as they haven't got termites here – what bliss – wisteria can run rampant along with every other climbing plant you can imagine and it does. Everywhere you turn at the moment there are roses just completing their first bloom of the season and vegetable gardens abound and run rampant and you wander how the owners can keep control of their vigorous growth. It is so rich and fertile here and it makes you feel young and fertile!

Chapter 23

It was getting late so we drove on to **Cygnet** where we just had to stop yet again for photos and to look at the views behind the main street and then on to Huonville where we stopped for some milk before heading home. The Huon River is long and Huonville is at the head of the river. We will be going back there again on our way to Southport and to do and see the famous local attractions but I'm so glad we did the coastal route first as it is not to be missed.

So today I am bogged down with so many photographs to download and it is so hard to get rid of some of them as they are such beautiful scenic shots. Did I mention that if you like Oysters you would be in heaven here? We keep passing Oyster farms and R.L is being very restrained. Or mussels – yes they have mussel farms here too. A first for Australia is the first Tuna farm ever developed and as the entrepreneur who has started it against everyone's advice as 'It can't be done' has said – 'They are funny creatures, you only have to look at them and they fall over'. I've had this weird visualisation of a Tuna fish standing on its tail, glaring at him ever since.

Tasmanian English language lesson: There are no such things as 'creeks' here, nor 'streams'- no, here they are called 'rivulets'. Isn't that nice? 'Rivulet' sounds much nicer than 'creek' and even nicer than 'stream'.

About two weeks later!

Time flies, especially when you get caught in a gale and your awning completely rips off at night! I think John got about four hours sleep that night but I won't bore you with it all. Suffice to say we are now awaiting a new one but that took some time to organise. I think this is the third time now that we have had substantial awning damage and we are amazed at the patience of our insurance company. It seems that this is the most vulnerable part of our motorhome according to the weather. We also had to do our Christmas mail and letters to everyone and with me alone having over a hundred relatives in England, plus friends, it is sometimes a daunting task. With the last one gone today and my 'other half' out at the moment catching up with an old friend from work, I have time to think and time to write. It's very difficult with him around as he talks all day long, mainly to himself, so sometimes I don't answer which irritates him but I don't realise that he's actually talking to me. He had an argument with me the other day with me sitting here listening and not saying a word. It's quite fascinating. He'll suddenly say something like 'Why don't we get in the car and go to …..? Okay, I suppose we don't have to go there but we could go to …….? Oh, I know, you say you want to do the washing today because it's stopped raining but I'm restless. You know how I am; I'm always restless; Yes, I know it's not your problem, it's mine but I can't help it, I've always been like that. Oh okay do what you want!' I sat there stunned and then asked him if he'd finished having an argument with me and then he suddenly realised that I was there! I tell you, he's completely nuts!

The last two days have been full of sightseeing. We went into Hobart for our second visit to the city centre, mainly to go and experience the **Saturday Salamanca Markets** which are a tourist destination in their own right. I have been to a lot of markets, including markets in cities and I reckon that the Hobart one is the best I've ever been to because it was a blast. There were superb street performers, two of whom were internationally known, plus several musicians. The markets are big but not so big that you find them exhausting (like the Brisbane City markets) and the setting, between the harbour and the old Salamanca settlement is superb. On top of that we were able to park all day in a multi-storey car park in the city for three dollars and it is a five to ten minute walk (depending on where you park) down hill to the waterfront. So we purchased fresh fruit and vegetables, had a coffee at an Italian restaurant which had pavement dining so we could 'people watch' and then walked back to town and dumped all our stuff in the car. We then explored the town centre, going up and down laneways and finding small squares behind the main street and marvelled at the beautifully restored original buildings and saw some beautiful parkland/flowers. With a couple of the main streets decked out with Christmas decorations it was also very pretty. Melbourne is a huge metropolitan city and Hobart reminds me of Melbourne but I like it much more because it is so compact and you can literally walk everywhere with ease. It is also the first time in Tasmania that we have seen so many different nationalities in any one place. John looked in awe at some women with ebony skin, amazing clothes and the weirdest hairstyles and said to one of them that he liked her hair. Her hair was sticking up and away from her head in the oddest style so in case

Huon Valley - Tahune Forest - River From Air Walk

she thought he was being sarcastic I hastened to explain to her that he was giving her a compliment as he thought she looked exotic and then she beamed with delight and thanked him! The Salamanca area is the 'arty' part of Hobart anyway and we saw some really weird and wonderful clothes. John was a bit blown away by the way some of the guys dressed. Anyway, we walked around so much that day with so much enthusiasm and interest that by the time I did sit down in the car my legs suddenly felt like jelly!

The following day we were off again, back to on the Huon Valley Trail and we stopped to purchase our tickets for the treetop walk at the Geeveston Information Centre and were told that there are several walks and three bridges so allow ourselves at least two hours without the other things they suggested we see. The weather was so cold that we sat in the car to have a cup of coffee from the flask we had taken with us and I told John that we were nuts to even think about doing it in the wind and rain because we wouldn't be able to see anything as the clouds were covering the hills.

At the moment Perth is suffering from 39C heat, there's been a tropical cyclone forming off northern Western Australia, at the Gold Coast where we live it is about 30C and there are fires in New South Wales and it's freezing here – what a vast country this is.

Anyway, I found out that the tickets last for thirty days so we decided to drive down to the end of the trail which ended with about ten kilometres of dirt road to reach the National Park at Cockle Creek. The scenery was stunning even if the weather wasn't all the time. We arrived in our mud-spattered car at Cockle Creek where many people seemed to be free camping and had to find a shelter to huddle in out of the rain to have our late lunch. Seeing the scenery from the other direction travelling back was awesome and we were actually stuck for words, pointing things out to each other saying 'Look at (silence)' and after a couple of minutes I would just say 'Stunning'. It just went on and on, beautiful scene after beautiful scene and I have virtually stopped taking photographs because everywhere we seem to go there are just too many enticing photographic shots. I'm really glad that I left my camera in the car in Hobart or I would have returned with over a hundred photographs and it was the same along that section of the Huon Valley Trail. I took a few when we stopped at places of course but you couldn't keep stopping the car or we wouldn't have been home for a week! Anyway, we still have to go back and do those treetop walks and it will be our third day trip just to do one peninsular.

Hobart - The New In Salamanca Place

We have a satellite navigation system in the car and we call her Kate. I put in where we want to go and whether we want the shortest time or never toll roads or we want motorways etc. Anyway, we ask Kate to tell us where to go and then we ignore her and make a sudden turn when we see something that looks interesting or scenic and she usually recalculates our route but if she keeps insisting we do a u-turn we turn her off or tell her to cancel the route and put her and the route back on later. When we were coming out of Hobart on Saturday we ignored her and went in the opposite direction to the route she had planned for us and although the map recalculated our route, she stopped talking to us! It was the first time it had happened. Yesterday we nearly drove her insane; actually she had a meltdown with frustration. First of all, earlier in the day, she stopped talking to us again and then out of sheer frustration when we were driving home she suddenly started to speak faster and faster instead of in her very well modulated English pronunciation. She said 'Do a U-turn…go left…at the end of the…keep right…at the next set of traffic…end of the road… turn left…bear right…U-turn….' all within about thirty seconds! We were driving down a straight road and we were so helpless with laughter I couldn't even turn her off.

We also enjoy changing our preferences with routes so on our return yesterday I asked Kate to avoid all main roads and we had a beautiful journey and found ourselves only twelve kilometres below the peak of Mount Wellington so we just had to change our journey and go back up to the top again! It is so cold and windy up there that trees can't grow but the sun was out and the city, sea and islands and rural scenery were bathed in that soft late evening light. By the time we reached a pub near our caravan park at around 8pm we were ready for the roast dinner we ordered.

Richmond Bridge - The Oldest Bridge In Australia

We have been to the beautiful village of **Richmond** twice. It is another main tourist attraction in this part of Tasmania. We were going to stay there for Christmas and first there was a mix up because they had forgotten to take our booking and then when the awning collapsed we realised we would have to stay where we are now, which is at Berriedale, not far from Moonah because that is where the company is that is going to replace it. We have been promised that it will be shipped over from Sydney and replaced by Christmas and we are so hoping that nothing goes wrong because we need to be back at Launceston for Christmas Day now. My friend's husband has had to have an operation and won't be able to travel for a while and we have been invited by one of their daughters for the family Christmas Day at her house and one of their son's has suggested that we park our bus in his back garden. That is one of the advantages of having a mobile 'house' - being able to move your home to a new City at the drop of a hat to fit in with altered arrangements! It will be lovely to be at a big family Christmas on that day though because we remember so well our feeling of sadness at being away from everyone we love when we were in Western Australia. This particular friend is like 'family' to me because we have been friends for so long and because she is the only person on this side of the world who knew me as a ten year old and knew my parents and my homes and we shared holidays and parents with gay abandon! She is the only 'sister' relationship I have in my life.

I knew I had a problem with horses (they like to lick me, particularly on the face, even if I've never met them before) and I was a bit perturbed about being temporarily adopted by a dog called Jack earlier during our tour of Tasmania but I never thought I'd have a problem with ducks! We were parked alongside the river but decided to move further away because of the wind. There is a public park next to the river and there are a steady stream of people who come to feed the ducks, invariably just with bread which, when ducks have ducklings is not a good idea as the ducklings can end up having malformed wings. We have just seen our first set of ducklings and the ducks have been mating furiously recently. One female duck looking a bit battered with feathers sticking up off her body decided to adopt us, probably for protection! I didn't feed her but did notice on about the third day that she was limping rather badly. She's got over that and her mate is now with us too all the time and he's still ravishing her several times a day. Whenever I go out the door she follows me and if I don't go outside often enough her mate calls me by croaking loudly which always makes us laugh. Another pair of ducks, obviously thinking that we have been feeding the first pair decided they too would adopt us so now I have four ducks following me around. Yesterday it poured with rain but as I cannot stand being inside all the time, I set up a chair under an awning attached to a row of ensuite toilets that are not being used. I can walk up and down the path under cover to stretch my legs and look over to the lake and mountains. The two original ducks live under our van or car day and night and appear on our step regularly and follow me over to where my chair is and the original female sits by my feet and her partner talks to me and within minutes the other pair of ducks come trundling over to join us. However, yesterday afternoon, I not only had the four ducks around me, I also had seventeen seagulls. This morning I went out to find that our 'sweet' ducks have crapped all over our awning mat which I didn't think was sweet and by the time I sat down with my coffee under the awning I was surrounded by so many seagulls as well that I hardly knew where to put my feet. Am I to become the 'free meal'? I often used to talk to the odd seagull just as I talk to the ducks but now I'm jumping up and down flaying my arms around trying to look like a giant bird to chase the seagulls away! I hope my fellow patrons of this caravan park don't spot me and suggest to R.L that I should be committed. Now if I was a duck and could get a free meal down by the lake, I wouldn't be hanging around someone who doesn't feed me just so I can hear her talk to me – how stupid is that! All they seem to be living on at the moment is grass and grit which is why they are crapping in streams all over our mat and the walkway I sit under. Helen had a pet duck once called 'Pluckaduck' and I know they are not eating properly. I don't suppose the park owners are going to like seeing all the marks on their path but seeing as we were told we could use these toilets and were then going to be charged to use them I'm really not that bothered! R.L was irked the other day when he told the gardener that the security lights had been off for about three days yet a light had been on in one of the toilets, only to get a grumpy retort 'You're not using the toilet are you?' The latter question was quite ridiculous anyway as the toilets are locked and we don't have a key! Not knowing that R.L had mentioned the lights, I also told the park owner the same morning and he told me that he didn't know how the security lights could have been off etc but he said it in such a way as to suggest we had been up to no good! He then added that the gardener had turned the light off in the toilet so he must have known the toilet had been locked all along. Help yourself ducks, crap over there but just keep away from our awning mat. How do you get rid of seagulls?

Well, our awning repair was done early and expertly and the guys were pleased that we had turned the bus so that we were not getting the wind on the side they had to install it. Within hours of them leaving we were in what felt like a cyclone. The only difference was that there was no rain. We both said in the middle of the night when we were terrified that it was worse than the cyclone we had been in when we were in Western Australia on a previous trip. Another couple put their kids in their car in the middle of the night as they were so frightened and they left today. Last night I decided I was moving out into a hotel but I'm still here and all is calm so far tonight. However, during the night we lost another awning! Obviously none of our four awnings were up. They all have heavy metal roller covers on them. However, as the motor home was rocking from side to side, despite the ramps being down and it sitting on six tyres and weighing seven and a half tons, the violent wind started to unravel one of the smaller awnings slightly and then pulled it sheer off the side, still rolled up and complete with all it's screws and metal plates that had been attached to the bus. My stomach did not unravel this morning so we took off into Hobart, back to explore the old area around the Salamanca Markets that were on again and did some Christmas shopping to try and escape our memories and we succeeded and had a wonderful day. My female pet duck was waiting for me by the step when we got back and her mate soon joined us for a chat.

We have at last completed our Huon Valley touring, having returned for a third time to see the **Tahune Forest** and do the air walk. That was another wonderful day. There were basically three main walks to go on so we did one through the forest first, trying to learn the different names of the trees and to learn how to recognise them. We saw Australia's heaviest tree which was impossible to photograph as it was so tall that we could hardly see the top without binoculars. It apparently weighs 405 tons. We saw hundreds of tall trees but walking through the narrow trail amongst the tree ferns and forest it was magical. At one point I mentioned the name of a tree and R.L was most impressed with my knowledge – I was actually reading it off a plaque. So another time I said that I liked the Nothofagus cunninghamii trees and he then cottoned on! Go on, Google it! Oh, okay – it's a Myrtle. What we both really wanted to see were the Huon Pine trees and when we did find them, R.L was disappointed that they weren't very big which was when I reminded him that all the big ones there were cut down and if it wasn't for the 'Greenies' we probably wouldn't have any left in Tasmania. They were much prized because they have an essential oil that gives it resistance to rot and marine organisms so was wonderful for boat building and the timber is light and soft so is easy to work with. One of the information boards told us that 'Pollen records indicate that it was growing 135 million years ago when the great super continent known as 'Gondwana' existed. Huon pine is slow growing and can reach an incredible age. Trees of 2500 years old have been found on Tasmania's west coast.'

Chapter 24

We also learnt about the world's tallest flowering plant – the mighty swamp gum Eucalyptus regnans. They can reach heights of over 100 metres. Apparently only the giant redwoods of California are taller but presumably they don't have flowers.

Port Arthur - Fabulous Rock Formations By Remarkable Cave

So, having completed our first walk we then set off to the tree top walk or 'air walk' as they call it here. It was okay but we are spoilt as we've done the one in Western Australia and have been on chair lifts etc many times in our lives so have seen the tops of trees fairly often. We both agree that it is so much more interesting walking beneath them. Our third walk was when we found the Huon pine trees. I have no idea what else we did that day other than a picnic in the forest by a scenic rivulet but we were out for hours. Oh yes, I remember, we stopped at **Geeveston** where I bought myself a milking stool. I haven't got any cows but have wanted one for a long time!

Port Arthur - Tasman's Arch.1

What will my pet ducks do when we are gone – it means their home will have gone too because they still live under our bus and any other duck that approaches is chased off with aggression. They did allow another duck to visit yesterday, along with her fourteen ducklings looking to be only a few days old. How could she possibly have fourteen babies? However, we will be so relieved to leave here. The park is in a beautiful setting and it would be perfect if not for the winds. Mind you, the toilet saga continues. Another family turned up and have been using one of the ensuite bathrooms and apparently they do not have to pay $5 extra! They suggested that we use it for showers too and they won't tell anyone!! It has caused a lot of mirth but it's quite inexplicable.

The company who repaired our awning managed to get it done quicker than expected and the very same night we were hit with ferocious winds – worse than those we experienced during the cyclone in Western Australia. We were both terrified and another coupe put their kids in their four-wheel drive vehicle for a few hours during the night as they were so frightened. We have three other smaller awnings with heavy metal roller covers on and the wind lifted up the ends of one of the metal covers and without unwinding the awning, lifted it sheer off the bus and it fell to the ground complete with all the metal plates and screws still attached. We then had to wait for the repairers to come back out again. The force of the wind actually bent both ends slightly. After only a few hours sleep we got up and decided to get out of the park for the day so went back to Hobart for the Saturday Salamanca market again and to explore **Battery Point** and the coastline down to **Sandy Bay** and beyond. We also did some Christmas shopping and came home exhausted having walked so much in a day. My camera had packed up and it turned out that I had run out of space which has never happened before as I have room

Doo Town - Amazing Cliff Walks

for two hundred and sixty photos! By the time I had finished culling and downloading the photos it was one o'clock in the morning. Then, having been so over-stimulated, I could not get to sleep. I had only had slept the equivalent of one night over forty-eight hours so the next morning I was walking around like a zombie. However, we had to get going on our 'big trip'. We still hadn't been down to **Port Arthur** and we were not going to just look at the penal settlement there (which many people take two days to do), we had a lot of other points of interest that we wanted to see. Places such as **Eaglehawk Neck** with **Pirates Bay** and the **Tessellated Pavement** (intertidal rock platform), then further around Pirates Bay to the highest sea cliffs in Australia. Next were the **Blowhole, Tasman's Arch,** the

Devil's **Kitchen** and the hamlet of Doo Town. At **Doo Town** it doesn't take long before you start spotting the house names such as 'Doo Drop In, Do Love It, Doo-Us, Doo-Little, Much-A-Doo, Just Doo It' and even 'Doo F#@k All'. I kept looking for 'Little to Doo' or 'Doo My Housework' etc but didn't find them. However, at one spot we did find a van called Doo-Lishus which sold seafood and bowls of berries with ice cream and cream and berry puree. The berries included strawberries, raspberries, blackberries, boysenberries and 'Silvan berries' and I have no idea what the latter berries are! Anyway, you could have a big dish of that lot for five dollars and there were a lot of people eating or hanging around waiting for their orders – all standing around in the parking area.

By the time we arrived at Port Arthur and the tourist attraction of the penal settlement. **Port Arthur** is near the end of a peninsular with many rural homes and grocery shop and petrol etc. Mind you, about half of the homes appeared to be up for sale which seems a bit odd as it is a lovely area. We were feeling tired before we even bought our tickets and sat in the car eating and drinking coffee, followed by mini bars of chocolate to try and give ourselves energy. We needn't have worried as once through the entrance building we were so delighted with the scene beyond that we instantly wanted to explore. The grounds have obviously been 'renovated' and they were beautiful. Facing us were acres of rolling green lawns, winding pathways, archways and flowers all leading down to **Carnarvon Bay** and **Mason Cove** and spread out over the whole area were the ruins of the original settlement and some buildings still standing complete – in fact we went into many of the houses and some were furnished in the common style of the day depending on who the occupants were. So we saw the church, the houses, the penitentiary, the Guard tower, the Asylum and museum along with many others. Actually, by the time we got to the asylum it must have been getting late because we browsed through the museum and went to watch a film and then every exit door we found was locked. We both went back into the museum and found the lights off. It was then that I panicked and told R.L we had been locked in the asylum for the night and he was looking equally fraught! We did get out eventually, when a woman called us through a doorway that we hadn't seen. By the time we had walked back to the visitor's centre I didn't have the energy to get up the one flight of stairs and R.L suggested we take the lift and I caved in and accepted.

We enjoyed our trip on the lake which was a complementary cruise with commentary and it was then that we heard that in Dickens day there was no such thing as 'childhood'. By the age of four or five children could be sent up the chimneys, by the age of seven they were tried in a court of law as an adult and would be imprisoned with adults and by the age of eight they could be sentenced to hang. By nine they could be deported to Van Diemen's Land (Australia). I had trouble coming to grips with this information. We saw the island where a bold experiment was conducted for the first time in the British Empire. The boys were separated from the men (most of them street kids from the slums) and imprisoned on this barren and windswept island where they were taught trades. It was no picnic however. If a boy lost his knife and fork he was put in a cell for twenty days receiving only bread and water. There was a chapel and a school room where 'attempts were made to teach up to 800 exhausted, hungry boys to read, write and do arithmetic'. In the early years they were allowed to play but that was stopped. By the late 1840's it was decided to keep the boys in Britain so they were put in prisons there and by 1849 the Point Puer island settlement closed.

Approximately 167,000 men, women and children were transported and of those about 73,000 came to Australia. The Port Arthur penal station was established in 1830 and by 1840 over 2000 convicts, soldiers and civil staff lived there. As more people arrived so more buildings were erected and expansions to existing buildings completed. Everyone had to go to church on Sunday, including the convicts but how everybody got into that church I have no idea!

Transportation to Van Diemen's Land ended in 1853 with this settlement closing in 1877. In the booklet given to us and from information on site there appear to have been several bush fires at the settlement, one of which in 1897 lasted for forty-eight hours. The Separate Prison was almost destroyed by bushfire in 1895 and the church was gutted by fire in 1884 with its spire already having blown down in 1876. However, it is easy to see the vastness of the occupied area, the size and proportions of the penitentiary with its four story's of windows still intact and some of the roofing still there. That appeared to be the biggest building on the site and it was vast and imposing.

There was also the dockyard – the only way to get here was by boat and they built boats for the colony here. We also passed by another island called appropriately '**The Isle of the Dead**' for it was the cemetery during our cruise.

We did not read about the convicts, nor did we do the nightly ghost tour. On the whole it was where the repeat offenders were sent and it would be lenient to just say it was a harsh and cruel life. I started to read the story of one man who had apparently not been exaggerating much when he claimed to have received about 3000 lashes in his lifetime. We knew that we needed to go to the **Memorial Garden** to remember those who died in a massacre in our own recent history and that is where we concentrated our personal thoughts. In April of 1996 a gunman killed 35 people and injured many more. Our gun laws were subsequently changed. We spent some time in contemplation in the lovely garden and read the names again of those that died.

After relaxing with a cup of coffee in the restaurant we set off to do some rather different sightseeing.

Just past Port Arthur there is a place called **Remarkable Cave** which I had wanted to go to before we went into the settlement. I had been concerned that I might be too tired afterwards. Well, here we were tired – too tired to climb one flight of stairs and needing to sit down and have a coffee after having to wait for a lift! I had been exhausted through lack of sleep before we'd even set out in the morning and now we had to tackle 125 steps down to this cave. So, I got out of the car, looked in awe at the magnificent view and reminded myself that it is just a state of mind and we can walk through our pain threshold and off we went. Perhaps my mind wasn't doing as it was told as I found going down quite hard and sort of hopped down rather quickly as my right knee was painful. It was well worth it – go do it! Coming back up was far easier! The next thing on our minds was food – dinner to be exact. However we had the long journey home to do first and by the time we got to our local hotel it was five minutes past their time of last orders. However, the managed to rustle us up a meal although it was not as good or as cheap as the meal we had had in the public bar at the other end of the building the week before. We could hardly complain though and my meal was half price for some special offer. The wine was excellent and by the time we got in our door and sat down we were like stuffed dummies – we couldn't speak or move – too full to lie down and too tired to do anything. However, when it did come time to go to bed I couldn't sleep and ended up in going outside for some fresh air at 3am – it's becoming a habit! I still wake up at a reasonable time though so it must just be over-stimulation. I'll probably collapse on Christmas Day when I'm supposed to be sociable and fall asleep at the table.

When we finally left Hobart to return to Launceston we travelled direct on the Heritage route and stopped at **Kempton** to have a look. It is a very quiet town and very neat with some lovely old buildings. It is a very pretty area within commuting distance to Hobart and surrounded by hills. Our next stop was at **Oatlands** which spun us out because it is absolutely beautiful. We sat by the river and had a look at **Lake Dulverton** which is being used as a wild life sanctuary and there is free overnight parking for motor homes and caravans. There were way too many beautiful old buildings to photograph! We went to the chemist there and had a coffee in **The Stables Café** and everyone was so friendly and we were told that the old windmill is being renovated and will be working soon. If you are travelling the Lonnie to Hobart road, stop and have a look and the locals will give you a warm welcome.

7 - I Was Quite Frightened Of Falling Rocks

2nd January 2010

Chudleigh - Where Mole Creek Residents Get Petrol

Happy New Year to you too and no, I did not collapse at Christmas – we had a wonderful day and my friends came to our place for Boxing Day so I could feed them for a change. We had to leave the park on the 27th as it was fully booked so we booked at a park that seemed to have plenty of space at **Mole Creek**. I should have realised that there might be a reason they had room when everywhere else was booked out but I was so worried about where we would stay for the week before being able to return to Longford, that we gratefully paid our weeks money in advance, in cash upon arrival. Sometimes you like a place and sometimes you don't and there is no rhyme or reason to these feelings if the surroundings are lovely as they are here. However, there only seem to be a couple of long term holiday visitors here. We have both been told off for various reasons by the park manager who, despite a gentle demeanour can be stubbornly determined that she is always in the right, and you do have to pay 40 cents for a hot shower on top of your rental which really

Lake Barrington Day Out - Simply Beautiful.jpg

annoyed some people who hired a cabin next to us for the night, and it is shockingly windy here yet very hot during the day and nobody has dared put an awning up for fear of losing it like we have already done so there is little shade.

However, it is a very pretty area and is within driving range to many attractions, not least **Cradle Mountain National Park**. We have done that and we thought it a bit overrated and preferred the day when we went out for a short drive and ended up driving all around **Lake Barrington**, calling into **Sheffield** for a coffee before facing the long, winding route home back over the mountain range. We had also called in at **Cradle Lodge** earlier in the day which was a lovely place – the sort of place you want to linger and perhaps book into for a few days. It's up for sale at present as are many other tourist ventures we have seen. Tasmania seems to be teeming with tourists so I'm not sure why. At present we are meeting a lot of people who live here and are exploring their own island and have met more people who have moved here permanently from the south-east coast of Queensland. I must say it is very tempting, the idea of moving here. However, whilst we have been having a wonderful Christmas my three kids have all had disappointments this year and we are so far away. Here at Mole Creek there is no mobile phone coverage at all let alone internet coverage! Our first morning we drove into Mole Creek which we had passed through on our way to this park and were told that we would have to drive to Chudleigh before we would get reception. So we were one couple who made no phone calls at midnight, nor sent any text messages. Actually we were shocked because all the holiday-makers in this park were asleep before midnight. We had had the television on which we could listen to even though the reception is so bad here we couldn't see the fireworks properly on it and after toasting each other we went outside and it was deathly quiet – in fact it was quite eerie. I have never been anywhere on New Years Eve that was so silent in my life. The following morning one of the managers said something to me (which is unusual in itself) and I replied 'Happy New Year' to which I got a surprised response. I mentioned how quiet it had been and was told that yes it had been and it was wonderful! Not one other person said Happy New Year to us although we did to them! I'm just grateful we had a good Christmas.

Devils Gullet Day Out - Extreme Windy Conditions

Alum Clifffs - River At Bottom

Today we went to **Devil's Gullet** which with walking conditions 'Easy, but includes a gentle uphill.' Rubbish!, it is quite a run up to the top. It's not a long walk from the car park once you get there along the dirt roads but the minute you get out of your vehicle and icy winds hit you. Down in the valley it was a very hot day but here we were getting jackets on. We met a kid running down who was obviously ecstatic and he was shouting 'It is so deep. You could throw a plate off the top and it would come back to you' and then his father added 'Take your hats of and hold them'. It was really quite steep in places going up and the air so cold it was almost hurting our lungs and then when we got to the top we heard the noise of the wind. There is a metal platform to stand on and the noise of the wind between it and the rocks it juts out from is so loud you can't hear each other speak. I put my sunglasses away and got the camera ready, held my hat in one hand and the camera strap in the other and stepped to the edge. The views were amazing, the winds awesome. John thought the wind had blown one of his contact lenses out of his eye! I managed to get a panoramic view using the video on the camera and tried to line up the camera for a photo but had to take it blind as I just couldn't see because of the wind passing over my eyes! Needless to say we didn't stop there for more than a couple of minutes and will rely on the video to have a look at the view! Coming down was tricky in places as it was so steep and the loose gravel made it a bit slippery at times. Yesterday John went to see **Alum Cliffs**, a sacred Aboriginal celebration place known as **Tulunpunga** which he enjoyed but he said that that wasn't always 'easy' with some 'gentle uphill sections' either and it annoys me that people might go to these places and then realise that they cannot climb up. I have some friends who I know would be disappointed.

One place we did go to that we enjoyed was the honey factory at **C**hudleigh where you can taste so many different varieties including chocolate. I ended up buying two different but plain bottles of honey and we also bought ice creams. There was a film playing about the bees which was really good until we were drowned out by the sound of a saleswoman's voice. As we were wondering back through the displays we stopped to look at the various ice creams on offer and were quietly discussing what kind we would buy before leaving when she suddenly asked us which ice cream we wanted and reached out for my two jars of honey and before I knew it we had them in our hands and were outside. On the way home I told John that I had meant to look at all the beauty products and would have done if she hadn't pounced on us like that! Once I had consumed the ice cream outside I had lost interest. However, it is well worth a visit and although there are a lot of honey outlets here in Tasmania, this one was recommended to us by a friend.

Cradle Mountain Day Out - Dove Lake

Anyway, we've enjoyed a lamb roast at the **Mole Creek Hotel** tonight which I needed having been blown off the steps of our motor home late this afternoon with a whiskey in hand! The wind was so strong that as I tried to open the door and step outside the wind caught the door which slammed back into me sending me flying onto the table below and the contents of my glass blew all over me. I am really looking forward to leaving tomorrow! On our return to Longford we will stop at Deloraine for what will be our third visit. We met the owner of a hotel there on our first visit who has lived and owned a restaurant in Byron Bay and also a motel after that at Bundaberg and who only moved here last March. He's a great guy who sells great coffee so we returned there a couple of days later to buy another one. There is a deli there which is worth visiting and you can taste test some of the products before you buy. There is also a caravan park which I would have suggested we moved to if we hadn't paid the week in advance here. However, we have thoroughly enjoyed the wonderful alpine scenery of the Great Western Tiers, Cradle Mountain and all the other mountains in the ranges in these wonderful national parks. John was so overcome by the beautiful scenery as we returned home through Paradise one day that he was driving at 40kph as though he didn't want to get back to the park. **Paradis**e seemed to have three homes surrounded by about seven acreage properties from what we could see from the road. I now have too many photos to download again.

LONGFORD, LAUNCESTON, PENGUIN

There's a reason for that heading – I am so shocked again to realise how long it is since I have caught up on this diary. Stayed another three weeks in Longford, did more touring in Lonnie and are now at Penguin. There we are – that's it!

During that time we considered buying some land in one village, spent time with our friends and went back to the Swiss village of **Grindelwold** overlooking the Tamar River, stopping on our return journey in **Launceston** to walk along the cliff walk which leads from a beautiful old bridge in town to the Cataract Gorge. In that area of town there are many very old buildings including the area where the Mill is and a tourist attraction which is presently closed for renovation called **The Penny Royal World** and **Gunpowder Mill.** The buildings are being done up and sold which is a pity as there were many backpackers and other tourists there when we were there – all looking through the closed gates. The attraction included a sailboat, barges, trams and historic gunpowder mills and the admission included a tram ride, plus a trip up Cataract Gorge and the Tamar River on the paddle steamer MV Lady Stelford. We clambered up and down the stairs to look at the internal renovations and found that fascinating.

We also spent the day visiting the Ben Lomond National Park and went up to the **Ski Village**. The journey was frightening as it includes switch-back roads with sheer cliff drops to one side and millions of fallen boulders on other side of the road. None of the mountainside looked stable! At just over 1000 metres above sea level there are still the tall Stringybark trees growing which is unusual but above that level there was just gorse and small alpine plants.

Another very full day was spent visiting some of the many lakes including **Arthurs Lake** and **Great Lake**, the latter which is 1034 metres above sea level. It has the capacity to cover 17,610 hectares – big! It is a natural fresh water lake and is very popular for trout fishermen with three kinds of trout to be caught. It's now managed by Hydro-Tasmania and was dammed in 1916 for the hydro-electric scheme. We drove right around that lake and ended up back at Deloraine again where we enjoyed yet another cup of coffee at the hotel. This was our third visit.

Chapter 25

On the way to the lakes area we had stopped off at the community village of **Poatina**. It is worth looking up Poatina, Tasmania on the internet as they do great things there and it is a wonderful scheme for what was a dying village. The day we were there, all the volunteers were doing shifts at tidying up the community gardens in preparation for their annual fund-raising events. Other towns and villages in the area also raised money and in our caravan park the Poatina volunteers held a sausage sizzle one Saturday night and a big breakfast the following morning.

Here Comes Our Ferry

A must see is a gallery at **Carrick** as not only is the place unusual and attractive from the outside but on entry you are treated to a feast for your eyes. It is called the **Tasmanian Copper and Metal Art Gallery** and there is metal jewellery, Australian animals and birds, wall art, sculpture, coffee tables and so forth and many of them in amazing colours. I cannot describe the place and suggest you find it. Which reminds me – my friend absolutely loves that shop I mentioned before called **Reliquaire** which I abhorred as I became claustrophobic there and she thinks I'm rather weird not to like it. I told her I'd rather do a sky dive which made her shudder. Never take advice when touring.

So we are now back on the northern coastline ready to catch our ferry back to the mainland but this time decided to stay at **Penguin** and that was one of our better decisions as we are parked facing the sea with views of it from our windows on three sides and it is a lot cheaper than the park we stayed at in Devonport.

It was an easy drive from Longford and it is not far from **Ulverstone**. We went there to have a look at it the other day and were surprised at how big the town is but when we mentioned it to a local he told us we would get a shock then when we saw **Burnie**. We did yesterday and it is not much further to there than Ulverstone so Penguin is ideally situated between two service towns. We didn't do Burnie justice as we mainly wanted just to see the sea front and were not in the mood for big towns. It is a big industrial town – well, big by Tasmanian standards anyway. It is the main town on this coastline. Penguin is a pretty, small seaside village.

Yesterday we drove down beautiful coastline to have a look at **Somerset** but didn't stop and continued on to **Wynyard** which we just loved. It is a lovely small town with the river and the sea to walk along and some lovely parkland. Between Somerset and Boat Harbour Beach there are several lookout points and many walks so we stretched our legs by climbing and walking up and down headlands to whet our appetite for lunch at a restaurant on the beach at **Boat Harbour**.

John had thought that we were going to buy fish and chips from the kiosk there but when I realised that there was little shade and that the restaurant had tables under cover on the beach front, I marched into the restaurant and asked to see the menus. He thought I was being smart and really only wanted to an excuse to use their toilets and was quite taken back when I sat down at one of the tables outside. I told him that he has the bank card and a wife that needed a decent meal.

A beautiful young lady approached to take our order and warned me by gesticulating that the meals were very large so I chose an entrée-size fish, chips and salad with home-made tartar sauce. She returned to ask me if I wanted dressing with my salad and at the same time she was nodding 'no' as if to warn me. I told her 'Yes. But separate' and after repeating it twice she nodded in agreement. I made a note to taste test it first. John chose the huge beefburger (including a fried egg) and chips. I asked the waitress for plenty of lettuce with my salad and she looked a bit puzzled as she was having a hard time understanding our English language. 'Extra lettuce please' – I had decided to use a different phrase She walked away with a slight frown on her face.

Then we tried to order the wine and I asked her what choice of house wines I could have because I just wanted one glass. That turned out to be a very wise decision. She reeled off a list of wines so rapidly in her (perhaps) French accent that I stared at her stunned and told her I wanted a red wine and off she went again and I only caught the odd word like 'Tasmanian' and 'Victorian' and a couple of other words but managed to order. John must have been oblivious to all of this because he then asked the same question and off she went again and I was looking at him trying not to laugh. He looked at me in astonishment when she had finished and I gave him the choice of two and he rapidly chose one of them so that he could relax. We both enjoyed the wines chosen.

The wine was good and I suddenly realised that John was slurring his words and had a 'silly grin' that I recognised. I suggested that he couldn't be sozzled already and then noticed that his glass was almost empty. He tried to tell me that he had felt it going down and sort of warming him and then he suddenly felt really happy when alcohol affects him and talks really slowly I had to guess what he was saying. It was because we were both drinking on an empty stomach and were probably dehydrated from climbing hills in the hot sun but I had hardly touched my own wine.

When our lunches eventually turned up I had a bowl of lettuce with no other salad ingredient so I asked if I could have some salad with it! A look of horror crossed her face 'You say the meal not good?' she exclaimed. I thought she was going to burst into tears and decided that she must be French because surely only a French person could be so offended, so I smiled and said 'A little other salad with my lettuce please' and she rushed off and returned with another bowl with a full salad. Now laden with enough lettuce to feed a thousand rabbits for a week, I realised that she had forgotten the tartar sauce so had to call her back again. As it turned out both the salad dressing and the tartar sauce were not to my taste. I think whoever had made the former had forgotten to add anything to the olive oil. We both admitted today that the meal wasn't that memorable (read chips soggy and almost white, beefburger not cooked enough etc) but we can recommend their wine!

However, I was so full with fish and lettuce that I just wanted to go to sleep and lay in the shade of the tree overlooking the turquoise sea and the soft white sand and was in seventh heaven. It is such a beautiful bay on a sunny day. We have been there before, when there used to be a caravan park there but although that no longer exists there have been great improvements to the area and we did notice that people were camping for free very close to the beach.

John sobered up following his lunch and went for a paddle (or perhaps it was the paddle in the very cold water that sobered him up) but I couldn't move, let alone drive. Actually, perhaps he wasn't sober because I do recall remarking on our return journey that when he drives over the top of a roundabout it is quite bumpy. Mind you, he had been looking at the beach whilst driving earlier in the day and I distinctly remember telling him that he needn't worry about the fact that he was driving on the right side of the road instead of the left as I would watch for any oncoming traffic for him. I blame the scenery here as it's most distracting.

Of course, not every day is wine, sun and sea. What a difference a day makes. The day before this wonderful day out had been quite out of hand! I had arisen beautifully relaxed believing that I just had to do some washing, cut my hair – which is growing as profusely as the flowers here but not as prettily to say the least – and that we had to make a couple of urgent phone calls.

The first call was to our real estate agent to tell her that we were giving our tenants the required two months notice that day as we need to return home for family reasons We had to phone our air line concerning tickets that we have booked to go to England in a few months time. Two weeks prior we had been promised the tickets the same day via email but had received a phone call to say there was a problem as our flight had been cancelled from Hong Kong to Australia on the return stretch. Although immediate action was promised we had waited a week and then called again. We were told a different date this time but no tickets arrived.

I was beginning to envisage us arriving in Hong Kong only to be told that we should have caught the flight two days earlier or that we didn't have a flight at all as it had been cancelled.

Originally we had also been told that we would only have a one hour stopover at Singapore where we were to change planes to go to London. I had subsequently realised that if our first flight had any delays we could be hard pushed to get to our second departure gate in time and even if we were on time, I doubted our baggage would be on the same plane as we were! Anyway, we still had no tickets to fly anywhere. However, before you get to speak to anyone at the airline booking office, you have to listen to the obligatory fifteen minutes of advertising.

We decided to phone the Real Estate office again but this time would leave a message to say it was urgent. The very efficient receptionist promised to send an immediate email from her desk to the rental lady's desk!

We finally finished the two calls but then I had to call two of my offspring concerning our family emergency. I still hadn't got the washing over to the washing machine, or our washing line out, let alone get myself properly dressed. We got the washing organised – I just forgot to collect it afterwards but luckily John remembered an hour and a half later. John had suddenly asked me where the photo was of the water rates that he needed to email. We had found it impossible to copy and paste or email this notice from the very secure Council email so we had printed it out and I had photographed it! In the meantime we been touring around and I now had about two hundred photos to download. That took me an hour (with the odd coffee thrown in, made by John out of sympathy) to find it, and email it along with a letter to our Agent. Of course, I had therefore opened our email file and emails were coming in and we had to check them! Every time I thought I had finished doing something, John would come up with something else.

He suddenly told me that we had to decide that morning how much we were going to increase the rent on our rental home in Brisbane. It was time for the annual rent increase and I hadn't wanted to talk about it because I like the tenants too much! He wanted to put it up five percent as we normally do every year and I thought that it was too much in the present financial climate. So we decided to look up all the rental properties that offered similar accommodation in the area to find out the rental prices. We had just got involved when our flight tickets arrived into our email account and John wanted them printed out! I was doing that when we both heard 'Hello' and it was our expected visitors but I sort of reacted as though they were aliens from outer space because I was already on some astral-stress planet myself!

I mumbled that I wouldn't be a moment and then I mumbled that I had wanted to get changed before they arrived and then I realised that my hair had blown all over the place again and then I just gave up and put the kettle on! I had thought we were going out to lunch but they had turned up with their own as they hadn't wanted me to go to any trouble and they like to treat themselves on their day trips out. I was more confused than ever by this time – totally addled really. Once they had eaten their cholesterol loaded treats to fill their wonderfully trim bodies and had had their cuppas they seemed quite happy but my head was still spinning with rental properties, flight tickets and thoughts of offspring. I was relieved not to go out to lunch as my stomach had been quite painful for a couple of days and I had been on a liquid diet so I grabbed another bowl of soup, chucking in a piece of grain bread to give my stomach something to work on and John grabbed a sandwich. When they left I felt sad that I had been far from relaxed but I didn't have much time to think because John had us both back on the computer looking at the rental properties. Decision made and email sent and then he asked me why I had a flight ticket and he didn't. I had wondered why we had a duplicate and had nearly deleted it! One email contained pages and pages of rules, regulations and advice about our travel. I have no doubt that a lot of people don't bother to read it because you feel swamped by it. I can't remember all the other things we had to do but I finally closed the computer at 5pm!

John went for a walk to clear his head and at last I had time to think - you know – just things you need time to think about for heavens sake – stuff. You file all the other stuff away in the cabinets in your brain and when there's a bit of clear desk to be seen again that's reserved for your own private thoughts to be laid down or for one of your own personal files to be opened and thought about. Sometimes it's relaxing just to have the chance to get to those files.

Yet there we were the next day tipsy with wine in glorious surroundings, not wanting to think about anything at all. Life's a ball isn't it?

SEVERAL DAYS LATER

We are now in New South Wales, back in **Narrandera**. The day we left started smoothly but after eating food from a fast food outlet things rapidly deteriorated for me. I've never experienced sea sickness but that's what I thought was wrong at the beginning so let's just say the voyage back was lousy for me and John, who had eaten about a third of my food told me that he had had stomach pains all night. Perhaps that is why, having found each others vehicles once off the ferry and went the wrong way! Eventually we made it to **Craigieburn**, west of Melbourne where we decided to book in for a night just so we could sleep. The heat was oppressive. The following day it was just as hot and my car air-conditioner didn't seem to be working. Having set off on the highway, John suddenly veered off into Craigieburn to get fuel which was quite beyond my understanding as there are places on the highway. So there we were in the car park of a suburban shopping centre holding up all the traffic that needed to get out of the car park as John was waiting to get to a pump and nobody behind could move! Believe me the situation got fraught with people pressing on their horns and shouts of abuse and I can't say I blame them. Then he had trouble getting out of the petrol station. Apparently, just up the main highway the gas was cheaper! So that was a good start.

We made it all the way to this tiny hamlet where there was a motel, pub, takeaway shop and a caravan repair workshop. The motel manager allowed us to connect to the electricity for ten dollars for the night and the gas hot water service is at last working having had the solenoid replaced. However, although my air conditioner ion the utility was refilled with gas, I was told that I cannot have it running whilst idling as the pressure is far too high. I have to have the radiator taken out, the condenser pressure hosed and the fluid replaced.

The following day I lost the plot with the heat and kept telling John to turn right instead of left and realised, by the time we arrived at a caravan park, that I was quite severely dehydrated. Then the rain came at last and we all felt wonderful again as it was so much cooler. However a couple of days later we crossed the border into New South Wales and it is so hot here that even with the air conditioner on full blast in one half of our van it is too hot to want to eat. Apparently they had a storm the other night here but it didn't bring the temperatures down and the only thing it's good for is drying the washing. I long to breathe fresh air again.

We did spend one day sight seeing. We were staying at **Cobram** and drove to **Yarrawonga** to see the huge lake and creek. It was interesting but the sight of so many dead trees sticking up out of the lake was rather chilling – a graveyard of trees. We did drive both ways around the lake and walked around an island a bit but we were disappointed with the area. The town centre looked tatty and the service in the two shops I went into to look for sandals was shocking. In one place there were no customers but the two staff wanted to resume their conversation! We also looked at quite a few of the caravan parks but there wasn't one that we would want to stay at that we could see. It seems that the townsfolk think that the lake is enough but it's not. Faded signage over shops, dismal shop fronts and few trees around – surely the local council or their chamber of commerce or whatever could do something to make the centre look more attractive. The locals need to take a trip to Bundaberg in Queensland and look at before and after photographs to see what can be achieved.

We couldn't find anywhere really pretty to stop and enjoy our coffee so went to the restaurant to the rear of the Information Centre and sat outside overlooking the water. The service was fabulous, the coffee superb and the berry muffins which are made on the premises were sublime. There were so many berries in them that it was almost like a pudding inside but the outside was crunchy. Topped with a sprinkling of coconut plus half a large fresh strawberry and served warm, with a bowl of fresh cream each – oh dear, I'm dribbling. I have never tasted a muffin as good as that and it was cheap.

That evening back at Cobram when it had cooled down, John decided to go for an evening walk. As there wasn't anywhere to walk by our park he decided to have a look at the adjoining retirement village complex. He got lost apparently! I asked him why he couldn't find his way back to a road and he said that in the end a man gave him a lift out of the place in his car and told John that he had lived there for four years, has all his marbles and still gets lost! Now, to my way of thinking, it is often the elderly who get age related dementia and for them to live in a place that can do that to someone without it must be a nightmare for them. You probably wouldn't want to go outside the door for fear of not finding your way back. Surely someone should have had a few bright ideas? All pavements can have a stripe down them in a colour and coloured signage can't they – at least something to signify different residential blocks and roads. At least they would be able to find their blue zone or red zone or whatever with some painted coloured arrows or signage.

We left Cobram before ten in the morning which is unusual for us. Perhaps we had a premonition of what was in store. We had a really easy journey on through **Finley** with no traffic on the road until we came to a junction at **Jerilderi.** John had also turned into the park entrance and went to get the Saturday paper whilst I got the kettle on and when he came back he told me there were a lot of shops or stalls or something that might interest me. We both ended up in going for walks in different directions and we were both delighted to discover that it was Jerilderie's annual **Ned Kelly Day**. It's funny how an outlaw can be so commemorated but he is. Not so different to Robin Hood I suppose. Anyway, there was a re-enactment of the hold up that took place at the post office and some of the townsfolk were dressed up in the costumes of the day and everywhere were stalls outside of shops and opportunity shops open, staffed by volunteers etc. The steam train was running and another mini train and a couple of guys were between the trains 'cycling' carts or whatever around the track. The children loved it of course. There was so much to see and it was such a happy event. I found John looking for me as

Adults Never Grow Up Do They

I headed back to look at the classic cars, motor bikes and old farm machinery. We ended up in staying there for some hours and even sat under a tree near the lake reading our papers until mid afternoon when the town was quieter. It was just beautiful there but we weren't sure that we could stay overnight where we were parked so came on to **Narrandera.**

Today has been all about washing and catching up on emails and photos etc. I've done three full machine loads of washing at the park laundry and still have another load to do tomorrow! John asked me how it was possible as we did the washing the day before we left Tasmania. Well, both beds needed stripping and the quilt covers needed washing before I change the quilts back to our summer ones, plus the weeks bathroom towels, flannels, bath mat and kitchen tea towels and towel. Then there are our clothes and I had completely run out of knickers! Because of the variable weather in Tasmania we would both have alternative clothes on the go, so I might have a light top plus cardigan and then for early evening a polo-neck jumper and then whatever heavy jumper that was currently in use lying around or in the back of the car. For sitting around in the evening I had some winter pyjamas as well as my dressing gown. All winter stuff now has to be stored – all we really need is swimming togs! And another thing – now that we have a hot water system that works at last, we don't need it as we are having cold showers to cool down and the water coming out of the cold tap is too hot anyway!

We've been told that we must visit a shop in Narrandera who's door faces onto a corner as they sell some really good items there and that there is an excellent coffee shop in town where they also sell sweets and home-made lemonade. However, once the washing is finished, our shopping done and all our computer work up-to-date I'm not at all sure what we are going to do with ourselves whilst waiting for the post because we've been here several times before. John mended a cupboard door this morning – only he could walk into a solid timber door under my cooker and completely rip it apart. The timber was actually split in a couple of places! He also caught up on other minor repairs.

Perhaps it will cool down and he can find a golf club and I can actually get my craft work out for the very first time on this trip!

Well it didn't cool down and our fridge was reading 18C on the fridge thermometer with the air conditioning on high from the time we got up in the morning. I didn't want to know the freezer temperature because I dreaded having to throw out all the meat we had in there! We didn't feel like doing much at all. In fact doing anything was an effort. But the post arrived on Tuesday and we congratulated each other on our good fortune because it meant we could leave the next day and get further north and then the coast. If we had had any neighbours in this park they would have thought we had won the lotto when the Post Office told John on the phone that it had arrived. We haven't any neighbours because nobody is staying put. The vans and motorhomes roll in at night, experience a sweaty night's sleep and are gone before we wake up in the morning!

However, we are both relieved that we didn't choose to return to Queensland via the coastal road from Melbourne through Sydney and beyond as there has been so much rain along the coast and many areas have flash flooding. We wouldn't have wanted to drive in that sort of weather and at least three couples we know, who are as far apart as Bundaberg to Portland in Victoria with the other couple south of Sydney, have all said that they are waiting for the weather to 'sort itself out' before moving on/setting off. We plan to hurtle on from now on until our feet hit the sea water!

Now the coin in my head has flipped and I wonder how an earth I can complain about this heat because all day, every day thoughts pop into my head about the Black Saturday bush fire victims. We passed some of the areas leaving Melbourne – the black tree trunks a constant reminder. Last Sunday Australia mourned for the victims and the survivors as the first anniversary came along and it seems it only happened so recently that I marvel that a year has passed. Some survivors were hoping it might help them to get beyond the first year. I hope some are helped but I cannot imagine how it will make any difference as each day must be a battle for so many people. Some are fighting to get their houses rebuilt, some are still stuck in grief and some say they are moving on but there are worries over the children, especially those who haven't reacted much yet. I read that 108 communities were affected, whilst many are fighting red tape and paperwork or insurance companies to re-establish themselves.

Some may keep going because they have something to fight for. It's when the struggle is over that the tiredness overwhelms or maybe in these cases grief hits like a tidal wave that has been held back. One old lady said that she is going to fight tooth and nail to get it built. She then added that she would probably put it on the market the week after but she won't 'let them beat me'

Chapter 26

MANY DAYS LATER

We stopped at **Dubbo** for one night arriving late in the afternoon and whilst John insisted on cooling down in the pool, I dashed off to buy the groceries and it was a good job I went immediately as the shops were already closing. However, having bought a couple of bottles of good whiskey I was then able to relax with a long cool drink. I sent John out for fish and chips. The following day we only drove as far as **Coonabarabran** for another one nights stop. We set off confidently and refreshed passing straight through **Tamworth** and then started to climb the ridiculously long hill out of town. Following John, I was alarmed as he drove slower and slower until he was driving at 19kph with his foot flat down. He tried to switch from gas to petrol and stalled. So there we were stuck on the hill and of course, once stopped, we couldn't move as the radiator temperature started to immediately climb. It didn't actually explode but we lost a fair bit of fluid from the overflow pipe and just had to stay put waiting for it to cool down. I was parked behind with hazard lights on and enormous semi-trailers were trying to get past with cars trying to overtake them. Our stomachs were knotted as we feared we would get hit. Once we got going again we decided to stop at **Walcha** for the night and that was an excellent decision. It is such a lovely town – sort of all neat and tidy and the people so friendly. We felt so relaxed at the park with the only thing dampening our enthusiasm being that the tar outside had melted in the heat and my expensive pair of 'special' shoes had tar all over them as I had actually sunk into it as I had got out of my car to go into reception. The heat was impossible but it was still a lovely place to stay and the following day I told John that I needed another night as there was no way I could go anywhere, probably reaction from the day before. We again ate out (so much for all that shopping I had done) at a local pub in one of the back streets. It was expensive and I wouldn't choose to go there again as the food didn't bowl us over.

So off we set again although I could quite happily have stayed on for a few days. I told John that I hoped this detour of his was going to be worth it. I had phoned a park in Port Macquarie and had booked in for a week. The park was near to an air conditioning mechanic and I had phoned him and left a message hoping that I could get my car done. Well he never returned my call despite having a very good web site and we never reached Port Macquarie!

A fellow camper had told me that it took about two hours to get to 'Port' as it is 173 ks. We were really relaxed about it and didn't leave until after ten in the morning. What nobody had bothered to mention is that the road from Walcha to Port is extraordinary. The scenery is absolutely stunning and I would go as far to say that it is the most beautiful scenic route we have ever travelled and it is loved by motor bike riders. It is almost all switchback bends. You have to drive with one hundred percent concentration at all times but all you really want to do is look at the view. There are very few places to stop and look with a sheer drop most of the way down. John stopped at one of the scenic lookouts but before stopping started shouting down the two-way. Annoyingly calm I told him to stop shouting, calm down and tell me what the problem was slowly. Then I heard him say 'brakes not working' and that shut me up instantly! I was so shocked I literally couldn't speak and got out of the car slowly to go and join him. He told me that just before the lay-by he had noticed the brakes had started to get spongy so had pulled in and now the foot pedal wasn't doing anything at all. He still had the hydraulic parking brakes thank goodness or he wouldn't be alive now. He said we'd have to call somebody immediately. I reminded him it was a Sunday. We set off in the car to find the nearest place where there were signs of life and thirty kilometres down the road came across a busy pub and a shop at **Long Flat**. As my air conditioning wasn't working I cannot begin to tell you how hot we were so we shot into the pub to seek air conditioning. They had none – not one room or area had any! We also realised how far we still were from Port Macquarie and how many more hills we had to climb up and down and switchback bends to navigate! I ordered a cider, which I found I didn't like but I needed to get rehydrated. We then ordered some lunch and no wonder this pub was busy because the food is superb, cheap and they serve you far too much! One meal would do two people but great for those with huge appetites. The theme in the dining room was Valentine's Day but as I did not know what day it was John told me that it wasn't until the following day. I told him that this would have to suffice and at least we were having a meal out together. He was actually wrong but it wasn't until the next day that my daughter told me on the phone that it had been Valentine's Day. We shared our woes with anyone who would listen which is quite a few people in a country pub and John was quite keen to use a local guy who was recommended, I suggested to him that on a scorching hot Sunday afternoon it might be a bit daft to use someone unlicensed who had probably had a few beers inside of him to work on the brakes of a seven and a half ton truck that he had to drive down the hills we had just passed.

I'm Right At Home Directing The Truckies

I've decided that those people who talk about having an angel looking after them are not actually talking nonsense. I believe I must have one but I wish to goodness I knew who it is so I can thank him or her! Where did the name Valentine's Day come from? Was it 'Valentine' who was looking after us? To start with and most importantly, the problem did not arise until just before a lay-by and as they are so infrequent on that route that is a miracle on its own. John kept starting to tell me what could have happened and I kept telling him to shut up and 'don't even go there'. At the pub I had used their telephone book and had found two truck repair centres further down at a town called **Wauchope** (pronounced War-hope), plus a mechanical mobile repair company at Port Macquarie. John only had to make one call and we were told help would arrive in two hours time. Again it was so easy, thirdly, he got us going again with working brakes and bravely drove in front of John with me behind with my hazard lights on in case traffic came up behind me. Fourthly, unlike the day before when John and I had to pull over often to let other drivers past where safe, not one vehicle followed us all the way to Wauchope. Lastly, as we drove into the truck repair centre my two-way radio ran out of batteries. Had it happened anywhere else en route I would not have been able to stop and change the batteries. Finally, we were allowed to plug into the mechanics electricity so we have air conditioning, fill up our fresh water tank and even use their kitchen sink to do some necessary underwear washing! I had planned to do the weekly washing when we set up camp for the week at Port Macquarie and we were running out of socks and pants. We went out to look around town after arrival and found a Country Club – with air-conditioning! We had a drink and then ordered their Monday night 'special' which was steak, salad and chips at a very reasonable cost.

Some asides to this story….when we were at the pub trying to find someone to help us we recalled a couple who had told us that they had driven up the hill towing their van and one of their air bags for their suspension on their fairly new and very expensive four-wheel drive had burst. At the pub someone else told us that a motor bike rider with a brand new Triumph had driven that road and his back brakes had failed the same day as we had our problems. A really helpful guy suggested that if we had no foot brake asked why we didn't go back the way we had come, up and over the mountain! Another guy asked me if John had been using the gears coming down. I told him he must have been because when we had previously stopped he had reminded me that I must use my gears and not my footbrake.

Another View Of Inlet At North Haven

Now we are at the truck repair centre and nothing has happened as yet because the mechanic has had to rush out to a petrol tanker who has broken down on the same road. I would tell anyone who would listen not to tow a caravan up or down that hill and for any large vehicle to ensure that their vehicle is in absolutely tip-top mechanical order before attempting it! However, it is a wondrous journey, particularly coming down with the vistas so glorious, especially when as green as it is now after all the rain they have had in this area. If we had gone on the coastal route from Melbourne to Sydney as John wanted to do and got quite cross with me for not wanting to do so, we would have stopped in favourite spots such as Narooma for a week. If we had done so we would have been in serious trouble because people are being told that the highway is closed with floods in so many places now that people would try and avoid the area between Nowra and the Victorian border. If we had continued on the inland route as I wanted to do instead of coming via Tamworth and Port Macquarie we would still have had to cross the Great Dividing Range and the Blackall Range to get home via Casino and if the brakes had failed there then we would have been very lucky indeed to have been on top of a lay-by! We also may not have been within mobile phone range to get help as we were on this trip. Okay, it is not great living in a yard surrounded by huge trucks coming in and out all times of the day, but our relief is so great that we have given the mechanic a whole list of things we want checked. We are beyond caring about the cost. He is a great guy and we trust him and we want this vehicle to be absolutely A1 mechanically. He's going over the engine thoroughly including engine mounts, the braking system, suspension, change the fuel filter and so forth. Everything is going to be tuned and timings checked. We are now wondering wether to sell the vehicle before going to U K. I would like to get a little van for short trips away and the odd weekends. You have to expect problems whatever you buy and a friend with a brand new caravan has found all sorts of odds and ends wrong and on his first trip that the dual gas/electric hot water system is not working on electricity. The company that made his van has a terrific reputation and high customer satisfaction. If you are a person who worries a lot, do not travel Australia! As for me, I remained blissfully calm outwardly but once stopped I went into the office to see if they had air conditioning (which they did) and then couldn't breathe! I still don't know whether it was the fumes in the bus as the engine cowling was still off, the heat or a stress attack. I was given a chair and sat down until I could get myself together. John had no idea I was like this and I didn't tell him what had happened until the following morning when I owned up. I'm not really very brave!

So today they got the engine mount off that needed repairing and damaged the condenser – told the owner he doesn't want to get rid of us! Suggested I cook dinner for him tonight because he didn't leave until about 7.30pm last night and was at work at 6.30am that morning. At least they close the office for their morning tea break and for forty-five minutes to share lunch together every day but it doesn't stop him talking to everyone who wants to talk to him on the phone which rings incessantly. I've sent John to golf as he's getting too restless.

AT LEAST A WEEK LATER

Actually we've been here two weeks and two days! You kind of get used to it despite being surrounded by trucks that are so huge that it makes our thirty-five foot bus look like a dinky car! We've had our down days – the worst when we were both fed up on the same day which rarely happens. The parts were eventually located and paid for but instead of the three day delivery, they took eleven days. Words cannot express the frustration and where they were nobody seems to know. Now we just await the repair!

However, **Port Macquarie**, which we didn't like that much on our first visit (other than the beaches which are wonderful) is now so familiar we are getting to quite like it and Wauchope is part of our home life now! I know which coffee shop serves the best coffee, which is the best Opportunity shop, where to get wonderful sausages, fresh fish, organic food, vegetables and where the town toilets are!

As for where we are staying – well I just walk into their kitchen or use their toilet like I own the place and asked why they haven't yet invited us to their homes for a barbecue. We are even getting to know the truck drivers who all arrive back on Friday night and leave again on Sunday night. The owners' dog thinks we live here permanently and comes to me for his tummy rub.

We spent one day at **Crescent Head** and just loved it there and I can recommend it for a stopover if travelling between Sydney and the Gold Coast as it is four and a half hours away from both. There is a huge caravan park there in two parts with one part being on the beach front and the other fronting the estuary. There is a cafe on site, the most amazing golf course right behind and along the beach where you are bound to lose some balls as some greens are right on the edge of the cliff. You also have other restaurants and a club and hotel in the small town, plus bowls etc. It is relaxing, very pretty and great for kids too with a good playground right next to the caravan park and skate bowl. It is also not very far to the large town of **Kempsey** for all the supplies you could need. The best views are from the top of town at the water tower lookout where you can see the crescent of the bay and south back towards Port Macquarie.

We finally left after seventeen days with repairs finished, fluid levels checked and even our tyres checked. Our first two nights were spent at **Nambucca Heads**. We should have booked into the caravan park beside the lagoon and beach because we spent most of our first afternoon there, sitting on the hotel verandah soaking in the glorious views. It felt most odd the first night and morning to wake up in a caravan park. Our second morning was a Sunday so we grabbed the newspaper and set off for the hotel verandah again! In the afternoon we drove to the stunning beautiful small township of **Sawtell** and I so wished more of the fashion stores had been open as so many items of clothing were tempting me to break down their doors. We enjoyed our organic coffee so much that we bought some and chatted to other visitors. So, we had glorious views in the morning and glorious views in the afternoon, especially when we drove up to the headland at Sawtell.

Whilst we were in town, I overheard a father say to his little boy (about 2 years old) 'Watch the road'. The little boy answered 'I am watching the road' and he was, with his two little fat feet firmly planted on the edge of the kerb. Still watching the road really carefully he stepped out into the traffic!, that was a bit too literal for comfort!.

The next day we drove to **Wooolgoolga** to a favourite caravan park of ours. This time we were given the most beautiful site, or rather two sites – one just for the car so it could be parked on a concrete pad! We have the tennis court to one side and the games room in front which is next to the beautifully designed swimming pool which is lit up at night and we go to sleep with the gentle sounds of trickling water from the pool waterfalls. We have nobody around us except for some permanent homes behind us on the other side of the road and we have already been given two home-grown cucumbers from one of the residents. The last time we came here we enjoyed the company of some of the residents and we have been told that they are really happy here and all look out for each other. There are some really pretty houses here. As there are few other temporary visitors, we can use the television in the games room if one of us wants to watch a different program to the other so no more having to negotiate when our programs clash! Not that I've felt like watching much as I spend a lot of time just looking at the beautiful lawns, flowers and bushes and the pool area. I've spent hours outside doing three weeks worth of washing in our small washing machine.

We have decided to stay for the week but I could quite happily stay a lot longer. Tomorrow we will check out some of the coastal communities that we missed on our way here and go to Coffs Harbour to do our weekly shopping and pick up some tourist leaflets. I've sent John out to find the golf club so that I've got some uninterrupted time to catch up with some computer work. As there is rain forecast for the rest of the week he might be playing aqua-golf. I've had my exercise for the day running up and down the stairs with buckets of hot soapy water to add to my washing machine and bringing in items as soon as they are nearly dry to hang them in our airing cupboard. I've had our rotary line on the go plus the clothes stand and I've been up and down swopping stuff around! Two items left to go and the pool is beckoning me.

After another beautiful day the rain set in but wasn't as bad as forecast so we decided to use our legs to explore. I'm surprised by how many clothes shops such a small town has and as there aren't many shops, I went into all of them. At one shop John and I entered together and I was talking to him whilst looking around when the salesperson suddenly realised she had customers and asked John if he needed any assistance but he told her he had stopped wearing women's clothes years ago. We found a vegetable shop with the freshest vegetables beautifully displayed and it was a joy to look at the produce even though I didn't need anything. At another clothes store I found a very unusual top for only nineteen dollars and considering that I've been looking for something to wear for a particular occasion for up to around two hundred dollars I was pretty happy. As we came out of the store I saw a guy around his late forties talking to a teenager and as I went past him I heard him say 'It is official – I have pubes'. I looked at him in amazement and said 'Congratulations' and then shook his hand. As I moved on I heard him burst out laughing so I guess he was talking about his son.

We walked to the RSL club and told two guys on the desk that we were strangers to the area and had come in to have a look around but they didn't bother to enlighten us as to what they could offer as they were too busy talking so we explored the place ourselves. There is a gym there if you come here and need one and I haven't seen any others in the area. We had intended to buy a coffee but the menu didn't inspire us much so we'll have a look at the bowls club another day. We really enjoyed our wander around and I reckon it would be a good idea if we used our legs more often. It's more relaxing too because if John is driving the car a short trip always becomes a marathon as he wants to explore everywhere.

Yesterday we had intended to go to a couple of the coastal communities and then into Coffs Harbour (which the locals call 'town'). We covered two areas and got the shopping at a third area in **Moonah** and explored that but then John went down every turn off the highway until I was so fed up with getting in and out of the car that I called a halt to his exploring and told him to get me back to the van and we'd do Coffs Harbour another day. Twice he disappeared over headlands and I ended up sitting in the car listening to the radio on both occasions as he was gone so long. He'll suddenly call out 'I'm just going to explore that hill' and before I can answer he's gone and there's no way I can catch up with him as his legs go on forever whereas I am blessed with very short pins. I always understand how tired little children get as they have to do seven steps to their parents' two steps. When he and I climb steps I have to tread on every one whilst he only has to do every other one but he did try once to do it like me and it was quite hilarious as he found it so difficult.

Well, I owe **Coffs Harbour** an apology because I didn't think much of it the last time we were here so we must have gone to the wrong part of it. Today we drove all along the beach front along Ocean Parade to start with and it was really quite lovely. There was a small headland at the northern end to explore with the surf club at the other end at the river inlet. You can sit on the balcony at the surf club and look at the glorious views both north and south and out to **Little Mutton Bird Island.** We continued on over the railway line and discovered Marina Drive where we enjoyed looking the boats and trawlers and realised that we could walk out to Mutton Bird Island which is part of the **Solitary Islands Marine Park.** We later returned here for a fish and chip lunch. We then continued along Jordan Esplanade and drove right out **to Corambirra Headland** and from there you can look back all along the coast. After lunch we went into the town centre for a quick look around and if you like undercover shopping and parking there is ample in the town centre. However, we loved the scenery we had seen along the beachfront so much that we returned and drove back along the coast road before returning to the highway to drive back to Woolgoolga. We were quite taken with the **Park Beach** area and wondered what it would be like to live there but decided to leave the enormous shopping centre near there just before the highway for another date. I've told John that I'd like to extend our stay here because we haven't yet seen enough although we are not going inland this time, along the Waterfall Way as we did on our first trip.

Apparently there was an earthquake seventy kilometres off the coast today further south but we didn't get a tsunami. A friend was telling me that the only trauma we haven't gone through on the road is being flooded but she'd forgotten about tsunamis!

John Timms

YAMBA

Well, what a difference time makes because last time we came here I believe I didn't like it – probably because the parks wouldn't accept dogs. Now we don't have any and are parked alongside the river, right in town with the beaches so close we can walk there. What with the myriad of boats and trawlers in the harbour nearby as well as not needing to get in the car as we can walk to everything, I just love it. So, this morning we walked around town and this afternoon we drove around the area. There are so many beautiful sea views to see, so many beaches and everywhere we go we sight the river as well. We are now orientated and always seem to need to drive around to get our bearings before we start feeling 'at home'. It's taken us less than twenty-four hours to get to that stage which is some kind of record for us! We had no idea that the Yamba area was so big until we discovered the housing estates and inlets today. Across the road is the bowling club with roast dinners on Sundays and weekly specials and there are so many cafes and dining facilities on offer that it is rather overwhelming. There are many individual shops in Yamba, not part of franchise groups and there are a number of boutiques with clothes that have asked me to go and try them on. I will get the opportunity as John has already found the golf club which again is so near he could actually walk there and it seems it incorporates a country club so I might actually be interested in paying the place a visit. It really is a stunningly beautiful area and we will do a river cruise as the boat departs almost in front of where we are parked. The Clarence River is spectacularly beautiful because it meanders around so much. We will also go back to **Maclean** just up the road because the last time we went there it was a Sunday and everything was shut. This time we'll ensure that everyone is awake to add to the liveliness of the place! As there are so many people of Scottish descent there they have adopted the Scottish theme over the area (can you imagine what it must have been like for the original inhabitants) I have to admit I would love to hear some bagpipes again in a 'Scottish' setting! Judging by the price of houses there in comparison to where we live, we might even be tempted to move there as, other than Tasmania, there has been nowhere else yet that has attracted us the way this area has.

We made our way back to Currumbin on the Gold Coast rapidly, because of the heavy rain via Evans Head, Ballina, Byron Bay, Brunswick Heads, Murwillumbah through Tweed Heads to a welcome rest from the road.

31/3/2010.

The Route-"The Big Lap'(Part 2) Diary 3

Jerramungup
Ravensthorpe, Hopetown
Esperance
Pink Lake, Bandy Creek Harbour
West Beach, Blue Haven Beach, Salmon Beach
Cape Le Grand National Park,
Norseman, Fraser Range Station
Balladonia
Caiguna, Cocklebiddy
Madura, Mundrabilla, Eucla

South Australia

Border Village, The Great Australian Bight Marine Park
Nullarbor
Yalata Mission, Nundroo, Ceduna
Streaky Bay
Port Kenny, Venus Bay
Elliston
Coffin Bay
Port Lincoln
Tumby Bay, Port Neill
Arno Bay, Cowell
Whyalla
Port Augusta, Port Germaine, Port Pirie
Nelshaby, Napperby, Weeroona Island
Port Broughton, Wallaroo, Kadina
Moonta [York Peninsular], Maitland
Port Victoria, Minlaton
Point Turton, Marion Bay, Corny Point, Stenhouse Bay, Warooka
Yorktown, Port Giles
Stansbury, Port Vincent, Hardwick Bay
Ardrossan, Port Wakefield, Adelaide
Port Adelaide
Henley, Grange

Glenelg
Victor Harbour
Port Elliot, Middlerton, Goolwa, Hindmarsh Island
Delamere, Cape Jarvis, Kangaroo Island Ferry, Second Valley
Lady Bay, Yankalilla Bay, Normanville
Yankalilla
Granite Island
Goolwa North, Strathalbyn, Wellington (free ferry), Tailem Bend
Meningle, Cape Jaffa, Robe
Beachport
Millicent, Mt. Gambier
Port MacDonnell
Mount Schank
Pengla
Hell's Hole, Nelson
Portland

Victoria

Port Fairy
Warrnambool
Great Ocean Road
Mortlake, Scarsdale, Daylesford
Ballarat
Castlemaine, Bendigo
Echuca, Moama
Cobram, Tocumwal

New South Wales

Narrandera
Peak Hill
Parkes
Dubbo
Coonabarabran
Gunnedah
Tamworth
Moonbi
Uralla, Armidale, Guyra, Glencoe
Glen Innes
Tenterfield, Casino
Wardell
Ballina

Nimbin, The Channon

Dunoon, Tweed Heads

This Diary continues with a further trip two years later to North Queensland, returning south by the inland route via Toowoomba, Goondiwindi, Narrabri, Dubbo, down to Melbourne to the ferry for a three months tour of Tasmania.

Queensland – 15/5/09

Gold Coast- Tallebudgera Creek

Armstrong Beach, Yeppoon

Airlie Beach, Bowen, Hillsborough, Seaforth, Midge Point

Mackay, Clairview, Bundaberg

Gin Gin, Childers

Toowoomba, Goondiwindi

New South Wales

Moree

Narrabri, Dubbo Zoo

Victoria

Whittlesea, Kinglake, Healsville, Marysville

Tasmania

Devonport, Port Sorrell, Longford

Sheffield, Railton, Latrobe, Promised Land

Imaginarina Science Centre

Spreyton, Launceston, Evandale

Bridport, Scottsdale, Windermere, Hillwood, George Town

Low Head, Beechford, Weymouth, Lulworth

Beaconsfield, Greens Beach, Yorktown, Beauty Point,

Gravelly Beach, Ross, Campbell Town

Classwood, Bicheno, Coles Bay, Scamander

St Helens, Bay of Fires, Binalong Bay, Lagoons Beach

Four Mile Creek, Falmouth, Cockle Cove Bay, Dora Point

Humbug Point Lookout

Swansea, Triabonna, Orford

Hobart

Cambridge, Sorell, Seven Mile Beach, Rosny Park, Rokeby, Kingston, Electrona, Snug, Kettering, Woodbridge, Flowerpot, Verona Sands,

Cygnet

Hobart

Richmond
Tahune Forest
Geeveston, Eaglehawk Neck, Pirates Bay, Tassellated Pavement
Blowhole, Tasmans Arch, Devils Kitchen, Doo Town
Port Arthur
Remarkable Cave
Devil's Gullet, Alum Cliffs
Kempton
Oatlands
Lake Dulverton
Mole Creek
Lake Barrington
Chudleigh, Paradise
Penny Royal World, Gunpowder Mill, Ben Lomond National Park
Ski Village, Arthurs Lake, Great Lake, Poatina, Carrick
Tasmanian Copper & Metal Art Gallery
Burnie, Wynard, Boat Harbour, Penguin, Ferry to Melbourne

Victoria

Graigieburn
Cobram, Yarrawonga

New South Wales

Finley, Jerilderie
Narrandera, Dubbo, Coonabarabran, Tamworth, Walcha
Long Flat, Wauchope
Crescent Head
Nambucca Heads, Sawtell, Woolgoolga
Moona, Coffs Harbour, Little Mutton Island, Corambirra Headland
Yamba, Evans Head, Ballina, Byron Bay, Brunswick Heads
Murwillumbah, Tweed Heads.

Queensland

Currumbin.

Printed in the United States
By Bookmasters